"Straight Inta Custody" – b

Author's thanks

Thanks to my parents for raising me well. As a parent myself, I now appreciate how difficult this was! And to my father, for not forcing the profession of police officer upon me but rather letting me discover it on my own. There's nothing quite as satisfying as saying "You're nicked!"

About this book

I've always wanted to write a book. I envy (and admire, of course!) authors with whom words come so naturally. But then, this is an authentic account by a serving copper of his time working in a police custody suite. I'm a copper, not an author! You should see some officer's statements! If you're an officer yourself, or perhaps work in CJU or CPS, you'll know what I mean!

The structure of this book is pretty simple. It is a day by day account of my first six months in custody. I would get home from most shifts and immediately write about that day. Sometimes, I'd go a few shifts. I made notes during my shifts to remind me what to include.

You've probably already guessed it, but Sergeant Custard is *not* my real name! I cannot see any reason why my home Force would take issue with this book, having respected confidentiality but needless to say anonymity was important to me. It keeps things simple. If anyone reading suspects they know me, or anyone about whom I have referred, please respect our privacy and perhaps keep your burning question until my retirement do! Should I make it that far, of course... Hope you enjoy!

Foreword

I'm a fifth generation police officer. Dad was a cop, granddad was, great granddad (and alcoholic by all accounts) and great-great granddad. Fifth generation. I think that's pretty spectacular, to be honest.

I never *wanted* to be a copper. It just happened. In my teenage years, I was adamant I would not follow what had become a family tradition.

I put a lot of effort into GCSEs and did pretty well. I achieved 7 A's and 4 B's. Being at private school, this made me feel completely inadequate compared to most other's results. They were all destined for greatness. They'd all get high paying jobs, as if it was their natural right to inherit them. I'd been to some of their houses. Mansions some of them. Millionaires. Was I jealous? Of course!

Trouble is, I had *no* idea what I wanted to do when I was older. I've *always* loved watching movies. I decided becoming a journalist may be fun. Perhaps a film critic. I reviewed *Romeo Must Die* for a local paper and decided I was a natural. I chose English Lit, History, French and ICT for my A levels. Trouble was, English Lit required a willingness to read books. I preferred watching the film based on the book. Quicker and easier. Reading was boring.

French became too difficult. Being able to request a table for four on holiday, ordering the standard moules frites avec biere was handy, but things had stepped up a gear. I switched to Philosophy, which I flunked but was fascinated by. Good old René Descartes' Brain in a Vat theory. I drew comparisons to *The Matrix*, which is, quite simply, the best movie ever made.

My increasing hate towards school work found me hanging with mates more, often by a particular bench next to the local newsagents. Twenty-pack of Camels was the brand of choice. Marlboro Reds followed. Golden Virginia, king skins...

I became, in my eyes, a bit of a rebel. Just about stayed on the right side of the law. Most of the time...

I recall walking the streets of a busy city centre one night, aged sixteen I think. We'd been drinking and smoking at a mate's and decided it'd be fun to check out the nightlife we'd soon get to experience for ourselves, without needing fake ID. We walked past a bus shelter, complete with advertisement poster. But this was not just *any* advertisement poster. This was a *Magnum* poster, with a "well-fit" woman posing provocatively with her ice-cream. We *had* to have this.

Trouble was, it was protected by state-of-the-art security. The glass-fronted screen was held in place by some sort of electromagnetic field. This would take some *Ocean's Eleven* ingenuity to acquire.

Nope. My mate used a bottle opener to prise open a metal panel and flicked the switch off, causing the shelter lights to turn off and the glass-fronted screen to swing open. Poster acquired.

Within seconds, a patrol car arrived. There were about seven of us. I'd not actually done anything but considered myself guilty as hell. My dad was a copper. I was going to get both of us in the shit. What had I done?!

So I ran. Two of us did. The others stayed put and for all I knew, were getting arrested and put in the back of "meat wagons" there and then.

My mate and I decided swapping tops would be an incredibly smart idea. Taking off a jumper, swapping it and putting another jumper on, all whilst running, is actually quite difficult.

I can't remember where my mate hid but I climbed over a metal fence and hid behind it. The fact it was less than a metre high assisted the copper who found me. He grabbed my jumper, pulling me back over.

He asked my details. Bollocks. I provided them. My *actual* details. I share the same name as dad too. He was a Superintendant at that time. Shit.

I confessed his occupation, name, where he was stationed, and asked whether he was going to tell him. His response was along the lines of "Would I tell your dad if your name was Joe Bloggs?" I took that as a 'no'. In retrospect, he probably should have, given my age, the fact I was out at 3am drinking alcohol, and had been associated with anti-social behaviour and a bit of criminal damage. Not to mention theft of Magnum poster.

None of us were nicked. Not even my mate, who masterminded the operation. Our details were simply taken and we were sent on our way. We considered ourselves 'cautioned' by police. We'd been given a caution. That's what we told people. Clearly not correct. But it *sounded* good and was, as far as we were concerned, not far from the truth.

I quit school at seventeen, deciding A levels were too difficult. I achieved AS level grades of B, C, D and E in History, ICT, English Literature and Philosophy respectively. I'd had enough. I wanted to get a job and start earning money. I had a new girlfriend too - a promising one this time, so affording a car was a priority.

By the time I dropped out of school, my dad had recently retired from the police, having served thirty years. He joined aged nineteen, so retired at forty-nine, with a massive lump sum and decent pension. Retired at forty-nine?! That sounded appealing. The seeds were sown, little did I know it. I got a job at the council, checking housing benefit forms. Very, very boring but I was earning money. I had an annual salary. I was earning £11k a year! Incredible stuff, I thought. To be fair, aged seventeen, it was pretty good. My parents charged me rent but I was able to save a decent sum during the five years I worked there. I packed in the smoking. My girlfriend became my wife and we bought a flat together.

I progressed into the council tax team, deciding appropriate enforcement action against non-payers. I never enjoyed this work, but became efficient at it. It would've been easy for me to stay there. I was in my comfort zone. My job was mundane but easy. But I *hated* being sat at a desk eight hours a day. I used to stare out the window and wish I was doing something meaningful. Something exciting...

I joined the police. The thought of being outside, on patrol, appealed to me. I saw the police as a career and as a good, stable job. Ok, the hefty pension was a big deciding factor. Being recently married, I started to think more responsibly, planning my future. A good pension was a priority. I'm glad to still have a pension but it's not the one I signed up for. Initial training lasted twenty-three weeks before we hit our stations. We paraded once a week, in number ones. This was a completely alien experience to me. I had never done *anything* like it. I enjoyed it but found it terrifying at the same time.

I achieved excellent results in my law based exams, often top of the class. In what would become a classic example of inconsistency within the job, one of the trouble makers in our intake was put forward for the high potential development scheme. It seemed they had achieved an excellent pass on the pre-joining assessments and despite only scraping passes in actual law based exams (and constantly getting into trouble for using his ID inappropriately outside of work) he was put forward. He was so good he ended up being back-coursed and left soon after that.

I enjoyed personal safety training (PST) we did. Handcuffing techniques, wrist locks, take downs, baton strikes, bleep tests... also the obligatory exposure to CS spray. Half of us huddled in a tiny shed, jumped up and down, and sang a song. As we did, one of the trainers delighted in spraying us with quarter strength CS. Once marinated, we had to run out the shed to our partner and perform a handcuffing technique. All while struggling to open our eyes through the painful effects of the spray and noses streaming snot. It truly is marvellous stuff. Arriving at my station was nerve wrecking but exciting. I got on well with my tutor, although we seemed to do a lot more traffic than most. I spent the next eight years with that same shift and station on response. I completed my Sergeants Ospre Part 1 exam after three and a half years service, achieving an exceptional pass. I started studying six months before, so put a lot of work in. I followed that up by passing Ospre Part 2 later that year, again achieving an exceptional pass. I started duties as Acting Police Sergeant (APS) shortly after passing Part 1.

I applied for promotion after eight years service but didn't make the paper sift. I was Temporary Sergeant at that time, on a three month stint, and felt hard done by. I sought feedback from the Superintendent, who was initially confused to see a Sergeant in front of him seeking advice on why they weren't good enough to be a Sergeant. I took the feedback on board and set about improving evidence. I was reluctant to jump through hoops the organisation wanted me to, just for the sake of promotion. With limited opportunities, I didn't want to move to a department I hated, only to get stuck there, with no boards in sight. Response was too much fun to take that gamble. Response was why I joined up but I had an underlying aspiration to make Sergeant. Anything above that gets too political.

I changed shifts. I'd become good friends with colleagues, who also, of their own admission, often needed a kick up the arse. Moving shifts provided me an opportunity to (not fall out with them and) work with other people and develop my leadership skills.

The next batch of promotions were announced and I applied. I passed that stage and subsequently passed my board. Almost eleven years in and I was nearly there.

I eagerly awaited my posting. I wanted to remain on response. I loved the variety of work and buzz of responding to jobs. I recalled that time I spent at the council, staring out the window, hoping I wasn't given a desk job in a department I knew nothing about, hidden from the frontline. I got custody. Ok, custody is frontline of sorts. But there aren't even any windows...

Day one of the four week custody course was my date of promotion. Stripes on shoulders, I started my training. The first week and a half was full on PACE (Police and Criminal Evidence Act 1984). This legislation governs how police must act when carrying out their duties. There's a PACE book we referred to throughout the course. PACE has its own Codes of Practice, which explains PACE (a bit) better and explains the correct ways we should carry out PACE. This is *another* book. Within the Codes of Practice, there's a section regarding dealing with persons detained by police, ie, those in custody. We were also lent an additional book, written by a professor and designed to explain *both* PACE and the Codes. Sadly, there was no fourth book to explain that one.

The trainer made the course fun, and full credit to him for doing so. However, it'd been some time since he himself worked custody. He certainly knew PACE well. By his own admission, he lived and breathed it.

The rest of the course consisted of computer based training, familiarising ourselves with the various screens we were likely to use daily. Frustratingly, this was taught by trainers with no custody experience, who were not au fait with current computer systems. This didn't provide me much confidence. The last few days of the course were 'live custody'. We travelled to our respective custody centres and, under the guidance of existing custody Sergeants, began booking in prisoners. Just before my first, it occurred to me we'd not been trained the "custody spiel". I winged it, based on my experiences as a PC when presenting prisoners. We tend to wing an awful lot of things in policing. Fortunately, this was well wung. Winged? I winged it well.

I soon realised the realities of custody. It *is* an extremely stressful environment. Duties (resource management) struggle to maintain minimum level of staffing at any one custody suite. Sergeants and Detention Officers (DOs) don't get annual leave they need. Hell, I've already had leave declined before starting!

The majority of Sergeants were keen to tell me how long they've done custody and how longer they anticipate being there. I'm told there's no set minimum length of time a Sergeant must remain in this post. However, it's generally accepted to be two years. On the flipside, they tell me it's nice to leave on time and only have one or two PDRs to do.

They say a death in custody is the worst thing that can happen to a custody Sergeant. It involves months or, more likely, years of intense pressure and stress, whilst you're investigated and, ultimately, you could find yourself prosecuted for corporate manslaughter. I tend to have a knack for going one further, so perhaps custody will simply kill *me*. From the stress people seem to be under, both Sergeants and DOs, it's surely only a matter of time before someone croaks it on the job.

I should be cracking straight on, putting training into action. However, I already had leave booked, so have a week off before I start. I'll read my course notes in preparation but the thought of working myself six feet under is an unnerving one. I decided to start this book to document my time in custody, so that, if nothing else, it'll assist the coroner when determining the cause of my death.

Chapter One – There Are No Windows In Custody

During my week off I decided I needed a new hobby. Sitting around the house watching movies was my idea of fun but some annoying voice in my head told me I should be doing something else. Ultimately, it was telling me I needed exercise, but I hate exercise. I do very little. I am blessed with a fast metabolism and tend to stay in shape. This doesn't mean I have a healthy body and I'm aware I need to do more to look after my health.

I don't tend to cope well with stress. I've never taken time off for it but expect like most people, those closest to me recognise the signs. My wife is awesome. She sees the tell-tale signs and lets me know I'm doing them. Mine tend to be fidgeting fingers! I can then do something about it. I get anxious on occasion and struggle with my breathing. I breathe in but it's as if the oxygen is not being absorbed. Becoming aware of this issue, means the issue worsens. This was more an issue in my teenage years but the jobs very stressful and there are times when I have to find somewhere private and try and calm myself. Not like that you degenerate! That's what we refer to as 'State Fourteen'. Someone on a training day once told us it's perfectly normal to masturbate in toilets at work, to which someone in the back shouted "so we are all a bunch of wankers!"

I drank far too much on my week off. I've resolved to drink less and save it for rest days once in custody. I find exercise boring and embarrassing. I have never belonged to a gym in my life.

I played a lot of Grand Theft Auto 5 on my week off. I found this great stress relief. I have owned an Xbox One for a few years but rarely play it myself. My daughter owns more games than I do. Still, like watching movies, this was fun (and perversely satisfying) but not really a new hobby. I enjoy playing snooker and consider that a hobby, but snooker requires two players and the nature of shift work means you rarely get opportunity to tie up with friends to do such a thing.

During my leave, I paid a chap to paint my front and rear doors and fence in my garden. I'd meant to get round to this myself for years, but ultimately am a bit lazy when it comes to such work and shy away from DIY, leaving my wife to put up shelves and sort flat-packed furniture. I did offer to paint, but the thought of me messing it up horrified her and she preferred to pay someone. My wife's recently become a PC herself. As such, she's busy studying, so this was another reason we paid someone.

However, there was a pot of woodstain left and I remembered the kid's garden bench desperately needed sorting. I took it apart and sanded it down. I painted it and left to dry. Probably shouldn't have rested on paper. Peeling that off was frustrating. I added another coat. The next day I went to put it back together. I realised a photograph of where all the bits had come from may have been handy. I managed to reassemble it, despite swearing some of the screw holes had drastically changed position. Proud of my achievement, I sent the family Snapchats to prove my new credentials. I found the experience rather therapeutic and I achieved a sense of DIY satisfaction. With the impending stresses of custody looming, I needed to find something meaningful to do outside of work. Perhaps that was something I could do more of in future...

A few days before starting, I played a game of poker with some mates, including a Sergeant who'll be my mentor during my first set. I discussed my training with him and that we'd been taught to use the NDM (National Decision Model) to document rationales in a variety of aspects, such as care plans, disposals and pre-release risk assessments. He laughed. As well intentioned as this was, there would be no time for NDMs, I was told. This seemed to be the general feeling amongst other Sergeants I spoke with, during my 'live custody' experience. Surely following a death in custody, one of the things they look for are well documented decisions? Maybe it's one of those things where you learn to 'cover your arse', aka use the NDM, in particular circumstances, rather than using it everytime. But there'll be times when someone appears normal, showing no signs of self harm intent, who then tops themselves on leaving custody. Where was your NDM, officer? As if the NDM itself would have magically prevented the death. This, I expect, will be a balancing act, perfected through experience.

Day One was the ideal start to custody. It was steady. Not too boringly Q (police officers try not to say 'quiet', seeing it as a jinx) but not too stressfully busy. Somewhere just over in-between. There were loads of sergeants on, more than we had rooms for! This, I am told, is a once in a blue moon type of situation and was no doubt responsible for the Q feeling, as work was shared more ways than normal. Oh, and I should clarify – there *are* windows in custody, I realised. But not ones you can see out of! And they have bars in front of them. So I'm not classing them as windows. They let a little natural light in but don't make you feel better.

I completed quite a few 'disposals'. This is the point where the detainee has been interviewed and the officer in the case (OIC) comes to speak to you to convey what evidence there is, what the detainee said in interview and seeks advice from you, the expert (allegedly), as to what should happen to them, ie, should they be charged and sent to court?

In order to satisfy oneself a detainee should be sent to court, the Full Code Test (FCT) must first be met. This test consists of the 'evidential' and 'public interest' tests. For example, an officer has arrested a male on suspicion of assaulting his wife. She provides a statement, detailing the allegation, and there's a photograph of bruising to her face, consistent with her account. There are no witnesses to the incident. In this case, the 'evidential' test is met, in that we have a statement of complaint from the victim and photographic evidence of an injury that's consistent with how she alleges to have been assaulted. There would therefore be a RPOC (realistic prospect of conviction). Without the injury, unless there's some other evidence to assist (a witness, CCTV, or perhaps a 999 call, where the victim can be heard trying to fight off her husband during the call), this would be unlikely to meet the 'evidential' test and the 'public interest' test would therefore be irrelevant.

So in the above example where the 'evidential' test is met, you must then consider the 'public interest' test. Sending people to court is impactive on the individual themselves and may not be proportionate to what is alleged. It may be an out of court disposal (perhaps a conditional caution, whereby the offender has to make good their wrong or is forced to address the cause of their behaviour) is more appropriate in the circumstances. Sending cases to court costs thousands of pounds but there may be a more beneficial way of proceeding. There are specified reasons why it either *is* or *is not* in the public interest to prosecute someone. An example of a *for prosecution* reason would be 'a conviction is likely to result in a significant sentence', or, 'A conviction is likely to result in an order of the court in excess of that which a prosecutor is able to secure through a conditional caution'. Examples *against* would be 'The court is likely to impose a nominal penalty', or, 'The loss or harm can be described as minor and was the result of a single incident, particularly if it was caused by a misjudgement'.

In the above DV (domestic violence) example, clearly it would be in the public interest to prosecute, as robust action needs to be taken in such cases, to show perpetrators the cycle of abuse they're subjecting their partners to is unacceptable and will result in prosecution. However, there are occasions when conditional cautions may be more appropriate. Perhaps the assault is minor, is not domestic related and is the first time someone has offended. A push perhaps, resulting in no injury. It may be a conditional caution is appropriate in such circumstances, the condition being the perpetrator has to write a letter of apology, pay compensation, or perhaps attend a victim awareness course.

If they're a regular offender, there's no point. Clearly they're set in their ways and are unlikely to change. But if there's a chance to change someone for the better, minimising further risk to victims, that's got to be a good thing.

So it's not as straight forward as charge or NFA (no formal action). There are other disposals available in your *tool kit*. Wait, that's too *Inspectory*. Hate that phrase. I've caught that from somewhere. Like a cold...There are other disposals available to you. As a custody Sergeant, you need to know them all. Some offences can be dealt with by fixed penalty notice, such as D&D (drunk and disorderly) and shoplifting. However, there are rules attached to these. Failure to comply with the rules could result in fines being refunded to offenders and having to simply write jobs off, as opposed to getting some form of formal action.

For a disposal review I completed on day one, I directed the officers to seek advice from the Crown Prosecution Service (CPS). Custody sergeants can make charging decisions on a number of cases but there are certain offences that *must* be referred to CPS. Domestic violence is one such area. In this case, the detainee admitted part of the assault but not all of it. They happily took responsibility for kicking their partner in the calf, but denied headbutting or slapping her. There was a photograph of swelling to her forehead, where she claimed to have been head butted. I completed my review, and off they went to CPS.

The day went amazingly quick. I managed to eat my sandwiches at my desk, whilst working. I get grumpy when I don't eat. One thing I realised on day one is that finding a gap in which to eat is tricky. There seems to be an attitude in custody where people are so busy that if you take a proper meal break, this is noticed and you'll be the one not pulling their weight. The knock on effect will be queues of prisoners at the back door and queues of officers waiting to speak to you to discuss disposals or other issues. These queues exist *anyway*, so they'd be uncontrollably long! Plus, as custody Sergeant, you are responsible for the block. You can't disappear to eat your lunch. If it can be taken, it seemingly has to be taken at your desk. Which is not hygienic. Your desk is where heroin addict's used needles and tourniquets are placed. It's where unwashed street drinkers' hats, gloves, scarfs, and scavenged fag ends are placed. It's where used tissues, hair bands and medication are placed. Being forced to eat my leftover barbequed pork loin and coleslaw sandwich in such conditions should be illegal. Let alone trying to eat a meal that requires a knife and fork. I expect such dangerous items of cutlery would be frowned upon in that environment anyway. Custody prefer plastic sporks.

Day two was much busier. Even the Sergeant mentoring me stated so and that was with others picking up the slack whilst I 'learn the ropes'. Not that I felt there was much slack, as I'm left wondering how you can possibly do all these things a hell of a lot quicker without compromising safety somewhere.

I booked in a couple of prisoners but completed far more disposal reviews than on day one. I was constantly occupied. There were occasions when I really needed the loo but my mentor had another job lined up for us. I have a small bladder, so this doesn't bode well.

I was put on the spot by an Inspector at one point, caught off guard and asked about a DP (detained person) and the current state of the investigation. I had no idea! My book with scribbled notes was in the other room. I thought on my feet. Nothing. "Sorry boss, I'm honestly not sure where we're at with that one. I'll need to pop next door and refer to my notes". To my horror, he followed me. I tried to decipher my notes but couldn't read my own writing! "I'll just check the computer and see if there's an update from the OIC, boss". Nothing. Shit. The Inspector said "If I was a particularly grumpy Inspector, I'd take issue with that", or words to that effect. Well, in my mind, he was taking issue with my lack of knowledge, massively. I'd simply not had opportunity to familiarise myself with the job, as I'd been manically busy from the get-go. What actually annoyed me most about this, was that he was the PACE Inspector. One of his responsibilities was reviewing each DP's continued detention, to ensure it was lawful and necessary. He had arrived to do this a couple of hours after some reviews were due. No mention made, no apology given. But on day two I decided I didn't yet have sufficient experience with which to make a stand and say as it was. Probably a good career move. I went for the more savvy, "Fair point, taken on board boss", which I felt was a happy compromise of not wanting to apologise to the man and also an admission that actually, despite having been busy, I should ideally have known a bit about the job.

At the start and end of every shift, custody Sergeant and DOs have to cram into a small room and discuss each DP in turn, so the incoming lot know risks associated with them and know sufficient about the job for which they were arrested. The time this takes varies depending on how many DPs are in and their individual needs. Typically I'm told they last up to half an hour. Some will be much quicker and some longer. During this time, the queue of officers arriving with prisoners increases exponentially. The queue of officers waiting in the corridor directly outside the room, waiting to speak to a Sergeant, increases exponentially. As a PC, I used to wonder what the hell was going on. Why was it taking so long? Were they just doing this to piss me off? I bet they were all stood around, having a laugh and a catch up. Probably eating their lunch. How wrong I was.

At some point, I expect someone has died in custody and upon close scrutiny, it was established risks were not handed to an oncoming team as not everyone was present. Every person present in custody will have had *some* involvement with a DP and so everyone will have their own knowledge that needs to be shared.

I now appreciate this and intend on sharing my new understanding with former colleagues. Ideally, the job needs to provide some form of custody awareness training for PCs, as they have no idea. It's not *their* fault – the job has never told them what goes on in custody, so they simply don't know.

I ate my lunch at home after day two. Probably just as well, as the stench of cheesy feet never quite dissipated from the moment a heroin user's shoes were removed during a search.

Lates were busy. I'd wanted to write something after lates, but just wanted to watch Bosch and play GTA5 once home. I'd then intended on writing something before my first night shift. However, I became addicted to Bosch and again found myself playing more GTA5. Bosch is good. Bosch is your typical hard-ass tv detective who won't play by the rules and just about gets away with it every time. Divorced, with a kid they are trying to reconnect with, having neglected them for their career. Seemingly never sleeps. It's an entertaining watch. GTA5 is pure escapism. I completed the story mode a couple years ago but recently got back into it by discovering the online mode, where you roam the city with 'randoms' and attack one another. You can also play missions with randoms, or with mates, which earns you virtual cash, with which you can increase your arsenal and improve your property portfolio. Love it.

I'm trying to remember what actually happened on lates. They're a bit of a blur. I recall them being busier than my first night shift. That started busy, as I had a couple of disposals first thing, which was challenging as there was a chap shouting and swearing in the charge room next to me. It made me laugh – the loud chap had been brought in for drink and drug driving. Despite his violent behaviour, you *still* have to go through the proper drink drive process. This involves working your way through a booklet, known as the 'MGDD/A', and asking all the relevant questions to satisfy the case, for example, had he consumed alcohol since the alleged offence (known as the hip-flask defence). That may seem pointless if the arresting officer has witnessed the driving, as they would know they haven't drunk anything since. But nevertheless it still needs asking. They still need to be asked if they've brought anything up from their stomach since the alleged offence. They still need to be asked whether they've inhaled anything since the alleged offence. Quite a few smartarses answer "yeah, air" at that one. To be fair, it *is* a bit stupid. And after all these questions comes the important one. Along the lines of "Do you agree to provide two specimens of breath for analysis?" If they answer "no", you're not done yet. Then you have to warn them that failure to provide them will result in their prosecution. From what I could hear, this chap was being pinned to the floor. It sounded as though he'd become extremely violent and may be trying to assault officers. And yet someone has to work their way through the booklet whilst officers are rolling round the floor with him, so the case will not be thrown out at court.

From what I recall of lates, I was non-stop. Everytime I finished booking in one person, another arrived in the holding cell. For the first late shift, I focused more on booking people in, so I could fine-tune the spiel. The day went fine but around early evening I became aware of several missed calls and voicemails on my phone. In custody, you have to leave your phone on silent. It can't start ringing half way through someone's rights. You're also lucky if you get reception. I did manage to just about hear what was on the voicemail. My young son's teacher. He had an accident, he's fine, but has an injury...please call us back asap. Text messages from my brother, my parents, my wife...I managed to excuse myself to leave custody and make some calls. Couldn't get hold of anyone. Luckily, my wife text me back soon after to confirm he'd been playing on the tricycles, had come off again, another face plant. Cuts to mouth, nose, just below one eye...wobbly tooth and bruised gum. No hospital treatment required. My brother, being an emergency contact, had rushed to the rescue, collected him and taken him to my parents. My folks said he disclosed to them a lad called Frankie had pushed him off the trike. My lad has previously accused Frankie of such callous violence. Upon questioning him later, I discovered they'd actually been playing police on the tricycles and, more specifically, a game of 'crash-bang'. I therefore think Frankie is absolved of any sole responsibility on this particular occasion.

What I do recall from the second late shift, is that I booked in a chap arrested on suspicion of sexually assaulting a fifteen year old girl. He was alleged to have touched her bottom, through outer clothing. Normally, this'd be a relatively straight forward booking in process. No dry cell was required under the particular circumstances of this allegation (a dry cell is one with no toilet or washing facilities and where your consumption of any food/drink is supervised – all to prevent you from destroying potential evidence on your hands or, um, elsewhere).

This chap spoke Punjabi. And very basic English. Only a few words. I do not speak Punjabi. In these situations, you therefore have to phone a language line for an interpreter. The booking in process is slowed WAY down. I got frustrated, as the person answering the language line call barely spoke English himself, and I felt a translator was almost required there too. Our chap was then being obstructive, which did not help matters. He pretty much answered every risk assessment question with 'I was just sat on the bench with my friend and did not do anything'. I got about three quarters of the way through the process, when the bloody phone line went quiet. I guess even the translator had had enough. Shit. So I then had to attempt to converse with the language line chap again, and fortunately got a much better interpreter this time, one that would just cut to the chase with the detainee and not get sucked into conversation. I was late to handover thanks to this chap, who took well over an hour and a half to book in, as whilst I had the interpreter handy, we got the HCP (health care practitioner) to see him, as he disclosed a recent heart attack.

The night shift was pretty Q. My mentor left me on my own with a DO, satisfied I'd grasped things well enough. They were still on hand to assist, when I inevitably had questions to ask. As I said, I got a few disposals sorted first thing and once that initial busy period went by, there were periods of time where I was actually able to chat with colleagues and learn a bit about them. Some stories the DOs told me made me laugh. One recalled a chap who'd been detained under Section 136 of the Mental Health Act and taken to the station. This used to happen quite a bit, but police stations are not places of safety and thankfully, bosses have started kicking back at other agencies and have made it clear we won't be doing this any longer (it still happens on rare occasions). The chap's mental health was, funnily enough, not particularly good and what did the DO find in his trouser pocket upon searching him? A dead hedgehog. The DO did the sensible thing, in placing the deceased road kill in an evidence bag, sealing it to prevent the smell escaping, and throwing it in the bin. Unfortunately, this was all done in the presence of the detainee, who, upon seeing his 'best friend' get treated in such a callous way, became extremely violent. You have to laugh in this job, or you'll become very depressed, however, this story, whilst amusing, is also a sobering example of how grateful I should be that my mental health is currently sound, as is that of my family and friends.

Another similar story told, was a chap who had a plastic bat in his pocket. He firmly believed the bat was alive and so became upset when it was placed in a sealed evidence bag, with the rest of his property. He then thoroughly appreciated the DOs humanity, when air-holes were pricked into the bag with a tip of a pen.

The gross-out story of the night has to be the DO who told me of a heroin addict he once searched, who had a dressing over a gammy wound on his leg. The injury had come about as a result of repeated injections in the same spot. Upon patting the addict down, maggots suddenly fell from under the dressing, where the wound had become infested. These were apparently scooped up and placed in the bin, to the horror of another DO / amateur fisherman, who suggested that they'd have made fine bait. I personally would not eat any fish caught using heroin-addict-gammy-wound maggots, though what you don't know and all that...remember *that* next time you're down the chippy.

My second night shift was actually a re-allocated rest day, courtesy of duties. A Friday night nonetheless! Despite being blatantly blacklisted, they did me a blinder there! All week has been glorious sunshine and I took full advantage of this by having my brother and his wife over for a barbeque. I declined to accept their offer of bringing food or drink, keen to show our gratitude for my brother's heroics earlier in the week. They told my kids their big news. I was already aware my sister-in-law was pregnant, as she'd told us a couple weeks beforehand. I missed my daughter's immediate reaction, but being the older one and having a greater understanding than my son, she appeared excited by the news. My son smiled and said, "I didn't know you had a baby inside you!" before resuming his burger. We put the kids to bed and stayed up playing cards in the garden and drank quite a lot. It was an enjoyable evening and a great way to let off steam after my first week's introduction to custody.

The next day, I travelled to meet a friend of mine for yet more drinking. He's on a career break from the police, though recently had a call from a Superintendant to discuss his future and opted not to return but rather continue his current business venture. In a week or so, he'll change from being 'inactive' to 'resigned'. It's a brave move for anyone to take and I respect him for having the courage to pursue other aspirations.

Many have become frustrated with the job over recent years, due to the current government constantly cutting budgets and being critical over things such as stop searches and crime classification. Some have fallen out of love with the police and no longer see it as a viable career choice. I still love the police and enjoy the work, but do share many of the frustrations felt. I still see it as a career but hope the public will support us and declare enough is enough in terms of cuts. We are limited in terms of what we can do to make a stand. We cannot strike (I would not choose to do so anyway, personally). Some take to social media to complain. They normally end up with written warnings. We just tend to grin and bear it. We make it work. Somehow. Just about. But for how much longer? As horrid as the recent terror attacks have been, they have resulted in some amazing support from the public and have highlighted that we need the same level of support from the government in order to be able to respond to these threats adequately. The MET (and GMP) have shown they can respond quickly and efficiently to such attacks but how would other forces cope? With just as much courage, dignity and compassion no doubt, but perhaps not so quickly or effectively, I would suggest. Purely down to resources.

For the remainder of my rest days I mostly drank a lot of cider, taking full advantage of the glorious sunshine by mostly only wearing shorts and staying inside playing GTA5.

Chapter Two – Flying Solo

So I was cut loose. I formed this weird mental attitude where I knew I'd be doing my best and hopefully well enough to get by, but wondered how the job thought it acceptable to dump people in the deep end at such an early stage?! With *these* kind of risks? Custody's the sort of role that you cannot master overnight. Other skippers have told me that it'll take at least six months to feel comfortable. Others said longer. I've still got an incredible amount to learn. My main concern is that from this point forward, I'll learn from mistakes, some of which may result in complaints. Complaints about PACE breaches. Such complaints are likely to result in at least operational advice from an Inspector. Surely that is an unfair way to learn?

Before the force started cutting back on a massive scale, we had custody suites in most stations. I've only been in eleven years but when I started this was the case. Hell, I even still had a bar at the station where I worked, albeit, that went after a few months. There's nothing more bizarre than being sat in a police station, trying to write up your day's jobs, with the smell of beer wafting down the corridor. I cannot imagine that sort of thing happening today. Things have changed *that* much in so little time.

Back when you had custody suites at every station, being dumped in at the deep end was the norm. Many of those suites only had a small number of cells. Mine had about five or six. There was only one custody sergeant and one detention officer for such a suite. Hell, even the twelve cell suite down the road had the same staffing.

I cannot imagine what it must have been like learning in that environment. Being the only Sergeant there. Unable to learn from watching others work. Having to literally wing it yourself. Okay, there was a telephone and I've heard people quite often phoned up other Sergeants for advice. But the phone would not always be answered. And sometimes you need to know the answer on the spot, as things move fast there.

And how would such suites have coped with so few staff? Well, there were custody suites left, right and centre, that's how. There'd be occasions where one suite was full and the one down the road empty, but on the whole, demand at each suite was far less than at current suites, due to being able to count the total number of todays on one hand.

So even though my shifts have so far proved to be busy, with little or no time to eat, I should at least be grateful that I have other Sergeants present I can learn from and go to for advice. On my first day back, I was back with my mentor. Purely as they'd been shown on duties as covering a shortfall in DOs. Normally, they'd move a DO from another site, but as is everywhere in policing, teams are running with little or no room for last minute sickness, courses, compassionate, or emergency leave.

As such, I had an experienced Sergeant at my side once more, to whom I could ask questions as and when I needed. The outgoing night shift handed over loads of prisoners. The stand-outs on my board were two in for conspiracy to murder. Whilst this sounded daunting, there was really very little for me to do with regards those prisoners. In fact, the only involvement I had with them was checking they were alive at the start of my duty. Oh, and helping the boss with language line when he needed to review ones detention.

I booked in more than we got rid of, so handed over more prisoners to lates than we walked into. Once again, I didn't have opportunity to take a meal break. The only time there was a lull was around nine in the morning and that's too early to eat lunch. And when I say 'lull', it seemed like an eternity but was probably only around twenty minutes, but such pauses in demand are heaven, I have already realised. They give you time to breathe. And use the loo in my case.

The next day I was flying solo. I know on my last night shift I was with a DO, but my mentor was still present in the block somewhere. On this occasion, he was on a training day elsewhere. This was me, with a DO, with no mentor in sight. Two other Sergeants present in the block, mind, and yes, I would go to them for advice on several occasions. I would rather that than make a huge error that resulted in heavy comeback. I'm a great believer in asking questions when unsure, provided you learn and don't repeat the same questions in future. There's nothing worse than when people do that to me and it grips my shit.

I felt that, on the whole, the day went pretty successfully. My DO was fantastic. I don't think she has long in the job herself, but she knew exactly what she was doing and when we had that 'lull', she didn't pull out her mobile and start browsing Facebook (not intended as a sexist remark – I actually think blokes are worse for this than ladies in the police anyway, the current favourite being to show off the latest Ozzyman review), she played catch-up with fingerprints and DNA swabs. And nights had left a whole lot of them for us to do. We worked well together and for the first time, I felt a slight feeling of confidence in what I was doing.

The main stress for me that shift was a gentleman from London who'd been arrested for damaging items in an amusement arcade, followed by a car, followed by accusing people in a local pub that they'd killed his mother, followed by damaging the till in said pub. Oh and apparently he was seen with a knife too.

Nights had said he was extremely demanding. When I did my 'alive and well' check, he would not stop speaking. In fact, I had a bit of a shock as I looked through the spy hole to check where he was before lowering the hatch and he was literally right there in front of me. Freaky. I managed to excuse myself without feeling I was being too rude (a skill I will need to master in custody), only to be called back by a DO an hour later when he was banging the hell out of the cell door requesting to speak to a Sergeant.

I spoke to him through the hatch and first off, requested he remove the cardboard from the CCTV camera, which he did (nights had marked him as 'leave no cups in cell', indicating this had been a running theme). He showed me his knuckle, which was swollen. He complained that he'd mentioned this several times and we had done nothing for him. I kept offering to get a doctor to see it but he talked over me. A DO went and found the onsite doctor and he examined it. He was satisfied it wasn't broken and the chap seemed to settle somewhat. Crisis averted. The next time I had dealings with him was reissuing his rights and he had chilled right out. He arrived in front of me panting and I was told he'd been jogging in the exercise yard. Whatever keeps these people calm is good by me.

During the shift, the Inspector called a team meeting and we were reminded that wherever possible, we need to ensure we took meal breaks. During the meeting, two or three prisoners arrived in the holding cell. I was then non-stop for the remainder of the shift and for the second day in a row, took my lunch home with me.

Lates were a bit of an oddity. On the first late, I was a DO. We'd dropped below MSL (minimum staffing levels), so as we had four Sergeants, one of us was selected by duties to cover the shortfall. It had been years since I'd done a duty as DO, so it was a useful refresher in logging prisoner property on the system. These DO cover duties used to be commonplace when I started as a PC but are unheard of nowadays. I am told custody Sergeants quite often cover this now. Best paid DO I was, yet I wasn't able to take fingerprints, not having received my password yet for the machine.

It was Friday and our late shift ran from 1400 to 2345hrs. There were quite a few prisoners to book in initially but then we experienced a bit of a lull around 1700hrs, which was when the response officers hand over from days to what is known as a lates plus. Friday and Saturdays are busier for police officers, thanks to one thing. Alcohol. To cover the increased demand of people getting pissed those evenings, late shifts for response are adjusted, meaning they work 1700 to 0300hrs. Nobody wants to be late off on Friday or Saturday days, and so unless it simply cannot be helped, very few arrests are made leading up to 1700hrs.

It picked up again a bit after that, once lates had started. Despite being told there were no bail returns that evening, we had a call through that someone was in the front office returning on bail. I could see no record of this on the computer, so went out front to clarify. The young lad wasn't actually returning on bail, but was attending to sign a community resolution for his involvement in a TWOC (taking a vehicle without the owner's consent). The OIC was supposed was be present to sort this but didn't realise, so I agreed to sort on their behalf.

I soon became fed up of flitting from the front office to custody and remembered the bail clinic lead directly to the front office. From custody, there's a door that leads to a waiting area in the bail clinic. From there, is another door leading directly into the front office. I got myself into the waiting area and then realised none of my keys opened the other door. I therefore turned to go back the way I came, only to realise none of the keys would open that door. Fuck. I looked around the counter for a buzzer. There was none. Realising my predicament would likely result in ridicule, I tried the keys one last time in both doors. No joy. I therefore banged the glass of the counter to attract someone's attention. However, the glass was thick and my hard bangs returned dull thuds. I then saw a CCTV camera in the corner. I bet someone is watching me, I thought. I bet someone is watching me and is gathering a small crowd to enjoy watching the new incompetent custody Sergeant having got himself locked in a small room. I formed a mental picture of them all sat round the screen sharing popcorn, laughing. Bollocks. I started shouting under the counter and a passing DO caught me in the corner of their eye and rescued me. I'm not aware that he has told anyone yet and am grateful for this! I sorted the paperwork out for the OIC and they were grateful.

There was then an unusual lull again. My colleague noted that it had been an hour and eleven minutes since our last prisoner and literally as he finished delivering those words, I heard the rear gate clang and two officers dragged a prisoner into the holding cell. The prisoner was screaming and shouting and being generally unpleasant. Lovely.

We were unable to complete the risk assessment or rights with this chap, as he was extremely drunk, unable to understand the process and also threatening violence towards officers. Route One it was then. Route One is the term used when a prisoner needs to be taken straight to their cell, without the usual booking in process being completed.

The arresting officer and their female colleague escorted the prisoner to their cell, followed by myself, the other Sergeant and a DO. As soon as the officers got the DP into their cell, he started violently resisting and had to be taken to the ground in a controlled fashion, so he could be searched safely, minimising risk of harm to officers and the DP themselves. The DP had been handcuffed to his front, which didn't help the situation, meaning we were unable to hold his arms behind his back.

As the DO that day, this was my responsibility. The others present held the DP down, whilst I started searching him as best I could under these conditions. I needed to check whether the DP had a cord in his trousers, as if so, replacement custody clothing would have to be provided and we'd have to wrestle these from him. I hate using this term, due to its sexual connotations, but I *reached around* and upon examining the top of his trousers, realised that his entire ballsack and penis had somehow escaped his trousers and were dangling loose. The female officer blushed, looking awkwardly at her colleague. I could tell she was considering leaving, no doubt feeling it inappropriate she should remain present with such a spectacle ongoing, however, fortunately she realised that holding the DP's legs to prevent me from being kicked was the better way forward.

The DP did have a cord but it was sown in and only appeared to be a short one for show, as opposed to serving a useful purpose. We therefore left the cell one by one, the last person holding the DP's arms behind his back and then making a run for the door, before the DP could get to his feet and offer them any violence.

Bang, bang, bang, bang, bang, bang, bang.

The first of that night's noisy prisoners was secure. The DP was put on level three, thirties (L3 30s) by the Sergeant responsible for him. This meant that he'd have to be physically checked by a DO every half hour, but that in addition to this, someone would have to constantly monitor a CCTV screen to ensure the DP wasn't harming himself. The arresting officer was told to do this. "But I need to go and gather the evidence", was their response. Now, I do feel for response officers in this situation and have only recently ceased being one myself. But now I have a greater awareness of the risks associated with custody, I knew the response this would bring from my colleague. The officer was (politely) shot down.

And for good reason. I was busy doing something else a few minutes later, when officers rushed to the cell upon seeing the DP on CCTV trying to rip out the lip piercing I didn't realise he had. In my defence, when we were restraining him on the cell floor, he was face down. Not being Clark Kent, I was therefore unable to see through his head and hadn't seen it earlier as he was Route One-d fairly quickly.

I am told that a taser was drawn but the Sergeant intervened and asked the officer to holster this, keen to avoid the situation getting out of hand. The chap's issues were likely mental health related and upon being told that he could actually retain the piercing, he calmed. Why he had therefore tried to rip it from his lip is beyond me.

Bang, bang, bang, bang, bang, bang, bang.

But no more lip piercing ripping, fortunately.

Handover to nights drew nearer and whilst my colleague handed over, I remained on my own, booking another in and covering DO. The prisoner was heavily intoxicated but compliant and I was pleased with how it went and felt that my new skills were starting to become more natural.

I spent the following late shift at another custody block. This happens occasionally, to cover sickness and other abstractions. Upon receiving the email from duties, some Sergeants set about trying to find someone to swap with, some being keener than others to work elsewhere. I didn't mind the prospect of working elsewhere, realising there was no escaping it and it'd be useful to get such a shift under my belt early on, rather than way down the road.

I received a handover from two Sergeants that'd been on my course. It was nice seeing them, albeit briefly, as they'd clearly had a busy day and were rushed off their feet. My late shift was less rushed. They had a completely different way of working there. This was a nice modern suite, better laid out, better grub for the prisoners (contentious), and a stapler on every desk.

Here, the DOs do the booking in and also the actual issuing of disposals. Sergeants hover over the desk initially, to authorise detention. They then review the risks identified and set a care plan for the detainee based on those risks. Such a care plan will include deciding how often a detainee must be checked in their cell, whether they need to be roused, whether there is a need for an officer to remain on constant observations of them, whether CCTV would be beneficial...the list of considerations goes on.

The theory appears to be that sergeants can then give more time towards reviewing jobs and deciding on the appropriate disposal. During my shift there, I was asked which way of working I preferred. I reserved judgment for now, not having even completed two full sets yet. I did comment on the layout of the block though and prefer this to where I work. It is more spacious and you seem to get bothered less, meaning you can concentrate more on the task in hand. Which is always nice.

With regards to the better grub for prisoners, there is a canteen at the nick that services officers and staff but also the custody block's residents. One prisoner complained he was not provided any ketchup with his freshly-cooked battered chicken. To be fair, his critique was well balanced. He was happy with how crunchy the chips were. And they were nice. The canteen sent some extras down for custody staff.

Nights were the busiest shifts I've done so far. A Sunday and Monday. What the heck was that all about?

Like, *seriously* busy. There were only two Sergeants on.

Before the first night shift, I was watching tv with the wife and received a text from someone on my old response shift, asking me to hurry up and get into work, as there was a queue of eight at the back door, four of which were immigration prisoners. So much for trying to chill before work.

I arrived at work and sure enough, the back yard was packed full of vans and officers spilling out of the holding cell, all desperately looking around, trying to sus out who was there before them to ensure there was no queue jumping.

After handover, I did my checks to ensure all my prisoners were alive and well. I then set about putting a log on each prisoner's custody record, formerly taking over responsibility for them. I had not even got half way through my list when I was already being bothered by officers keen to update me on their interviews. I politely asked them to wait outside but could feel their eyes burning into the back of my head as I continued typing my logs.

It became clear that there were a number of prisoners who needed releasing. My colleague started processing the incoming prisoners, whilst I started booting some out. The first of these was there for a serious sexual offence. They were a first timer in custody. His pre-release risk assessment would have to be good. These are essentially done to cover one's arse, should a prisoner be released and go kill themselves. You have to ask yourself before someone is released whether you think they're likely to go and kill themselves. Now, I don't know about you, but I'm not a psychic. Unless someone tells me that they are going to kill themselves, I have to guess. But my guess is based on information available in their initial risk assessment, any comments handed over from custody staff and how the prisoner presents and answers questions during their pre-release risk assessment. Should someone say they are likely to go and top themselves, we would seek to keep them in for a mental health assessment, even if it meant breaching PACE to do so. As organisationally, and personally, we prefer to be criticised for doing something unlawful than being responsible for someone's death. Fortunately for me, as this was a serious sexual offence, the OIC confirmed they'd already done a very in-depth RA with him post interview. I still did mine, but the fact theirs didn't raise significant concerns made me feel better about releasing this one.

Once I booted a couple out, I started booking in and there was a constant flow of prisoners in the holding cell until three in the morning. Time to breathe at last. More came in but having that slight pause felt so good.

Surely the second night wouldn't be as busy? Well, it was busier to start with, that's for sure. Not quite eight queuing, but close. I started off accepting back three suspected transient drug dealers, all juveniles, who'd previously had their detention authorised by lates, only to be sent straight up to hospital suspected to have swallowed or otherwise concealed drugs.

None of their RAs had been completed, and so apart from authorising their detention, everything else needed to be done. Which, I am told, is a bit of an arse as far as figures are concerned, as I did all the work but get none of the credit. But that's fine by me, as I refuse to play the figures game.
None of these three caused me any trouble and were well behaved. But the x-ray result on one was inconclusive, meaning they could not rule out rectal concealment. I therefore authorised a strip search, which had to be ratified by an Inspector, given the DP's age. This was negative. However, as concealment could still not be ruled out, the doctor in custody screened them and directed they should remain on 'poo watch' for the remainder of their stay. Basically, this meant two officers would have to remain on close proximity observations of the prisoner and should he go number two, one would have to watch him take the shit, whilst the other would have to sift through any turds laid. Such pleasant jobs land you an extra fifty quid bonus payment. I'd be happier without, personally.
Just as we thought we were about to clear the queue, rumour spread there were seven DPs on route. Great.
The rumour was true. Traffic had nicked seven juveniles, following an incident where a stolen vehicle failed to stop and crashed. It became official...I was running a kindergarten.
"Would you like anyone notified of your arrest?" I would ask. "My mum", they would reply. Could I get hold of half their mothers? Could I fuck. Which was, no doubt, the reason these twelve to fifteen year olds were out stealing cars in the middle of the night. The parents literally had no idea where they were. Or likely had any care either. It was well past their bedtimes and fortunately, they seemed to realise this and all went to sleep fairly quickly, meaning the block was quieter than I'd feared.
Once the days nursery workers had arrived, I was out of there, completely knackered.

Rest days mostly consisted of the same old things, except for Bosch, which I am now up to date with, having finished it earlier in the set.

I say *mostly*, as on one of my rest days I accompanied my daughter to a sporting event, whereby the best schools in the county compete against one another at a variety of sports. My daughter's school had entered the annual competition for the first time and represented the most sports there. They had basketball, tri-golf (don't ask, I've no idea) and swimming teams. My daughter was in the swimming team.

I'd paid for her place on the coach and then managed to blag myself a spot too. With this free seat came a condition. I would be a 'parent helper' for the day. Fine, I thought.

Cue hilarious tales of children winding me up no end, losing one or two along the way...? Actually, not at all. They were all weirdly well behaved and there was very little for me to do responsibility-wise. Occasionally, both teachers would wonder off and say, "You're in charge now", leaving several bemused children staring up at me, waiting for some form of instruction or merely sussing me out to see what they would likely get away with. I went for the 'crazy-eye' approach, which seemed to scare the kids into obedience. This worked for me.

My daughter came first in her front crawl-with-float and 'mushroom float' events. Her team came second and third in their relays, though she powered through *her* lengths. I was extremely proud of her and now I've seen her up against others in competition, I realise what an excellent swimmer she is. I had my suspicions from swimming lessons, but this put any biased parent doubts to rest. I did my embarrassing dad bit, shouting her name as loud as I could and was asking her for the other kid's names so I could support them in equally yobbish fashion.

Her school came seventh out of nine schools overall at swimming, meaning, sadly, she didn't get any medals, as they were done for overall 1/2/3 places only. Seventh out of all the schools in the county was a more accurate way of looking at it and it was quite an achievement for a school entering their first such competition, and which, unlike many of the others present, does not have its own swimming pool or squad.

I thoroughly enjoyed the day and it was great to see schools embracing a variety of sports. I went to a private school at my daughter's age, and whilst I hated many things about that experience, daily sport was a definite positive. Sports are too often overlooked in schools and I'm pleased my daughter's school appears to have finally caught on and hope this continues.

I finished the rest days with an impromptu barbeque at home, taking full advantage of a surprisingly nice hot evening.

Chapter Three – Insomnia

Well, that's a bit of an exaggeration. I don't *really* suffer from insomnia. The dictionary defines insomnia as 'habitual sleeplessness; inability to sleep'. I can sleep but find it extremely difficult on occasions. Some nights I lay there, staring at the ceiling, absolutely knackered but unable to get to sleep. I check the clock regularly and watch my opportunity for sleep reduce by the hour. This normally happens before day shifts, as I get up around 0500hrs and cannot go to sleep generally before 2200hrs, so because there is a smaller window for sleep on those nights, I feel more pressure to go to sleep, which does not help the situation. Other times it's because I have something important the next day and cannot switch off my mind. The night before my response car course I got two hours sleep. I was climbing the walls, going insane. I was so tired that morning, I produced an awful practice drive but somehow managed to pull it out the bag when it mattered.

I envy people who can sleep easily. Those people tend to have a knack for napping. I cannot nap. Never have been able to. Colleagues often say how they enjoyed a quick nap before a night shift. I don't bother trying anymore. Whenever I do, it never works and I just end up feeling more tired than I did before.

My wife gave me her old watch on my last rest day. It's one of those smart ones that helps you keep track of your fitness. Her battery life had reduced to *only* two to three days from around five to six, prompting her to complain and get sent a replacement. I therefore got the old one, which still worked perfectly, just needed charging slightly more often.

I try and write this book as I go along, after every couple of shifts. I've slipped slightly this set, in that I've now done days and one late. Being so tired, I'm struggling to remember what I did each day and there's a danger they all merge into one if I leave it too long.

Looking back over the last four nights, the app on my phone (that links to the watch) tells me I got 6hrs 25mins sleep before the first day shift, 5hrs 55 before the second, 7hrs 16 before the first late shift and last night (before my upcoming second late) I got 6hrs 24. The kids woke me up this morning and I never got back to sleep. Very frustrating but it's a fact of life that kids don't have a volume switch.

We have to start days at 0630hrs. This gives nights enough time to handover so they can be off by 0700. Anything over 0700 would incur overtime, being the first rest day and therefore the Queen doesn't get her free half hour. The job clearly doesn't want that extra cost. This is no doubt the real reason it's done this way. I used to start at 0700 on response and was always in half an hour early anyway, so it makes little difference to me, and means I can leave earlier in the afternoon.

I was in around 0620hrs and two of the other Sergeants were already in and noting down the prisoners. There were four Sergeants on duty. Two of us therefore concentrated on binning remands to Saturday morning court and sorting disposals the remainder of the day. Getting my head round disposals is good practice. I didn't mind that. Picking up the pieces to rush people off to remand court *did* bother me. On weekdays, files are sent electronically. On weekends, we still need the paper files from the OIC. I checked through one to find there was only a prosecutor copy. There is supposed to be a copy for the defence too, containing less forms, as some are not disclosable. I therefore had a photocopying exercise to do first off.

There were also people in for breaching bail conditions that had not yet had the information laid. 'Information laid' is the term given to breach of bails that would normally be referred to as 'charge wording', only breach of bail is not a charge as such. Nor had the breach wording been added to the custody record, meaning I had to pick the bones out of each job and work out exactly what condition they had breached and how. This takes time. Time that I didn't have. The knock on effect meant DOs were releasing prisoners to the courts without me considering their pre-release risk assessments. I gather there's a process whereby DOs will do these RAs if they are low risk, but I'd have liked to have had the opportunity to review them myself. But there was simply not enough time to do so. I am left hoping this does not come back to bite me in the arse should one of them decide to harm themselves following release. Not having had enough time would no doubt not wash with PSD (professional standards department).

On the second day shift, I saw one of the prisoners was still in, who I'd sent to CPS the day before. I had reviewed a job where a local drunk had gone into several charity shops and masturbated in the changing area, leaving the curtain open. He'd been arrested outside for all the exposures and gobbed off, leading to a further arrest for a public order offence.

The jobs were largely not up together in terms of evidence. There were key statements outstanding on the majority. This chap was clearly a danger to society and even his behaviour towards female custody staff was concerning. I was told how he had reached out with his foot towards one female DO as she checked him. A female custody sergeant told us how she completed her initial check on him at the start of her duty, only to find out he'd gone straight to the toilet afterwards to knock one out.

Fortunately, there was a key statement on one of the jobs, evidencing not only the indecent act, but having witnessed the same person get arrested outside a short time later. Another staff member had yet to be statemented but we knew roughly what they'd say and their statement was achievable in a reasonable period of time, ie, over that weekend.

I had therefore directed the OIC to send the job to CPS for charging advice on the Threshold Test (THT). I have previously explained the Full Code Test (FCT). I see the THT as being halfway to the FCT. The THT requires certain things. It still needs to be in the public interest to prosecute. You need to believe that the outstanding evidence can be obtained within a reasonable period of time and that it will bring the case to the FCT. You need to suspect the offender has committed the offence. And the THT can only apply to cases where the suspect has denied an imprisonable offence (including a 'no comment' interview). Most importantly, if you are sending a job to CPS on the THT you should be seeking to remand the prisoner. Otherwise, they would argue that you should simply release the chap under investigation (RUI) for those further enquiries to be completed, with CPS advice sought slow-time. It should be noted that some jobs that do meet the FCT have to be sent to CPS for a charging decision anyway. Such jobs include anything domestic violence or hate crime related. There are also specific offences such as ABH/GBH, terrorism offences and anything involving a death. There are others too and I have a list somewhere to help me!

I read the job and saw CPS had agreed to charge with one offence of exposure and the public order offence. I wrote 'pubic' in error just now, correcting my mistake, then realised 'pubic' was actually rather apt here. CPS had also supported the decision to remand.

The day shift was steady but not over demanding. I was booking in, with the odd disposal in-between.

I was back with my mentor for the first late shift. We had five custody Sergeants on duty. *Five!* Unheard of. They acted as my DO but did the occasional disposal too whilst I was reviewing jobs. The 'spare' Sergeants were on disposals, but whenever they were hit with a couple at once, they sent OICs back to me, meaning I then had to concentrate on them rather than booking anyone in. Fortunately, we were very Q in terms of DPs arriving that afternoon, so this mattered not.

I reviewed a job involving a female who'd been nicked D&D at a local hospital and subsequently nicked for two assaults she was outstanding for. I was told on handover she arrived during the night bound by limb restraints to a wheelchair. She was not disabled, fortunately. Someone would have had some *serious* decision making to record there. She was in fact *so* intoxicated that they needed to use the wheelchair to get her into custody. It appears she was also likely lashing out, hence the limb restraints (made out of extremely strong Velcro).

I was able to make a charging decision on the D&D and one of the assaults. The other assault was DV related and so needed sending to CPS. My understanding, as was that of the other Sergeants, was that all the jobs would therefore need to be sent to CPS. The Director's guidance on charging (5th edition May 2013) acts as an aid for police officers and prosecutors to determine when and how CPS advice should be sought. It makes reference to 'in a case where any offences under consideration for charging include an offence which must be referred to a prosecutor under this Guidance then all related offences in the case will be referred to a prosecutor to consider which should be charged'.

The key word here is *'related'*. The D&D and other assault were not *related* to the DV assault, other than it was the same DP and she was under arrest for all three at the same time.

However, we were under the belief that all three should be referred and that *related* simply meant they related to the same DP. The OIC came back a short time later, saying the prosecutor refused to provide advice, as only the DV case should have been referred. We quoted the guidance as we understood it and sent them away. They returned, very distraught, saying the second prosecutor had said the same thing. I was not prepared to mess about any longer and said I'd charge the other two myself and sent them away to get advice only on the DV matter.

The advice came back just before handover to nights, authorising a charge. I remanded the DP, as she was under a suspended sentence for GBH-ing the same DV victim a few months earlier. Her offending history was poor and she had markers for offending on bail. On top of all this, she was homeless and an alcoholic. She made no representations to me about the remand decision, but did express her annoyance, being her birthday the following day. She would be celebrating this waking up in a police cell and being transferred to court. Happy Birthday! The DCID evidence review officer (ERO) saw me afterwards and said he shared our interpretation of the guidance and said he'd email the Chief Inspector to seek their views on the matter. I await the outcome of this.

Once again, I have let things slip. Four more shifts have now passed. I made notes on my phone to help me remember what happened each day.

The second late shift was bonkers. Absolutely banzai. There were five of us Sergeants on duty. Yet even *that* was not enough. Quite frankly, we would have been completely fucked with only two on. That would have been dangerous. But it happens. Luckily, not on my shift very often, as we are flusher than others.

I had a different Sergeant DO-ing for me this time. She is extremely near to retirement – only a few shifts left. One bloke, Mr Wettimself, was in for breaching a restraining order concerning his neighbour. When he was presented to me by the arresting officer, they told me he had urinated in the holding cell cage. He was obnoxious. Very rude to me. Drunk elderly bloke. "You're going to fucking bang me up. Aren't you sergeant? Aren't you". "Yes, I am", I replied, much to his disliking.

He refused to answer any of my RA questions. He got on slightly better with my colleague, so she took over those, with mixed results. I was able to get him to complete his rights, funnily enough. People usually seem to want those.

Then there was Mr Colostomy. I can't even remember what he was in for. I just remember the unfortunate disgusting smell that came with him. Nope, got it – he was in for shoplifting. I remember him being sat on a chair for the booking in process, as he was hammered. I thought it was drink at first but I gather from the nurse it was opiate-related. I ended up NFA-ing him without interview, as there was no CCTV and the statement from shop staff showed he'd not passed the last point of payment and had offered to pay on being challenged. Indeed, he had sufficient cash on him too. The fact that items had fallen out his pockets into the basket he was carrying was a consideration for pursuing a theft, but given the evidential difficulties, I decided we'd be better off creating an extra cell space, and allowing this chap to get back to his tent.

There was an AA (appropriate adult) cock up. Juveniles and vulnerable adults require an AA to help facilitate communication, to ensure they understand the custody process, from their rights to the questions posed in interview. When people have been in custody before, you can check their last few records to see what came up on past RAs. These may show they previously required an AA. Adults suffering mental health issues such as bipolar or personality disorders, or those with learning difficulties are examples of when an AA may be required.

One of my DPs were interviewed without an AA present. Custody gets so busy sometimes that OICs head down and retrieve prisoners themselves, taking them into interview without your knowledge. They are supposed to check the custody record as to whether an AA is required. Had they done this, there wouldn't have been a cock up. The prisoner they interviewed had been displaying erratic behaviour in custody, causing us to question his mental health. He was seen by our in-custody MH (mental health) liaison, who has access to patient records to research their history and what support may be in place for them. They believed he was of sound mind, however, to be fair to them, it would have been difficult to judge this particular person, as they were Romanian and only spoke Romanian or Italian. The officer on constants spoke some Italian. The Romanian interpreter was also present. There would therefore have been a mix of English, Romanian and Italian going on during the liaison's assessment and no access to the DP's home country records.

Fortunately, this job was going nowhere. The OIC abandoned the interview, explaining the DP's mental health had deteriorated rapidly. The liaison worker therefore called for a full mental health assessment. The DP was on constants the whole time he was in. Initially, this was on close proximity observations, which means an officer sits outside the cell with its door open, staring at the DP. I'm told that before we started our duty, he'd been running out his cell on several occasions, so they had to close the door and revert to constant obs via CCTV monitor. Two officers were utilised, one watching the monitor and one stood outside the cell, in case they needed to get in quickly, dependant on what the DP would attempt to do next. I was being pestered periodically by officers asking if I felt it was still required, assuring me he had calmed. I totally get why officers were keen to get back out on the streets, and indeed I would've been the same on response, however, being as busy as we were, I had to delay assessing the situation several times to concentrate on the more pressing matters of either getting people into custody or getting them out. I was later able to reduce this to just the officer watching the monitor. The chap ended up voluntarily going to a local mental health unit to be further assessed.

Then there was Mr Arrogant, a transient drug dealer from London. Mr Arrogant knew it all. He had no desire to play the game. My risk assessment was of no importance to him. Weirdly, he wasn't even cared about his rights. I pissed him off by still going through each question, like you would during a 'no comment' interview, just so they can't argue later they hadn't been given the chance to answer. Mr Arrogant's response to most questions was "Why don't you just take me to my cell then, innit". He'd been brought to custody, along with two mates, for a Section 23 Misuse of Drugs Act search. The officers had done a roadside search but believed they'd concealed drugs, and so brought them in for a strip search. We provide a cell for this, but have little else to do with that process. No drugs were found but he possessed a large quantity of cash and a phone that constantly rung. In addition, the circs in which he'd been seen was suspicious to say the least. A drug deal was suspected to have occurred. A knife was found in the car the DP was in. He was arrested after the search on suspicion of being concerned in the supply of a class A drug, possession of criminal property and possession of an offensive weapon. Mr Arrogant was fairly confident that he'd be getting released NFA. Mr Arrogant was also wanted on warrant for failing to appear at court. It seemed Mr Arrogant didn't know everything after all and that'd be a nice surprise to wipe clear his smug look later.

Mr Anxious was brought in, following disclosure from his young niece he'd sexually assaulted her a couple years ago. Fortunately, I've forgotten what was alleged. Mr Anxious was extremely quiet, worried, nervous and tearful. Mr Anxious did not deny the allegation once during booking in. He didn't request a solicitor. He'd brought minimal property in and when I asked him to put any property he had on the desk, he produced a pair of boxer shorts and flung them a little closer than I'd have liked, explaining he'd been sleeping between night shifts when arrested. I later asked whether he had a cord in his jogging bottoms (standard stuff, to ensure one has as little chance as possible to hang oneself). He stretched the elasticated waistband out as far as he could forwards, reminding me instantly I'd forgotten he disclosed he was wearing no underwear. I caught sight of his flaccid penis and returned to my desk. I decided to recheck the cord situation once he'd put boxers on.

Mr Perv was in for a few sexual assaults - it appears he feels the need to run up to women and smack them on the arse. For good measure, Mr Perv had also attempted to rob people, threatening them with a knife. Mr Perv was in good spirits and having a whale of a time in custody. Mr Perv was no trace on PNC (the Police National Computer database), indicating he'd never been arrested before. He'd certainly chosen a serious set of offences to pop his cherry. Mr Perv was picked out by all victims in the photographic identification procedure. It was nice knowing you, Mr Perv. Enjoy prison.

Dinner was not meant to be. But then I've got used to that already. However, there were cakes. And *really* awesome ones too. It was the birthday of a colleague and they'd chosen to celebrate by working this truly horrific shift. The amazingly delicious millionaire shortbread was literally the sweetest thing about that day.

I got 7hrs38 sleep before my first night shift, according to my wrist gadget. This was only the second time this set I'd broken what I like to refer to as 'the acceptable 7hrs sleep'. Anything under seven is a disaster, anything over acceptable. Over eight hours is brill. Most of this set was a disaster, sleep-wise.

I got a few jobs done round the house and, of course, played some GTA. I decided a walk to the supermarket would be a good way to rack up much needed steps on my wrist gadget. I then walked to the bus to collect the kids. My daughter saw there was no car with me and said "Aren't we going swimming today then?" Bollocks. It was Wednesday. She swims on Wednesdays. My son complained about the pace of the return walk home, giving his usual go-to "My knees are hurting". This tends to be what he says when he can't be arsed to walk, although the amount of times he uses it does make me worry that he actually has a knee problem and I'm an awful parent.

The half hour swim session gave me time to finish last month's Total Film magazine. My son watched Paw Patrol on his DVD player – a guaranteed way to ensure half hour's silence. I looked up every now and then at the pool to try and catch my daughter's eye to give the illusion I was watching and paying interest. I do enjoy watching her swim and get real pleasure from doing so - watching something you have created do so well is quite special after all. But I don't often get time to read, so this half hour is bliss. Albeit, unbearably sweat-inducing by the pool and in exceptionally hot weather too.

I booked in a couple of people that night. No big deal. There was leftover cake. I took full advantage. I was given advice by a DO and fellow skipper I should try and get in there first and handover my prisoners to days before the other Sergeant did so. They hinted otherwise I'd be there all day, as she tends to go into *a lot* of detail. I took their advice, gave my handover and shot off. I then managed 6hrs43 sleep.

After a cheeky Nandos, I was suitably nourished to get through the second of three nights in custody. It turned out we'd shot off a bit *too* early that morning - our colleague realised after handing over her prisoners she'd been left the remanded ones to hand over too, of which she had no knowledge. I had none either, as it was another Sergeant that'd sorted those. But I felt guilty nonetheless for leaving her in that predicament.

I was on disposals. There were four of us on again, so I had another skipper with me. She'd developed a cold overnight and was coughing and spluttering. A fair amount of sneezing too for good measure. Like a trooper, she explained she preferred not to go sick for colds, as you can muck through them. Whilst I share her work ethic here, it wasn't much consolation, as I felt myself breathing in her germs, wondering how soon it'd be before I too was producing mass amounts of mucus.

I released a chap under investigation for firearms offences, so some in-Force expert could examine various component parts officers had seized and determine whether they were legal. I charged a homeless man D&D. And I sent a case to CPS whereby a nineteen year old living with his elderly grandma damaged property and assaulted her by pushing her.

I'd been told the latter chap was really cocky in interview. He'd never been arrested before and such arrogance makes you more determined to get a job home, to see the look on their face when the realisation dawns this matter will be going to court. Indeed, CPS authorised charges of damage and assault. I was informed by the OIC he'd admitted the damage and assault too, albeit, for the assault he said he pushed nan on the stairs but she over-exaggerated her reaction.

On being charged he made reply admitting the damage but saying the assault never happened. There was a look of complete shock on his face when charged. But his cockiness began to creep back in and he asked "If she decides to drop charges, will I still have to go to court?" I reminded him of his bail conditions and that he was not permitted to contact her directly or indirectly, sensing he was already planning his way out by 'encouraging' her to drop the complaint. I informed him we'd likely still pursue a victimless prosecution, given we still had statements detailing the assault and his admissions. He asked "What if they admit what they said never happened?" This guy did not give up. He was a nineteen year old car salesman, driving a brand new BMW or Audi. Typical car salesman. "I'm not interested in buying your car, thank you". "But we can offer interest free credit..." Always a comeback.

Being on disposals meant no direct responsibility for the chap brought in for trashing a pub, who staged a 'dirty protest'. A dirty protest is the phrase given when a DP decides the best way of 'getting back' at police is to shit in their hand, throw their shit at the CCTV camera, use it as a pen and write on walls and smear it over themselves to make rousals more disgusting than ever. For good measure, he also urinated under the cell door, leading to a flood of yellow in the corridor outside.

Every now and then I'd pop into the main office where the CCTV monitors were and get live-time updates. There wasn't much to see on CCTV, as he'd done a cracking job of smearing excrement all over the lens, hence why an officer had to also stay outside the cell all night. Every now and then, an officer would lift down the hatch to check the DP was still 'ok' and close it quickly before Mr Hanky was acquainted with their face. I'm told every time the hatch was dropped, poo could be seen hanging off the other side. Quite what brings someone to do this is beyond me. This is far from normal behaviour. I know the guy was pissed but I've been pissed countless times in my life and never once felt the need to behave in such a way. Ok, I've never been arrested. But if I was, I'm pretty sure I wouldn't turn my cell into a coprophiliac paradise. Please don't Google that word at work. Or at all, for that matter.

I managed 5hrs35 sleep before the third night. This had been one knackering set and I was ready for rest days. But they weren't ready for me. I was down to perform the role of DO, to maintain MSL. However, on arrival, it became clear there was a MASSIVE queue of prisoners, spilling out the holding cell into the yard outside. I never counted them but believe there were around six to eight, some had been waiting in excess of three hours.

There were only two other Sergeants on. They asked me to remain as Sergeant, booking in DPs rather than act as DO. Given the backlog, I had no issue with this.

I started booking in without a DO to assist. Much to their annoyance, having been queuing for so long, I used escorting officers to search DPs and log their property. I had to give quick refresher courses to some, where it'd been years since they completed a 'gaoler duty'.

First up was the homeless man nicked D&D. He'd actually been arrested for assault but upon being transported to custody, the officers received update there was no complaint, so they decided to de-arrest and re-arrest D&D. Not ideal, but given the chap was argumentative and aggressive, I got him booked in. After a few hours of sobering up, I binned him NFA. He had extensive previous for theft but nothing for D&D. Being homeless, I decided it highly unlikely he'd have means to pay a £90 fixed penalty notice. I informed him of my decision and he was grateful. I provided him a hot drink and sandwich, before he hit the streets, headed for his tent. It did make me laugh when I retrieved his property, pulling out a wad of notes, remembering I'd booked £183 into his property earlier. No means to pay? Think I missed a trick there. Hey ho, decision already made and given the dodgy circs, probably for the best.

Then there was the nineteen year old girl in for assaulting her boyfriend. She was a timid, pretty young thing, experiencing custody for the first time. In fact, she was completely unknown to police; the officer had to create a computer record for her.

She'd recently given birth and had her first night away from baby. She got home from seeing friends to find her boyfriend missing. Boyfriend then returns drunk, having been done the pub. An argument occurs. She twats him over the head with a plate, causing a gash. There was no complaint from boyfriend but he'd confirmed the assault to officers on BWV (body worn video).

She needed an AA for interview, as disclosed she had a borderline personality disorder. I only realised this after I had released the escorting officer and didn't have opportunity to update them. The officers almost cracked on with interview without the AA. Fortunately, a DO realised and told them. What did then happen is the officers cracked on with interview, but without first bringing the AA and DP to me, so I could complete her rights with AA present. As it was, I couldn't see this being a massive issue, as she'd already opted to accept a solicitor and have someone notified of her arrest, and so this wouldn't have made much difference in the grand scheme of things.

The officer came to me after interview, clearly hoping for an NFA decision, given the lack of support and 'no comment' interview. And it being almost home time. However, she hadn't denied the offence. We still had photographic evidence of injury, corroborating the victim's verbal account. I decided the FCT was met and instructed the officer to seek CPS advice. They got everything set but then received an email from CPS warning of a minimum ninety minute delay. Only the day before I'd been emailed policy in relation to this issue, stating we should try for at least thirty minutes, then hang up and bail, unless seeking a remand. The officer forwarded me CPS' email, stating he was passing it to nights to get the advice. I phoned the nights response sergeant, who didn't have an officer to allocate it to and it was their intention to keep for days. I was not happy to leave for days and decided to treat this the same as the half hour rule. I therefore bailed her for that advice to be obtained.

Then there was the cool-as-a-cucumber GBH man. Little did I know it at the time of booking in, but this chap was believed to have caused some serious injuries. "Injuries consistent with GBH" was all I got given but on reading the job ready for handover, one person was blinded in one eye and another had a bleed on the brain. You'd never have guessed it. He was calm, polite and given all the various mental health conditions on previous custody records, you'd have expected something different. I authorised his clothing be seized, allocated a dry cell and informed the DOs he was 'supervise all'. A dry cell is just as it sounds. No toilet, washing facilities and if they want food or drink, a DO has to remain with them until finished (hence 'supervise all'). This is to preserve forensic evidence, ie, to ensure they don't wash their hands etc.

The fourth and final guy I booked in was a Turkish taxi driver, who had arrived home to find out a neighbour had had a go at his missus. As in, argued with her, not shagged her. They started pushing one another about and he was alleged to have punched the other guy in the face. He spoke basic English, but requested a translator. I knew what to do, having done this before, so it was easy but slowed the process down. I told the escorting officer to tell the other sergeants I'd be out of action for a while. I was aware I was booking in less prisoners than them, but mine all had complications associated with them, and I had no DO support. I therefore didn't feel guilty for taking more time.

It was slightly farcical, as I'd ask this guy a question in English and before the translator had time to repeat it in Turkish, the guy would often answer me in English, having fully understood. I decided to continue, as otherwise he'd no doubt turn around later and claim not to have understood anything and land me in it.

Having binned two of my prisoners throughout the night, and another from lates, I only had two to handover to days. I asked my colleagues if I could go first, keen to get home and have some much needed sleep. Only having two prisoners, I knew them well and felt pleased with the handover I gave. However, the room fell to silence when I was asked whether I had completed the mandatory form for foreign nationals and done other relevant checks such as Immigration. I had not. I should've known to do this, as I've done these before with my mentor but it never once occurred to me. All I could do was apologise and ensure I remember for next time.

On my way out, a DO completing his final check of the night asked me to assist, as he'd just realised a DP still had cords in his shorts and was refusing to hand them over. I entered the cell with the DO and another and this guy was clearly keen to fight. Great. This was all I needed. Absolutely hanging out my arse and about to have a fight for a pair of bloody shorts. We asked him several times nicely. "Fuck off you cunts!" So we fought him for them. Or rather, danced around the cell for a minute or so, with no real coordination or conferring with one another as to what we were trying to achieve. One of the days DOs came in and took a no-nonsense approach in getting him straight on the floor. Worked a treat. Off came the shorts. I left annoyed that my lack of mental alertness had resulted in such a pathetic struggle. It was clear the fully refreshed, just-starting-his-shift DO's decision making was much better than mine at that hour.

After a pathetic 4hrs9 sleep, my rest days finally started. Jumanji was my daughter's movie choice that night. Nutrition came via the wonder of pizza delivery.

I slept 8hrs40 that night. Finally, a brilliant sleep. My wrist gadget awarded me a green star.

The next day, we caught an 1100hrs showing of Spider-Man: Homecoming. Brilliant. Very funny. Do love Michael Keaton. I found the idea of Batman playing the baddie amusing in itself. My son was glued to the screen throughout. When it finished, he said "I want Spiderman toys for my birthday". I knew holding out this long was a good idea. Less than two weeks till his birthday and I finally know what to get him.

Straight after the cinema, we headed to a colleague's barbeque. The weather was perfect for such a thing. Perhaps a little *too* perfect, as sun + lots of alcohol meant that on the drive home, my exhaustion caught up with me, and much to my wife's annoyance, I fell asleep.

We got home and it was time to bath the kids. I needed a dump, so she started the process. However, I then went from the loo to our bedroom and fell asleep on the bed. I woke up when my wrist gadget vibrated, showing a text from the wife basically saying I was taking the piss with how long I was taking on the loo.

I showed my face just as the kids were getting out the bath and offered to sort our son. I then proceeded to fall asleep on his bed as he got himself dried, dressed and read me his bedtime story.

Probably should've gone straight to sleep myself at that point, but the thought of missing out on Sunday night's GTA extravaganza with mates gave me a second wind. However, I had to excuse myself after a couple of hours, as my head began beating hard and I realised my body was failing me. I broke 9 hours that night. Well impressed with that.

The third and last rest day went by very quickly and before I knew it, I'd had 6hrs27 sleep and was back to work again.

Chapter Four - The Take Over

With one of my colleagues retiring this set, I officially take over the two DOs they supervise. During my brief stints as Temp Sergeant, I never really had chance to get my teeth into performance issues, as these often require longer term management. I certainly had my fair share of welfare issues to sort, but the only performance issues I sorted were the sort that required a word-in-the-ear response there and then. Not the longer term development plan kind, as these are usually reviewed after three months and that was about the length of my stints.

Having been promoted straight into custody, I knew I'd only have responsibility for a couple of staff, which is great in terms of workload but bad in terms of developing *myself*. Ideally, I need to master these things by the time I leave custody, otherwise I fear I'll appear very incompetent.

I'm certainly not the sort of person who would do things for the sake of it, just for practice. That would be ethically wrong and unfair on staff. I like to apply a bit of common sense wherever possible. Provided it's in areas the job will allow this. Things such as sickness triggers are fairly rigid in terms of what you must do, supervisory-wise. Once the trigger's reached (in terms of periods of sickness, or amount of days sick), you must arrange a meeting with the officer/member of staff. The same process applies to unsatisfactory performance, though depending on severity, you should've already tried to address that by debriefing incidents as they occur and through regular 1-2-1s. Not just saving the evidence up and hitting them with it all at once.

I was with the outgoing Sergeant the first day back, as their DO, making up MSL. In-between prisoners, we discussed the DOs I was inheriting. All in all, they were both very good, hard working members of staff. Like anyone, each had their own slight issues I needed to be aware of.

One had failed a fitness test and needed to take another. This was due to an injury they sustained whilst training for the test some time beforehand. Since then, they'd been undergoing physiotherapy.

The DO heard back from occupational health, who arranged for them to attend that same day to complete their second attempt. We were short of DOs but this was important, so off he went.

I therefore spent much of that day supervising showers, taking the nurse to cells, taking the drug and alcohol worker to cells...all on a sergeant's wage. I did book in one prisoner myself at handover, so my colleague could handover their prisoners and we weren't keeping the officers waiting too long in the holding cell. The officers looked sheepish as they wheeled in the DP's suitcase of belongings, aware it would require searching thoroughly and items booked into property. The sheepish look turned into one of veiled annoyance when I tasked them with booking the property in. To be fair, I instructed them to go through and only remove valuable items and book the rest in as a job lot, so in reality it wasn't *that* bad.

The following day, I was with the same sergeant again, but roles reversed. I learnt the DO had failed their fitness again. Being the second failure, we therefore checked protocol. Guidance was clear – I needed to hold a meeting with them. They already had training and nutrition advice from the job recently and together with their own physio techniques, they had everything in hand. But I needed to set a development plan, reflecting the need to continue those things, with a view that after three months we review the situation by arranging a further test, by which time hopefully things will have improved and they will pass.

The correct way to arrange such a meeting is to issue a standard-worded letter to the individual, amended to reflect whether it's for attendance or performance issues. The annoying thing is their performance at work is brilliant. They are extremely knowledgeable, calm, polite, helpful...the list goes on. They've been a massive help to me in my first few sets in custody. The letter is worded in such a way that it comes across as a big FUCK YOU. It is supposed to be SUPPORTIVE. It reads like their world has just ended. Now, this chap is pretty chilled. I explained the letter to soften the blow, with extra emphasis on the word 'supportive', aware that someone extremely sensitive may read it and throw a wobbly. They took it well, knew I was only doing what I had to, but, quite rightly in my opinion, expressed their disgust at its wording. And they are right. I could only change the bits in red. Most of it was in black. They were never going to like how it was written. It doesn't take into account individual circumstances and is there to serve one purpose...ultimately, leading the way to UPPs should performance not improve. Or in their case, fitness was their only performance issue and even then, they were able to still get on and do their job as they did before. The fitness test was the only barrier. This was a frustrating situation.

I had to give them five days notice of the meeting, so set it for the first day next set. In the meantime, I need to work out what I'm doing in terms of setting a development plan. I checked the intranet for advice and it said to email HR for assistance. I emailed HR and asked if they perhaps had any examples of similar plans that may assist. I received a response saying they were unable to send me anything and provided me a link to the site I'd already read. I had hoped to write it in such a way the job preferred. A water-tight plan that would stand up to scrutiny if challenged later. I'll just have to blag it.

I'll have a go at that on lates, I thought.

(In Les Dennis voice) "Our survey says...uh-uh".

My first late was relentless. Non-stop all shift. I'd actually started three quarters of an hour early, hoping to get on a computer and start the meeting prep, but none were available. There were 4 sergeants on. Two in the main charge rooms and two of us in the third, doing disposals. There was an endless line of people waiting to enter custody and a constant stream of people needing turfing out. I was under constant pressure to take post-interview updates from OICs but how many can you take before you have to turn them away? I'm no superhuman. I can only deal with one job at a time. I was basically taking one job, working on that...would then take a second and queue that up, and would turn any further ones away, requesting they speak with their own supervisor. When I cleared the first and started the second, I was then able to queue another up. But then turn people away again. And so on.

One of the jobs involved a prolific burglar. I knew the chap from where I used to work and knew anything short of a charge and remand would be heavily scrutinised by the nine o'clock jury. This chap would never last long out of prison. His M.O. was get released and get sent back as soon as possible. Probably spent more time in prison than out. Another H-Plan customer.

There were six jobs on him. None were completely up together, but there were a couple I felt met the FCT, with only trivial bits outstanding. There was a RPOC on those jobs as they stood. One was a dwelling burglary whereby a debit card was stolen and used several times within hours of the break. No evidence linked the DP to the scene, however, he'd been identified from CCTV using the cards within hours of the crime. Due to the 'recent possession' of those cards, I argued there was a case for him to be charged for the burglary itself, as it was unlikely that within that timescale, they would've been passed or sold on to him but rather, more likely, he stole them himself.

The other was a non dwelling burglary, where he'd actually been identified from CCTV within those premises. A much more watertight case.

There was another dwelling burglary similar to the first but not quite as up-together. I believed it would be within a reasonable timescale, so considered that at the THT.

The three other jobs were all circumstantial and based on the suspicion he was solely responsible for the first dwelling burglary. There were several outstanding enquiries on those jobs and this chap had already had one Superintendent extension. I would RUI those offences.

I sent the three others to CPS. The OIC had completed a fantastic summary of each job but in order for me to work out which I was sending to CPS I still needed to know the jobs inside out, as CPS guidance states the custody sergeant should only send those cases that are at FCT (or at THT where seeking remand) for pre-charge advice.

Getting my head round the jobs took time. Time I was being pressured not to spend, by the sheer demand placed on us. But time I realised I must spend nonetheless, and so batted away people. I refuse to do a half-arsed job that will attract criticism and prefer to get (unfair) criticism for turning OICs away. It's not my fault that we are made to work under such conditions and I take pride in doing the best quality job I can, not in achieving high quantity of mediocreness.

Between disposal reviews, I would release DPs who'd had a NFA decision made elsewhere. Once it's been decided to take no further action against a DP, they should be released as soon as possible.

I was working in overdrive – like I'd been doing this for years. I think sheer adrenaline had taken hold of me. I felt my anxiety creeping in. It felt like I had no time to breathe. But I was *so* busy, I had no time to pay much thought to this. I was aware of feeling anxious, but was too busy to focus on that. It cannot be a healthy way to work. I only wonder what long term harm it does to my body or what strain it puts my heart under.

There was a five-hander job, where five teens had been nicked for theft of a motor vehicle. Some for other offences too. None were at FCT and all required RUI. Some of the nippers were the same as the night shift I'd recently worked that felt like running a crèche.

The race was on to bin all five before nights started. The OIC helped by phoning each chap's mother, who attended the station in clockwork precision to collect each DP as I was ready to release them. It was going so well...

...until the fifth little shit. His mother arrived and I sat her in the holding cell, whilst I retrieved her son from his accomodation. I reunited them in the charge room and went through the pre-release risk assessment. I formerly released him under investigation and was about to return his property. But then his poor attitude broke his mother's patience. They argued. Big time. He made it clear he wasn't going home with her. She made it clear she wasn't having him back. She demanded I release her, saying I had no power to keep her there and Social Services would have to take her son. I told her she had parental responsibility and must take him. She refused, looked close to tears, was starting to shake and he was still arguing. I was on my own. I called for a DO and asked they take the teen back to his cell. I tried to reason with his mother, who was not backing down. She would not even provide details of friends or family who may take her son that night. He was a 15 year old chap. Whilst I hear many of you thinking, *sod it, just release him on his own*, I'm a police officer and this is a child in my responsibility. I cannot release him to nobody. If something happened to him after I released him, there goes my pension. That's on me. However tempting it was to do so, I was not satisfied that was the correct thing to do. Yes, his mother should've taken him. But it was crystal clear to me that was *not* going to happen. I quickly went to confer with my more experienced colleagues but both other sergeants were busy. This I would have to sort out on my own.

Mother wanted out. It was as if she was claustrophobic and couldn't stand being in that room any longer. I let her out into the holding area, which is a bigger room but she walked outside. I had hoped that once in the fresh air I could try again to reason with her, but she simply stormed off.

Great. I was now unlawfully holding a teenager in a cell. Breaching PACE. However far from ideal this was, and it was fascicle, I felt I was at least doing so for the right reasons.

I went and discussed with another sergeant, who, funnily enough, was now free. It was if someone was looking down at me, having a laugh at my expense.

They tried phoning the mother, hoping that female-to-female, they may get somewhere. Straight to voicemail. She left a message, encouraging her to make contact.

The DO updated me that her son had provided a number for their aunt, who may have him. I managed to locate said aunt on the computer and phoned her. Landline didn't connect and mobile unanswered. I left a voicemail.

In the meantime, I phoned out-of-hours Social Services. I was fully aware they were unlikely to get involved, but felt I'd little other choice at that stage. I explained the situation to them and they advised a social worker would review shortly and call back soon.

I also called the Force control room, and requested the next available unit assist with attending the aunt's address and see if she could assist. I got the usual, "We have no free units and six jobs outstanding".

I received an update from the control room a short time later, saying they'd managed to get through to the aunt by phone and she could not assist.

I decided to call the nights PACE Inspector. I informed them of this ludicrously embarrassing situation I found myself in. They were great and told me to contact the control room and say they wanted a unit to collect the chap straight away, take him to mum's and if she refused to take him she would be nicked for child abandonment.

I updated the nights custody sergeant, who was happy with this result. I went home, frustrated with how the shift had ended. I could've done without that.

I came into work three quarters of an hour early again and managed to find a computer. I didn't achieve much, but enough to locate some useful information which would get me started.

There were three sergeants on. It was the outgoing sergeant's last day. We delayed handover to see her off. We'd all clubbed in to get some jewellery and booze. She brought in donuts. There were tears (not from me, I'm emotionally stunted). There was laughter. There were memories shared. I thanked her for being patient over the last few weeks and providing me support.

I was in one of the main charge rooms that afternoon. My colleague was under extreme pressure on disposals first thing. I helped bin a few. The other Sergeant receiving prisoners had taken responsibility for a really loud Scottish chap, whose accent was a mix of Scottish, American and only God knows what else. He could be seen on CCTV putting a top round his neck and then, in a Golden Raspberry worthy performance, dramatically falling to the floor (breaking his fall carefully) and then playing dead. I knew it was a performance but suggested we go check. Then, as soon as I said that, clearly uncomfortable, he reached out, grabbed the mattress and placed it under his head before continuing to play dead. We left him like that.

The majority of the afternoon and early evening was steady. It would seem Q enough to start working on the meeting stuff, only for someone to arrive in the holding cell. That was how the day went until it got busy late evening. Once again, it was clear meeting prep would not happen.

One chap landed early evening, very drowsy. He'd taken a clear disliking to the escorting officer and was aggressive towards him. I didn't manage to quite finish the RA Q's or complete any of his rights.

We escorted the DP to his cell and once the escorting officer was out of sight I asked if he wanted any grub. He seemed pleasantly surprised by my kind offer given his behaviour and accepted. I said I would fetch his grub as soon as he completed my Q's. This bargaining worked and he answered the remainder of my questions. Good thing too, as he accounted for his drowsiness by explaining he'd taken lots and lots of pills prior to arrest. I asked what these were and he said diazepam and temazepam. I asked how many and he again slurred "lots".

I got the escorting officers to hang fire and monitor the chap on CCTV whilst I requested a nurse. The nurse didn't even bother seeing the chap and said based on what he said we should transport the DP straight to hospital, as worst case scenario could be fatal. Off he went to hospital. It turned out my colleague's prisoner, who had arrived around the same time, also needed hospital treatment for a gash to his head. He had sprayed blood everywhere and so the cage in the holding cell was out of action, pending a professional clean. There was another brief lull but then four people arrived in quick succession. It's how it goes sometimes. The holding cell will be empty one minute and overflowing the next. The cleaner arrived and sorted the cage out as the prisoners all clustered on the same bench.

I booked in a very polite, softly-spoken young girl accused of domestic assault. She caused me no problems. I had volunteered to take this prisoner when it had been just her out there. Almost immediately after the other sergeant agreed, a vile woman was lead in, screaming and shouting. I was accused of having planned that tactfully. I hadn't – it was pure chance. But I had chosen wisely, for sure. I had to close the charge room door to drown out the noise the other woman was making as she was bundled down the corridor, Route One style.

The next chap I booked in was wanted on recall to prison. They'd been released on licence only a couple of weeks ago but had displayed 'poor behaviour' according to the paperwork, and so were being recalled to serve the remainder of their sentence. Or, more likely, another few weeks until released on licence again. That's my impression of how those things tend to go. He was polite and caused no issues. Result. I handed over to nights and helped bin another prisoner, before logging on a computer out of custody to start my meeting prep. I stayed on late to make a decent start and felt better for doing so. I certainly wasn't going to kick the arse out of this thing for reasons already stated, but wanted to at least know what was needed.

Before my first night shift, it was my lad's soft-play birthday party. He was celebrating his fifth birthday prematurely, as I was keen to get it done before the holidays. I dislike awkward chit-chat with parents I've never met. The event was also poorly organised. Most staff looked under twenty. I was constantly chivvying them along. But my son enjoyed it, which is the main thing, and did quite well present-wise.

My first night began with a prisoner spitting at me. It went nowhere near me, just set the tone for the shift. There were only two Sergeants on. It was a Saturday night. This was always going to be a disaster.

Sure enough, early on, the post-interview updates started flooding in. There was a queue of prisoners at the back door. Myself and my colleague both had around three disposal reviews to complete each. There were other things going on in custody also requiring our attention. This was where the balancing act skill really comes into play.

I informed the Inspector early on of our predicament. He was happy for prisoners to queue outside and wait. I felt sorry for the officers with them, as I was there myself only a few months ago, but there was nothing else I could do.

Before I could even get on with disposals, I was made aware one of my prisoners (linked to one of my colleagues') had been in since 1100hrs that morning and had not even been interviewed. His co-accused had just been and the solicitor was due to represent the other too, but declared a conflict of interest. I was informed another solicitor couldn't be found at that time. They were juveniles, in for about five non-dwelling burglaries. One was 15, the other 17. I released both under investigation there and then. I was too busy to pay it much further thought. My first reaction was it was ridiculous how they had not both been interviewed by this point and it was pointless bedding them down to the morning, as the PACE clock would be close to expiring.

One of the disposal reviews was a domestic assault, whereby the victim had been twatted across both arms by his partner, armed with an oar. There was no complaint and the victim hadn't allowed officers to photograph injuries, but the officer had done a statement describing these and they did appear to be defensive in nature. She had also made admissions on arrest, confirming they'd not been assaulted themselves. In interview, they claimed they'd been hit first and were defending themselves. They said the injuries described were already on her partner's arms, from a charity wrestling match that morning. We had a photograph of the broken oar. At first, I instructed the officers to seek CPS advice, as I believed the FCT met and there to be a RPOC based on the above circumstances. The officers went away, dejected, knowing they would either be off late or nights would not be impressed to inherit this. Then, I had a brainwave. There was a legitimate line of enquiry for days to complete, in re-attending the victim and obtaining details of this wrestling match and seeing if anyone present could confirm whether those injuries pre-existed. As the DP had brought this up, I was sure CPS would want this covered. I bedded her down much to the relief of those officers.

During all this, I had officers coming to find out what the delay was all about. I politely explained the situation and that they needed to be patient. The cheek of it! I get it, but having done this for four sets now I get custody too.

Then there was Mr Angry-NFA man. I read the officer's summary of the job and interview and decided this domestic was going nowhere. I went to get him out his cell and he went through the fucking roof. I genuinely thought this chap was going to assault me. He was super aggressive and how you expect people to be when they arrive, not as they leave. I considered closing the cell door on him but decided it unlikely he would ever calm and, quite frankly, just wanted him out so I could crack on.

He would not stop shouting abuse at me. I calmly carried on with the process, aware of how ridiculous he would come across on the CCTV when his inevitable complaint was investigated. He was one of those people who kept demanding my number. I explained I would write it down for him before he left. In his anger, he tried to storm off and leave without it. I reminded him as he did so, and took satisfaction from the look of annoyance on his face, as he realised his dramatic storm-out was ruined, as obtaining my collar number was more important to him. I had yet to write it down, which annoyed him more. I carefully wrote it down, taking time to ensure neatness, on the NFA letter he'd refused to wait for.

I found the next disposal an interesting one, from a geeky point of view of trying to work out what offence to charge and how best to proceed with bail.

There'd been a public order incident at a school, whereby the drunk offender had attended, hoping to verbally abuse his ex-partner working there. She hadn't arrived for work, so he verbally abused a colleague of hers, witnessed by another. He then went to his ex's address, by which point she *had* left for work, and was alleged to have broken in and stolen items.

In interview, the chap admitted having a go at school staff but denied verbal abuse. He said he did go to his ex's but it was unlocked and the damage described was old. He took the items to cause annoyance and didn't intend to permanently deprive. Indeed, the OIC confirmed he was now living back with the ex and she has the items back and wishes to retract her complaint. I NFA'd the burglary, and considered the public order incident. I read the victim statement. Nowhere in her statement did it detail any upset caused to her, let alone harassment, alarm and distress, which was the key point to that offence. Without being able to show he intended to cause such emotion, I was reliant on the witness statement, which confirmed they were shocked to see such abuse offered. I decided a charge of Section 5 Public Order was most appropriate in the circumstances.

I checked his previous convictions. None since 2016 but that was for witness intimidation and he had been given a prison sentence, suspended for eighteen months. That was still valid. This meant there was every chance he may be sent to prison for committing another offence during that time. I considered refusing bail on the basis I believed a custodial sentence likely, but decided against this, being a minor offence in the grand scheme of things. I bailed, with conditions, not to contact either of the school staff or go to the school itself. I did this given his previous for witness intimidation. I bailed to the not guilty court, given his lack of admission in interview. Considering all that, he took the charge well.

I had now caught up and could start booking in prisoners. Prisoners kept arriving. There was about a twenty minute pause at one point. Enough time to eat leftover pizza from the party. I offered some round in a quick effort to keep the team motivated. It appears most on the team are watching their diet, as I was left to eat most. Which suited me fine.

Then they all started arriving at once again. One chap had been CS'd, as he refused to let police into their house to search for a guy who'd just caused damage nearby. He was arrested for obstruct police. They reversed the van into the rear yard, getting the cage as close to the holding cell as possible. I was expecting a right old melee. Instead, the DP casually walked into the charge room and although cocky, was calm and cooperative.

The guy who had caused the damage was next in. He was more pissed and less cooperative. He played silly buggers and didn't last as long in the charge room. I did have to try extremely hard not to laugh though. It's awful, as he'd been shouting "Oi, fucking Ed Sheeran!" in the holding cell, which seemed odd but then in came the escorting officer with their *very* ginger hair and it became apparent. The DP continued referring to the officer as 'Ed Sheeran' and they did very well to keep their cool. I released them as quickly as I could.

I refused my first prisoner. A lad had been nicked Section 5 Public Order and brought into custody with a suspected broken knuckle. I never even saw the guy, but one of the officers came and saw me for advice. They explained the DP had calmed right down. I said on that basis, given the offence, to transport them to hospital and report for summons. They could pick the bones out of it later. Job done.

We somehow managed to clear all prisoners seconds before handover to days. The cell block was pretty much full. It had been a cracking bit of team work. However, you cannot sustain such stress levels and the job needs to learn, fast. Quite simply, it is not healthy.

I returned to my car, which I'd deliberately not parked under a tree, to find it had been bombed overnight. Tone had been set at the start and this topped things off nicely. Spat at and now shit on.

Thank god the second night was much better. I was DO for the shift, making up MSL. I even found time to finish prep for the meeting.

A drunk DP was brought in for assaulting a random member of public. The escorting officers informed me he had loads of cash and they believed he was a car salesman. Once they'd resumed, I located a knuckleduster in his bag, along with what appeared to be around thirty to forty car keys. I also counted around £2500 cash. No wonder he had the knuckleduster with him but that's a shitload of cash to be carrying around when inebriated.

I put my response skills into action and created a job for the offensive weapon, booked it into property and did a statement.

A DO showed me the shoddy work of a fellow DO from another shift, only half doing the PER forms. These are national standard forms, which follow a DP as they leave our custody to either the courts, jail, immigration and so on. The main purpose of the PER is to ensure any risks associated with that DP are shared. I asked him to show me examples of the poor work and it was clear there were several shortfalls. Apparently something was previously said to the person but there's been no improvement. Another thing for me to monitor.

I got home that morning, emptied my pockets and found a set of custody keys. Bollocks. I phoned in and explained my mishap and that I was too knackered to return. Fortunately, there are several other sets and a mate was working overtime that evening, so I arranged for them to swing by my gaff and collect them. That evening, they did just that, arriving outside my house in the biggest police van possible, leaving none of my neighbours in doubt as to my profession. It would've looked extremely dodgy, as I was in shorts and t-shirt, opened the passenger door myself, and passed them the keys in return for a litre bottle of Jack Daniels. Yes, I'd finally been given my leaving present from my response team!

After that, I went to see War of the Planet of the Apes with my brother. At last, after about nine POTA films, an ape finally throws shit in a human's face.

Chapter Five – Blagging

My next set began early. I'd previously made the stupid but financially sensible decision to stick in for a nights overtime, as custody sergeant, mid rest days. There's generally not much overtime available for sergeants. I used to blag overtime regularly but since the wife joined the job, I've been unable to, given we work opposite one another for childcare reasons. When I'm off, the kids are with me. It's actually a handy way of ensuring that work-life balance. Kids do have a detrimental effect on your bank balance though, so it's nice to top it up on occasion with some ovies. Especially when there's a holiday booked...
I've actually got a couple of shifts booked in with response too. I went through the overtime spreadsheet and it was all 'PC required for this' and 'PC require for that'. Nothing for skippers. Rankist bastards.
I went through and found a couple of PC shifts that fall on my rest days. I had a look at my old nick on the duties page and saw that on both those dates, they were reliant on a PC covering the Acting Sergeant role. I stuck a cheeky email in, suggesting they give me the overtime as skipper and the APS could revert back, thus creating that extra PC they needed. They bit my hand off! So I have two of those booked over the next month. Probably won't be too popular with the respective Actings but needs must!
When it came to the night's overtime, I was kicking myself. What had I done?! Why was I not at home, enjoying another evening with the Captain (Morgan, not the wife)?
Actually, it was easy money. It certainly didn't look that way when I arrived to see we were pretty full. We were told on handover investigations hadn't had anyone free to interview that afternoon and the response Inspector had essentially stuck his finger up. Very few had been interviewed! Like the situation would get any better on nights!

Sure enough, the nights Inspector caught wind and started binning prisoners that had been in for hours without a single thing done. What a ridiculous state the job has found itself in, that it comes to this!

I booked in a few prisoners that night. Nothing to shout about. I did refuse one, but for very good reason – there was no offence! The officer had stop checked them and believed they'd been told he was wanted on warrant. I checked PNC but the only thing there was a marker to arrest for failing to return on police bail for TWOC. Further evidence needed putting to the DP, following his failure to return on bail. However, he'd since been nicked for something else and the TWOC matter had been dealt with. Not only that, he'd been charged with the TWOC and gone to court. Even the courts had already dealt with it! I informed the officer that someone appeared to have cocked up by not removing the marker. They gave the young chap a lift home to mummy.

In the early hours we caught wind of a fantastic job in the town centre. It was pretty close to where we were and the response officer in me wanted to throw my body armour on and run out. But I was a custody sergeant now, so would have to stay put.

We heard the "one detained"…"two detained"…possibility of a third. Someone suggested it may be one of the usual teens we seem to see in custody regularly. There was some suggestion it was indeed the usual crowd of teens and that once again, we'd be running a crèche. I instructed the DOs to set up the ball pit.

Then the two DPs arrived. "Cancel ball pit", I said, realising the faces on holding room CCTV were not those of teenagers, but rather the weathered faces of heroin-users.

I sent my DP straight to hospital. He had a swollen ankle and nasty cut to finger. I was certain an x-ray would be required and decided not to mess around by booking in first.

There was a last minute prisoner arrival but I left my DO logging them on, whilst I completed handover. Boom! Cha-ching.

After then wasting half my final rest day sleeping, I proceeded to waste that afternoon too by sorting out my wife's flexible working application. I'd had no time to sort this previously.

I was on disposals the first day back. There were three skippers, so I got those DPs remanded ready for court, by completing their pre-release risk assessments and ensuring PER forms were satisfactory.

One DP complained he'd been injured the day before, when officers kitted up in riot gear. He'd completed a dirty protest and needed moving cells but wouldn't do so compliantly. He told me he would not be going anywhere, certainly not court, until his complaint was taken.

He alleged one officer had kneed him in the face, knocking his tooth out. Sure enough, he then showed me a tooth he had in his hand. He slotted it back into a hole in his top gum. He'd already previously had a top tooth knocked out, so now had a massive gap.

We'd already been warned that any delays may result in prisoners not being accepted by the courts, due to staffing issues. I was keen to avoid this chap remaining with us longer, as his dirty protest had apparently come about from being informed he wouldn't make court the previous afternoon. I therefore found an Inspector who attended and took details of his complaint. This kept him sweet and he went to court.

It seemed to be a day for complaints. One DP showed me bruising he sustained on arrest. He reckoned the level of force used hadn't been proportionate. I'd just about convinced him to give it further thought, when on retrieving his property, he saw the state of his phone. It was smashed to shit.

I recalled from handover they mentioned he'd been allowed to retrieve a number from his phone, but refused to give it back, so they had to fight him for it. I'd forgotten they said the DP became *so* angry, that he squeezed his hand tight over the phone, literally crushing it, like Oddjob with that golf ball.
He was also angry to learn cash had allegedly gone missing, and his watch was also damaged. Along came the boss again, to take details. No doubt CCTV would be reviewed and DP invited to see how much of a tit he was being on arrival.
This was also the day of the meeting. I didn't kick the arse out of it, keen to stress this was simply something that I had to do and that otherwise their performance was excellent. Job done. The DO does a cracking job and is well thought of by the team. I've said I'll review in three months by which time I'm seriously hoping he'll have passed, as the procedure following a third fail is one step harsher still.
I took a charge room the next day. Once again, we were almost full. Just one cell free from recollection, but we were officially shut for business. The last remaining cell was reserved for any drink/drivers, or something serious. Neither happened and only one person would get booked in that entire shift, once we reopened early afternoon.
There was a morning lull. There were no quick disposals. Usually there's the odd D&D that can be ticketed or charged and binned. The majority appeared to be domestic assaults. There was a six hander burglary – all juveniles. A few rapes – clearly not something to rush.
The majority of the morning consisted of officers popping their heads in asking if I was free to give rights. Whenever a DP first arrives, one of the important things to cover is their rights. They have the right to have someone notified of their arrest. They have the right to a solicitor, free of charge. And they have the right to read the Codes of Practice – a book that police officers barely understand, let alone criminals.

These rights will be covered with everyone on arrival, unless, for example, they are violent and taken to their cell, or they require urgent medical attention. Even then, they must be completed as soon as possible. Sometimes, rights have to be reissued. Perhaps someone was so drunk on arrival they were unlikely to understand them. Juveniles and vulnerable adults requiring an AA will have their rights reissued, once the AA has arrived.

There seemed to be an endless stream of prisoners requiring reissue of rights. It seemed the majority in custody required an AA.

Late morning therefore saw the usual sudden change in atmosphere. Having been no investigating officers in sight, they all arrived at once, all wanting to use one of the few interview rooms, all wanting to use the same AA that is provided via a scheme for people who have no family member or friend that can perform the role. All wanting the same Duty solicitor...

It goes from Q to C very quickly...the C being chaos.

If I were an investigator, I'd want to get down as quickly as possible and get my interview over with, before the rush. But the cynic in me reckons it's likely people avoid that through fear of being handed another DP to interview. In fairness, their workloads are massive and stress levels high. Some jobs will also have outstanding enquiries they are waiting for response to complete before interview. But the result is definitely chaos for sure.

After handover, I raced home, got changed, headed to Tesco to buy them out of cider and then headed to a mate's for a barbeque in the rain.

When I first arrived, I'd been saved a space in front of the host wife's car. I proceeded to reverse my car back, carefully, and then the wet sole of my shoe slipped on the pedal and I hit her car, causing no damage to hers fortunately but a minor reminder of the faux pas to my rear bumper.

I needed to catch up – others had started drinking at noon. I certainly caught up quick enough, thanks to free reign of a seemingly bottomless keg. One mate disappeared and was found upstairs throwing up in a sink. WHY NOT THE TOILET YOU MORON?! Nobody wants to be washing their face the next morning with bits of half digested burger painted over the enamel.

The host fell through the bottom of his garden chair, ripping the canvas support. Naturally, I tweeted the photos within seconds.

A couple of other guests disappeared and returned with dilated pupils and giggles. I was later told they'd been informed of my profession, and should they wish to indulge in their weed habit, they should do so away from the address, so as not to cause me embarrassment. I'd rather have not known at all, quite frankly, especially as the location of choice had apparently been their vehicle.

I was lates the following day, which provided sufficient time to recover but I was still tired.

I sat with the investigators, as we had the luxury of four sergeants, so I was primed to take disposal reviews post interview.

I took four in quick succession and had to draw the line there, to play catch-up. Once I had, the remainder of the afternoon was a steady stream of reviews, one after the other.

One OIC was running out of time. The DP arrived the previous day around 1900hrs. It was gone 1700hrs and they sought pre-charge advice from CPS for a victimless domestic assault, only to be asked to transcribe the attending officer's body worn video to show why the victim didn't support. They also wanted her contacted to clarify this. By the time they had done so, it was around 1815hrs and they couldn't get through to the same prosecutor, as they'd taken another call. It would take another prosecutor too long to familiarise themselves with the case. I had to make a decision.

A DVPN (domestic violence protection notice) had been authorised in case of NFA decision. However, I released the DP under investigation. Therefore, it was my understanding, and of my more experienced colleagues, that the DVPN could not be served.

I had considered bailing the DP for the advice, with conditions of non contact to the victim. However, as CPS declined to provide advice, wanting the victim re-contacted (yet to be completed), I decided we couldn't be at the FCT and couldn't therefore bail under what is called S37(7A) bail. I therefore considered bailing under new bail legislation, but decided it was not proportionate or necessary to do so – two things it must be in order to satisfy the requirements of new bail legislation (an Inspector also then has to believe this to be the case). I decided it was not proportionate or necessary, as there would be substantive offences such as witness intimidation or harassment we could arrest the DP for, should he return and cause further issues. I therefore released him under investigation. This is the current working practice for the overwhelming majority of cases these days, and they are warned on departure of consequences of interfering with the victim.

I received a phone call from the Superintendent, who had authorised the DVPN. They were clearly not happy with my decision, even questioning my 'mentality'. I kept my cool, explaining my rationale, which they disagreed with. But even they had to concede that ultimately it was my decision, as custody sergeant. This is what I am paid to do – make such decisions. I documented my decision thoroughly. I couldn't see what was exceptional about this case over any of the other thousands that we deal with in a similar fashion.

Of note, the Superintendent did inform me I could still have issued the DVPN, even though the DP was not being NFA'd. This is completely new news to me. I questioned this and he said he would have preferred to have lost it at court the next day than to simply not issue it at all. He said he'd check with the Force solicitor and I requested he email me so I can learn from this, and can share that learning with my colleagues, none of whom believed this to be the case either. Watch this space!

I kept taking reviews right up to and just past handover. I went home, knackered and with mixed feelings. Other than the awkward phone call, it'd been an alright shift. Busy, but quite useful in terms of experience. Just when you think you're doing an alright job, someone comes along and makes you question that. And even more annoyingly, it's someone quite high up the ranks. Someone that, in my view, should be more tactful in how they communicate with officers and staff. Someone that should be more aware of the pressures and stress that people in the organisation are under. Not questioning my 'mentality'. What does that even imply?! That I simply don't give a shit?! Because I do. And to have that questioned does genuinely hurt. Frustrating and annoying.

I woke up the next morning, realising I now had a five year old son. Where had the time gone? I gave him his Spiderman and his Vulture action figures, only to then say he couldn't play with them as he needed to go to school. The wife took both kids to school and I climbed back into bed. I'd taken the late shift off as annual leave. We went out for a meal that evening and I was late to bed playing GTA. It was a fantastic bit of leave usage, missing what I was since told was an extremely busy and stressful shift.

I took a charge room the following night. It was a pleasant surprise to walk in and see around 10 people in custody for a change, if *that*. Prisoners, that is, although to be fair, even 10 DPs outnumbered staff.

I probably booked in around four people that night. We had two sergeants on disposals, so it was a nice change of pace. I caught up with sergeanty paperwork. I made a lever-arch file for custody procedural matters and one for everything else. I'd been keeping bundles of course handouts, certificates, etc in my workbox on response for years. I don't have a workbox in custody, so now was the ideal time to arrange this. Much of it got binned. If I hadn't needed to refer to it thus far, into the confidential waste it went.

Half the people I booked in (sounds better than 'two') were domestic related. Both these were slightly unusual cases, in that an independent witness phoned them in, with the respective victims telling attending officers nothing happened, denying any assault. But in any case, as an assault had been witnessed, the suspect came in, much to their partner's annoyance (or secret relief, as the case may be).

One chap came into the holding cell extremely angry. He was sat on the bench hurling abuse at the arresting officer, demanding to use the toilet. Another sergeant went out and he assured them he'd calm once used. When he'd got what he wanted, he continued with the aggressive behaviour and was placed in the holding room cage until I was ready to accept him.

I went out, opened the cage door and asked the chap whether he was going to be fine with me. He said "I WILL BE FINE WITH YOU, AS LONG AS YOU'RE NOT GOING TO STICK UP FOR THIS CUNT", pointing at the arresting officer. "YOU STICK UP FOR HIM AND YOU'RE A CUNT TOO AND I'LL CAUSE YOU PROBLEMS".

Normally, I wouldn't entertain this and he'd probably have ended up Route One. However, this was a drink driver and I was keen to ensure nothing gave him the opportunity to wriggle out on a technicality. I wanted to give the procedure the best possible chance, so I skirted round his comments and said he'd only have to deal with me, not the officer.

Once circs were given, the officer hid in the corridor, out of sight and I managed to get the risk assessment and most other bits done surprisingly well. Off to the breath procedure he went – 77Ugs being his lowest reading. Whilst in the procedure, the officer returned looking slightly chuffed and explained he'd read the original call log and it turned out the bloke had committed at least one racially aggravated offence prior to the drink driving. Once he was safely in his cell, the officer went to wish him goodnight, further arresting him. The DP took this surprisingly calmly, only giving a thumbs up in response. I think the realisation of losing his licence had dropped its usual bombshell.

I was a DO to make up MSL the following night. I have two more of these next set. Whilst it's pretty awful they utilise a sergeant to do this (from a cost perspective), it's certainly a nice break from the relentless responsibilities of performing the sergeant role. Not that DOs aren't busy – I don't mean that *at all*. It's just nice to mix things up.

I still stepped forward and took a few disposal reviews. I'd decided one chap needed to be NFA'd. He was under the responsibility of the other sergeant, but they were busy and I was available. However, just as I made that decision, two DPs arrived and the sergeant I was working with decided we'd book those in first between the two charge rooms. Once this was done, I then got distracted by arranging a dry cell, sorting the DP's property and other related things. I then got distracted by another skipper informing me there were plenty of out of date sausage rolls up for grabs, in the fridge door (where such items get placed, to ensure poor criminals aren't subjected to them).

I went straight to the kitchen and heated my sausage roll in the industrial strength microwave, nuking it. I ate it, cautiously, at my desk, enjoying every bite of its greasy deliciousness.

I then twiddled my thumbs for a bit and chatted away. We had a laugh about this, a laugh about that. Talked about upcoming holidays and the like...

A bit later on, the other sergeant came in, "I thought you were going to release that bloke?"

Bollocks. One sausage roll distraction and I'd breached PACE. I suggested that next time, we bin the NFA before taking new ones, so it didn't happen again. A similar situation arose later, but as the arriving DP was compliant, I used another desk to release the outgoing one.

Neither of the two DPs I released overnight had money with them, nor did they have bank cards or anyone they could call to collect them (allegedly). Overnight, clearly trains and buses don't run, so people do effectively get stranded, often miles away from where they live.

Response officers used to get called upon to give people lifts home. It was something I always hated doing. Why were we giving these criminals lifts home? Then there was a mindset of if they were charged, they should sort their own travel arrangements. If they were NFA'd, we would give them a lift. But sometimes the NFA'd people were clearly in the wrong, it was just we couldn't find sufficient evidence to charge. Why should they get a lift home?

In the end, response just couldn't keep this up, due to dwindling officer numbers and service demand. The Force started using taxis overnight, to get stranded people home. A policy was drawn up, whereby each situation would need to be justified and written up accordingly on the custody record. Particular priority would be given to ensuring vulnerable persons were provided a taxi home. But most people in custody are vulnerable in one respect or another, hence their very being there. Most people have some element of risk attached that causes the releasing sergeant to keep their fingers crossed they don't kill themselves after release. A taxi home is another tick-box in ways we minimise the risk of that person coming to harm. I don't make a habit of dishing them out willy-nilly, as that doesn't sit right. But where the risk is there or they've been stranded miles from where they live (where, in my view, the arresting officer probably should've done more to ensure at least a wallet came with them to custody), I'll call a taxi.

The Force has an account that these are billed to. I'm told that originally, we were just using the same taxi firm, known for their reliability. Others complained we were giving preferential treatment, so in typical police fashion, we had to show impartiality and a taxi firm rota was made. However, some of these firms are predictably shit, with usual hour waiting times. Someone with a history of self-harm doesn't need an hour wait to dwell on the consequences of their actions. The chances of them sticking around that length of time are slim. Often, therefore, we revert to the usual reliable firms.

Both DPs I released overnight had some element of risk, no funds of their own and received a taxi on the house. Neither thanked me.

After a wasted first rest day catching up on sleep, I was back at work on overtime. This was not custody overtime, but rather the first of the two response shifts I'd booked in.

I was back at my old nick, working a Friday day shift. It was a pleasant change of pace.

There was very little for me to do that morning. I popped out in a response vehicle with someone from my old shift who was also blagging. Naturally, I drove to keep my response ticket valid. One drive every six months keeps it going.

We were sent to what turned out to be a verbal domestic and then called on a few addresses to sort jobs on my colleague's account.

Later that afternoon, we were sent to take a misper (missing person) report. Sure makes it easier to review as supervisor, if I'm witnessing the report being taken first hand. However, before we could, we were diverted to an ongoing domestic assault. Information passed was that the caller's father had assaulted her and was pinning her down by the front door. As we arrived, someone from within tried to open the front door but it could only open a fraction. It soon became clear the female caller was still on the floor by the door and as the door opened a little further, I could see a male stood over her. Both had blood on their faces.

I was a little confused initially, as judging by the apparent ages of both occupants, I assumed they were partners. It took me a few minutes to establish they were the only persons present and the male was in fact her father. He certainly didn't look all of his 81 years. I'd placed him at early 70s and her at late 60s. I was pretty spot on with her, maybe a few years on the harsh side.

She was extremely upset and tearful. I sat her down in the conservatory, whilst my colleague spoke with the chap in the kitchen.

From what she said, it transpired that things had gone wrong for them in the typically ridiculous domestic fashion, in that something really stupid caused an argument. In this case, they'd been unable to locate the jug for the iron.

She hadn't been home long from work and so following the tense iron jug argument (?!), she'd then walked upstairs to take a shower. He was alleged to have stormed up after her, grabbed her hair and dragged her downstairs, pushing her up against a wall, hurting her elbow. She then said he kept hold of her hair and dragged her towards the front door, pinning her up against it. Whilst pinning her against the door, he then punched her several times in her face. She had a cut to her eyebrow and chin, which corroborated this. She said she'd lashed out at him during this, to try and get him off her. She showed me her long nails and said she thinks one of these most likely caused the cut on his face, which is why he'd been bleeding.

She said he then got her on the floor and pinned her there by her throat. Whilst on the floor, he stamped on her hand and kicked her in the shin. She showed me what appeared to be early stages of bruising to her shin and was clutching her right hand in pain.

I could also see spots of blood on the mat by the front door where she'd been lying on our arrival and her phone screen was smashed, though she said it was already like that.

I updated my colleague, who informed me he had claimed *she* assaulted him. Given the severity of what she'd disclosed, her injuries and the fact they both appeared to still be in the alleged positions of the attack on our arrival, I believed it more likely *he* was the aggressor in this incident. Our domestic violence policy is quite clear. Regardless of whether a complaint was forthcoming, positive action must be taken, which would usually involve arrest. She most certainly did not support arrest, stating her brothers wouldn't forgive her. However, they both lived together and neither had anywhere else to stay. The assault was also rather nasty in nature. I suggested we should nick him.

It was then my colleague broke the news he was 81.

This bombshell caused me some hesitation. Could I really nick an 81 year old? I now work in custody, so what would I think if someone brought me an elderly prisoner? The sergeants on duty at that time were people I hand over to. What would their impression be of me? Would they even accept him into custody?

I asked the daughter a few questions about his health. It appeared that he was generally a very fit and able person. He'd recently had a urinary tract infection, which, she told me, can cause people to go a bit doolally. However, from what she said, this appeared to have subsided a week ago and the catheter he'd been fitted with, removed that same length of time ago. He was on anti-depressants, as his wife had passed recently. Otherwise, he was of sound mind and capable. He even drove himself to Newcastle and back within the last week.

This caused me to question why I was hesitant about nicking an 81 year old, over, say, a drug or alcohol dependant thirty-something year old, who fits on withdrawal. The same drug or alcohol dependant person would no doubt have self harm markers, markers that they conceal drugs up their arse, markers they were suicidal...As custody sergeant, I know which I would be more twitchy about, all things considered. Yet, I was pretty sure despite the inevitable custody load of addicts, it would be *this* DP that made staff twitch nervously. Why should this chap get away with not being arrested, purely down to his age? If he were a younger person, we wouldn't have hesitated but to get on and nick. As police officers, we shouldn't be discriminatory. I wasn't going to start discriminating with him due to his age. He had no obvious current health issues and was alleged to have committed a violent assault. They both lived together and had nowhere else to go. We couldn't leave them both there, to pick up where they left off. He needed nicking.

We waited to break the news he would be arrested until the van arrived. Sadly, we had none available locally, so had to wait an hour for one to arrive. He was quite a feisty individual and of stocky build. The last thing we wanted was for him to turn angry and be wrestling with a pensioner for that length of time.

As it was, he took the news calmly, even cracking the odd inappropriate penis joke here and there.

Upon returning to the nick, I started uploading photos of her injuries and then thought to check the custody record. He'd been accepted. Phew! The sergeant accepting had been on my course. I sent her a text saying 'thanks for accepting – good work', justifying my decision with the drug addict comparison above. She said they'd been deemed fit to detain by the nurse and their interview was being expedited. Sounded fair enough to me.

The next morning, I caught a showing of Dunkirk at my local cinema. I was only aware of one bad review, courtesy of *The Times*. 2/5 stars they'd given it. It seemed to have almost universal 5/5 elsewhere. Someone at work had spoken poorly of it too the previous day. Their main gripe appeared to be Tom Hardy's face was covered 99% of his screen time. I pointed out Tom Hardy's best role was when he had his face covered – Bane, prompting me to unleash my (slightly incorrect but still awesome) Bane impression on parade, covering my mouth and saying "Oh, you think the dark is your ally. I was born in the dark!" He was awesome in Mad Max too, and had a garden fork covering his face for a good portion of the first half.

I digress.

Wow.

It was absolutely amazing.

The film is Christopher Nolan's shortest but is the culmination of all his efforts to date. The film is beautifully shot and the musical score literally hijacks your emotions from the get go. The film is extremely tense throughout and I felt myself welling up several times, fighting back the tears. It was simply stunning.

I was really worried at the start, as two bald-headed chaps were directly in front of me. I do get easily distracted and found their shiny, polished tops rather amusing. The moment I caught sight of them, I had the horrible realisation that was probably going to be the only thing I could think about throughout the movie. I even considered moving seats, but thought the wife would think me mad. I'm pleased to say once the film started, the noggins were forgotten about.

I cannot wait to see it again and, dare I say it, it may even rival *The Matrix* as my favourite ever. But I'll save that judgment for the post Blu-Ray viewing. Anyone who knows me, knows how much I like *The Matrix*, so I need to consider my position here carefully.

Chapter Six – 9 to 5

Well, not quite 9 to 5...but the police custody equivalent, being 6.30am to 3.30pm or thereabouts. But once I thought of it, Dolly got stuck in my head. Hate that song. Film pretty average.

One thing I really like about policing is shift work. I have no idea how I ever coped working nine to five, Monday to Friday. Hated that Sunday evening feeling you got about the next morning. You just don't get that with shift working. The days go far quicker too. Even though there's more of them. There are six shifts in a typical set. Two days, two lates, two nights. Then four rest days.

This set, I'm working four days, followed by two nights. This was my own doing, as the wife passes out on my fourth shift this set. This isn't a pre-planned faint-a-thon, but rather the celebratory event marking the end of fifteen weeks initial training. Although there is still the possibility of it turning ugly, as the bar *will* be open.

I therefore arranged to swap shifts with another skipper. I'm working their days; they're working my lates. Or rather, they've since been abstracted to do something completely different, leaving my team in the lurch. Well, leaving two sergeants, which is all many other teams typically have anyway.

This appears to be the set of abstractions. Several sergeants are currently off sick. Stress, sickness bug, etc...

One of our sergeants is on holiday. Another was called on rest days by an Inspector, requiring them to vary duties to cover sickness, meaning they're now working four lates. This leaves just myself and another skipper on days. Which is fine until the late morning rush inevitably happens, when all investigators want to update you at once, leaving queues at the back door.

Fortunately today, there were no such queues. We had a couple early on, one of which had assaulted three officers prior to arrival. There was talk of one on route in limb restraints but when they arrived, he casually walked in, unaided. My colleague booked him in, keen to even things a bit, as I'd taken more prisoners at the start. They'd already booked another in too, meaning I felt I was lagging a bit.
I booked in a chap wanted by another force for stealing £37000 via the skilled technique of computer hacking. He was calm as you like, minimal risks attached. The sort of prisoner you like.
Still no disposal reviews to complete.
Another prisoner arrived, which I insisted on, to keep things fair. He spoke no English, only Vietnamese.
A member of public had reported a male on top of a lorry. On police arrival, he jumped down, hurting his ankle.
Paramedics had seen him; no suspected breaks.
He limped into my charge room, clearly in pain. I jacked up the interpreter and started booking in. I got the nurse to check his injury. She shared the paramedic's view and sorted some pain relief.
The Vietnamese chap had provided a date of birth indicating he was 15 years old. He certainly didn't look old, but I'm always sceptical of age, as Social Services are the lead agency for juveniles, rather than Immigration. Their age verification people would decide his fate.
Booking in took ages. During this time, my colleague had taken a few disposals for my DPs. He made this known in his usual direct way and I was probably rather short back but made it clear I hadn't just sat about doing naff all.
Before I knew it, handover arrived. There was a prisoner waiting in the holding cell, so I offered to give my handover first and book them in to help lates.

They'd been nicked for theft from motor vehicle dating back two weeks. ID'd from stolen bank card usage. This wasn't disclosed to them. They wanted to keep that bombshell for interview. All this dude needed to know for now was "police enquiries" linked him.

I let the escorting officer resume and continued booking in. My DO had the arduous task of searching his bag; a minefield of needles. She, understandably, took time, sticking them all in the sin bin as she went.

She found a hammer, a small bladed object and a torch. Items criminals typically carry with them to steal. The bladed item was something I hadn't seen before. It looked like a miniature squeegee; indeed, the DP even claimed it was such. However, the metallic end lifted off to reveal a blade. Such an item could be used to cut rubber seals of car windows. I directed them to leave those items in a separate evidence bag, ready for the OIC to seize. I wasn't popular, as I then instructed them to complete a statement, detailing their find. But evidentially, we needed this for continuity, to show how those items arrived at custody. They needed to be attributed to someone. Clearly, the arresting officer hadn't searched the bag. Possibly aware of the hazards inside and knowing it'd need checking in custody anyway.

I went home and did very little. What made my day was the book my five year old had made me. It was a book called 'The farm haze all sorte of anermalls'. It was five pages long, and each page had a different animal drawing, with a sentence explaining what it was. My absolute favourite was ' Theis anemall is a griarf', followed by a picture of what looked more like a red duck, with a beak longer than the width of its head. I shall treasure it forever. It's moments like this that remind you why you work hard and provide for your loved ones.

Then before you know it, you're back to the daily grind, having kinder eggs thrown in front of you by a colleague, informing you it was found in the corridor one of your DPs had just used to go to court. Seemed an odd place to deliberately dispose of drugs. He went to all that trouble stuffing it up his arse, only to get rid in the police station, rather than take through to court and then, dependant on outcome, to prison. I suggested perhaps he farted and it shot out his trouser leg.

My main priority that morning was getting rid of the Vietnamese lad still in. His twenty-four hour clock expired at eleven and Social Services had told nights they'd get someone there by nine to verify his age. My understanding of the process was corrected that morning, as apparently Social are supposed to do these checks off site, if there is any suspicion they are a juvenile. He should've been collected long ago. I got my DO to chivvy them along and sure enough, on arrival, they took one look at him and he was gone. Problem sorted.

I got a Route One guy out to the charge room to issue his rights and go through their risk assessment. This always makes me wary. They'd arrived extremely violent overnight, with several officers mucking in to get him to cell. Then a few hours later, there I was – retrieving him from said cell on my own. He was quiet, swore occasionally at his shoes (yes, you read that right) but caused no issues. Another customer who should clearly never drink.

I sent a domestic related criminal damage to CPS. The DP was a forty-something alcoholic, living with his seventy-six year old mother. She was trying to help him combat his alcoholism but upon realising he'd snuck out to buy booze, the switched-on lass locked him out. He was peed off on his return, so put the window in.

She wouldn't make a complaint and was adamant she wanted him back. He admitted it in interview and I sent the case to CPS for charging decision. I recommended a charge of damage, and as he was not a remand candidate, explained I'd look to bail without conditions, given this wasn't a violent incident, he had nowhere else to go, and his mother wanted him back to help him through his addiction and sort him accommodation elsewhere. The OIC was satisfied this suited the particular circumstances of this case.

The advice came back authorising he be charged with damage but suggesting bail conditions of non contact and not to go within one mile of her address. I decided to stick with the original plan and hope for the best.

There was a guy who'd been stopped by police with a kitchen knife. No comment interview, but no denial and no reasonable excuse offered. Due to this, and given it was an officer who stopped him and found the knife, I anticipated a guilty plea at court. As a not-denied either way offence, suitable for sentencing in the Magistrate's court, I could therefore make the charging decision. I charged and bailed him to court.

There are summary, either way and indictable offences. Without complicating things too much, generally summary offences are only heard in Magistrates' court and indictable offences in Crown court. Either way offences can be, well, you've probably guessed. They depend on level of seriousness, as to whether they are likely to be heard in one court or the other.

In addition to this, we must make sure we bail to the correct type of court. It's not a simple question of clicking a button and the case goes to 'Magistrates' court'. That would be far too easy. They separate different types of cases, so CPS know how much work they have to do prior to taking on a case. The length of time between a DP being charged and appearing at court depends on their anticipated plea. If it's anticipated they'll plead guilty, they go to a 'GAP court' (guilty anticipated plea). These court dates are much sooner. Where a not-guilty plea is anticipated, they go to a 'NGAP court'. Domestics have their own domestic court, irrespective of plea. Remands have their own remand court. Youths go to youth court.

Custody sergeants are bound by the Director's guidance on charging (5th edition May 2013), which enables officers to determine when CPS advice should be sought, as opposed to sergeants making the decision themselves. In the kitchen knife example above, I was able to make the decision, for the reasons stated.

I took an update from an OIC, who'd interviewed someone for going equipped to steal, possession of a bladed article (lock knife) and possession of cannabis. They'd been seen on CCTV happily hacksawing a bicycle lock. They failed in their attempt and walked off, only to be stopped by police five minutes later and arrested.

The OIC updated me post interview that he'd initially been asked whether he was guilty of all three offences, to which he replied "yes".

Then he went on to deny the going equipped, stating he'd only been bending down to get something out his bag to give to a homeless person. He was then shown the crystal clear CCTV and conceded there was no doubt that was him, or what he was doing, but that he couldn't recall it. Complete bollocks, of course, but not a denial and based on this, a guilty plea anticipated.

Regarding the lock knife, he stated he always carries his tools with him, as he works DIY by trade and never knows when his missus will kick him out. He didn't realise this was an offence but stated he should have and conceded he is currently living with his missus, so could've left these items there (he also had hammers, screwdrivers etc on him). He also conceded he was not working at 3am when stopped. No reasonable excuse offered, no denial, guilty plea anticipated based on him conceding he shouldn't have had with him.

The cannabis was the easiest to decide on. He had cannabis on him. It was a small amount, consistent with personal use. He admitted what it was and for his sole use. The only flaw with the cannabis was the seizing officer hadn't identified it as such. A small oversight that could be corrected that night when back on duty.

Based on the update, I anticipated a guilty plea in respect of all three offences. Once again, I was therefore able to make the charging decision as a not-denied either way offence, suitable for sentencing in the Magistrate's court, under the above Director's guidance. I set the disposal on the computer, clicking the 'GAP court' option. The officer said they'd go back to their home station.

What the guidance does not cover, is what to do when you start to read the charge wording out to the DP and they make it clear they don't agree and will be contesting one of the offences at court. And the going equipped, no less! The one on CCTV clearly showing him using that item to try and steal something.

I paused.

I considered my options.

Option 1 – The 'Fuck It' approach: Carry on regardless. You've made your decision already.

Option 2 – The 'Gut Instinct' approach: This was now a not-guilty anticipated case. CPS would be required. Stick him back in his cell and direct the OIC to get the advice.

Option 3 – The 'Double Check Instinct' approach: As per Option 2, but run past the other sergeant first.
Option 4 – The 'Fuck My Life' approach: Walk out the custody block without saying a word, get in your car and literally fuck off home. You don't work there anymore. These situations cannot keep happening to you. Don't take this shit anymore. Go play some GTA and have a beer.
I have to admit, Option 1 did cross my mind. I ruled out Option 4 very quickly, deciding I'd need to stay employed to fund the GTA and beer long term.
I considered Option 2, but decided this was probably such an anomaly that I wanted to ensure I dealt with it correctly. Otherwise, I'd simply not know for next time.
Option 3 it was then. They agreed that DP would have to return to cell and OIC seek CPS advice. In fact, they added that they wondered if CPS would run the going equipped or whether they'd go for attempt theft of pedal cycle instead.
Now when I first retrieved him from his cell, it suddenly dawned on me who this was. I'd arrested him a few times as a PC. On two-thirds of those occasions, he'd put up a fight. I had been single crewed every time. I won these, but they were hard fought. He even said to me "Ah, it's you! You've had some fun arresting me in the past haven't you?!"
I gave him the bad news and he said he'd just plead guilty then, if it got him out quicker. He had things to do that afternoon. I said it'd be morally wrong for me to proceed based on what he'd said and that it was clear he was going to contest this matter, which meant 'NGAP court', which in turn now meant CPS advice whilst he returned to cell.
I anticipated a fight, or at least some shouting. But then what do I know?! I'd anticipated a guilty plea but got the complete opposite a lot earlier than expected too! He was clearly unhappy but went back quietly.

I gave my handover and explained the farcical CPS situation. I found a quiet room to log on and get some supervisory bits done and then headed home to play GTA and drink beer. Only I wrote this instead. And realised we had no beer.
The next day was my third day, instead of first late.
The shift was nothing but stressful. Working with another team always takes a bit of adjusting, but they work very differently. The DOs do *all* the booking in. I think this is how they want all the teams working but that's a subject being looked at by those with pips.
I was once again covering DO MSL. I was asked to sit with a sergeant, which I did. Rumours came from upstairs the boss had seen two sergeants sat in the same room and questioned this. I was told to be prepared for a challenge. That would've been easy..."Boss, I'm a DO today. Not a sergeant". That's certainly how duties view me. Otherwise, keep me as sergeant and employ more DOs!
Of course, I still mucked in and did plenty of sergeanty stuff. In any case, I still haven't got access to the fingerprint machine, so am reliant on DOs doing those. I therefore have to do what I can to help move things along, so if disposal reviews are needed, that's what I shall do.
I had to swap with a DO doing DP checks, so they could take outstanding prints. I was met with resistance – they were frustrated that sergeants are not trained to do this. I can't answer for others, but I assured him I'm doing my utmost to get my password through so I can do these. This was requested pretty much on day one and still nothing. It makes you wonder if anyone in the back offices are actually still employed.

There was fingerprint chaos. It seems we get this an awful lot these days. They should be taken when a DP first arrives. That is the perfect vision. However, if a DP is too drunk, too violent, or requires an AA, they cannot be taken on arrival (unless, in the case of an AA, one happens to be readily available...but overnight this is almost unheard of and even daytime this is rare, as the sole AA via the scheme is being utilised).

The boss had put an email out only yesterday, stating his expectation that prints should be taken on arrival. The first chap we booked in was shouting, swearing, drunk and aggressive. My colleague actually booked him in, whilst I logged his property. I'm surprised he wasn't Route One'd, however, I think they knew him and realised better than I did that this was pretty much normal behaviour for him sadly. He was bonkers. That is the best way I can describe him. He clearly required an AA and there was *no way* we were able to take prints at that time even if one was available.

Between jobs, I was able to check the job from yesterday, where I'd put the DP back in their cell for CPS advice. To my delight, CPS had ratified all three of my charges. But to my surprise, they had recommended he be bailed to GAP court. Well, I knew the evidence was there...but he was clearly saying he was going to go 'not guilty'! Which is the sole reason I sent it to CPS! If I'd known CPS would've considered it a 'GAP court' case regardless, I could've just binned him there and then! Hey, ho.

There was the usual AA and solicitor chaos. Every OIC arriving downstairs at once, all expecting to use the same AA. OICs were asking me where AAs were, as their solicitors were on route or already there.

I booked in a BTP (British Transport Police) prisoner. Theft of pedal cycles from two train stations. He was alleged to be part of a gang of youths going round the area doing this. The custody environment is daunting for most people when it's chaotic, including investigators who attend daily...but some of the poor BTP officers looked like rabbits in headlights. One of their DPs needed the AA scheme and they kept missing out to other officers, who knew better, and loitered near the interview rooms. I advised them to do the same.

I NFA'd a coercive and controlling behaviour job. This is a relatively new domestic related offence, requiring several factors present in order for points to prove to be met. I won't bore you with those here (saves me looking them up again) but needless to say without this particular victim wishing to give a statement, the *numerous* points to prove couldn't be satisfied. That was a quick easy review and bin.

I managed to get the slightly crazy man's disposal sorted just before handover. They'd attended a police station with two samurai swords to hand them in. And got arrested for doing so. There is really no other way of viewing the incident. I have no doubt his erratic behaviour is what got him arrested but at the end of the day, he offered no violence to officers with them, threw them to the ground when approached and was arrested. I NFA'd that offence. He'd been further arrested for an outstanding assault, whereby it was alleged he'd been directing traffic (I am told this is a usual pastime for him) and then pinned an elderly lady up against a wall before telling her to "Fuck off". He denied this (admitted directing traffic) and so I directed the officer to organise a Promat, which is a video identification procedure. They'd also been arrested for a malicious communications offence, for phoning 999 a couple times and being abusive towards the call taker, for no apparent reason. For these, he said he was sorry, though I'm told the solicitor then reminded him of his right to silence, which oddly he found the ability to do for the first time that day. He was to be released under investigation for these offences, so further evidence could be sought.

After handover, I logged on to the computer in custody that is well hidden from the chaos. I read one of my DO's PDRs. It looked remarkably similar to last year's one, which the outgoing sergeant had emailed me prior to retiring. In fact, apart from the date, my name as current supervisor, and various other minor tweaks, it *was* exactly the same!

The paragraph they wrote about *Professionalism* talked about how they'd volunteered themselves for an upcoming move to the shift they were already on and had been for over a year! Under another heading, they talked about the fifteen years they'd been working for the Force, yet at the top of the PDR, it clearly stated they had been in post for 17 years. I suspect this PDR has done at least *two* years now!

I fully get why some DOs do not wish to put much effort into PDRs. Many see it as a job, not a career. There is *no* progression. Don't get me wrong – some go the extra mile. But as long as people are doing their job and not underperforming, that is all we can ask of them. I sent a polite email back requesting they make it a bit more relevant to the *current* year.

I then took the opportunity to start an E-Learning. We get emailed about these periodically, and I tend to get them done and dusted quickly, so I don't fall behind. Falling behind with E-Learning leads to Inspectors knocking on your door. I don't like Inspectors knocking on my door. But this one said it'd take *two* hours. It referred to it as 'protected learning time'. I'm quite sure in the chaos of custody, I won't find two hours to sit and watch videos. No time in custody is 'protected'. Time escapes you. There isn't enough of it. I managed to get a couple of short videos done but the main bulk remains outstanding. It was home time.

I was a DO-Sgt again the next day. I booked one in whilst the morning handover was still ongoing. They'd done an early morning arrest for possession of indecent images of children. The guy was 'no-trace' and middle aged. He was understandably very quiet and shed the odd tear. Clearly what he has done, or accessed, is disgustingly wrong. But, ultimately, my job involves being responsible for his welfare whilst in custody and minimising the risk of him topping himself upon leaving. Despite what he's done, I see it as a professional and moral responsibility to do this.

Therefore you offer the same amount of reassurance and support you would for anyone. He said he needed help and I provided relevant contact information for support agencies that can offer counselling for persons with such thoughts.

Part of me was thinking I should feel sorry for the guy, but the majority of me was remembering what he'd done and whilst I'll do my best to ensure their welfare and be perfectly polite towards them, I cannot bring myself to feel any ounce of compassion.

He was released under investigation later that morning after interview, for further enquiries to be completed. The OIC went through their usual enhanced pre-release risk assessment for suspects of such crime, and they came out low risk. Fingers crossed we should be okay with that one.

A short while later, a mad man arrived. He was presented to me by the arresting officer, stating he'd randomly attacked two staff from a local bank, who'd been waiting outside for it to open. The guy was bonkers. He was very polite, calling me 'Sir' throughout. He was built like a brick shithouse. I had no doubt if we had a ruck, he'd have the upper hand and I'd have to use quite a high level of force. Fortunately, he remained calm throughout my dealings, though I could tell he was the sort who had potential to snap randomly at any minute, which appears to be what happened outside the bank, when he asked one of the victim's names, shook their hand, and proceeded to beat the crap out of them.

He was placed in his cell, with his copy of the PACE Codes of Practice as requested, and before long all I could hear was screaming from down the corridor. I checked CCTV and he was doing the Maori haka dance. He'd told me he was Maori, although born in Britain and British. But then he'd also told me he'd spent the whole summer locked away in rehab, only to be let out and was allergic to the sun.

We referred him to our in-custody mental health liaison, who informed us he was well known to local mental health teams. It seemed they'd been seeing him in the community recently and noted their concerns he was deteriorating. Shame it'd come to this. I couldn't see the victims getting any real justice out of this; the bloke needed sectioning.
They called the crisis team to come and assess him.
There was another argument about fingerprints. Same DO, different sergeant. I walked in on the argument, realised what it was about, and couldn't be arsed to listen to the same shit again. The tirade was directed at the skipper, but it's not *our* fault. The job is quite prepared to use us as DOs to make up shortfall. But we're *not* DOs. We're *sergeants*. Of course this is going to create tensions and additional stress for DOs. But this is an *organisation* issue, not anything the sergeants have created. I made the other sergeant aware who had direct supervisory responsibility for the chap as this was getting ridiculous.
It was clearly a day for mental health, as the next person I booked in was just as mad. Or at least, under the influence of drugs. The referral we made for her came back that she was previously detained under the mental health act, assessed when sober, and deemed to be of fit mind.

She'd gone up to someone in the street, spat at them, bit their hand and scratched their face. On arrest, she was found with suspected Class A. I could see her acting bizarrely on CCTV in the holding cell. She couldn't stay still and was constantly fidgeting. She came through to the charge desk and was dancing about, moving her head from side to side, eyes fixed open, hands flailing about – clearly not right. She wasn't being violent, just appeared under the influence of something that disagreed with her. It was extremely difficult going through her risk assessment. Getting her attention was almost impossible. She was searched at the desk and another wrap was found concealed on her clothing. I authorised a strip search. This was negative but at least I knew there'd be no further drug consumption today. On CCTV, she could be seen dancing around her cell, never staying still. Needless to say, I got the nurse to see her to determine fitness to detain. Ironically, her cell was next door to the man doing the haka. It made me wonder what would happen if we placed them both in the same cell. Would this result in a Strictly Come Dancing Custody Special? I doubted it. I don't think she'd have lasted two seconds in there.

I handed over my prisoners to lates (my normal colleagues) quickly, so I could book in one that was waiting in the holding cell. My colleague had disappeared, so I was left to do the whole lot, property included. This delayed lates getting on their computers, so whilst I'd taken it on with the best of intentions, I'm not sure there was any real benefit to lates that I'd done this. At least the response officers were able to resume quickly.

She was wanted on warrant. Fairly straight forward. Recovering alcoholic. Hadn't touched a drop in over eight months. Had loads of medication with her. I doubted she'd get into court that afternoon but informed the lates DOs as quickly as I could, so they could make the call through to the courts and start the relevant paperwork.

As I finished off her care plan, I heard an argument down the corridor. It took me a few moments of eavesdropping to realise no DP was involved – this was a heated argument between two DOs, one from days, the other from lates. I recognised the voice of the one from lates, being my normal team. He remained calm and politely told the other guy to stop throwing stuff about and acting childish. It was quickly diffused by another sergeant, whisking the days DO away to debrief. Tensions are high. Everyone is stressed. This was just yet another reminder.

After this, I made my escape. It was my wife's passing out ceremony that evening. I collected the kids from holiday club and bathed them. My daughter put on a new dress and I stuck my son in the gear he'd worn a year earlier, for my brother's wedding. It just about still fit. My brother had sown a police badge into the inner lining of the waistcoat, as an additional incentive for him to wear it. He thoroughly enjoys showing this off. Sure enough, the same trick worked again. We arrived at training headquarters in good time. My wife had been asked to sort the seating arrangements, so we were near the front. Both kids were well behaved. I was especially proud of my five year old son for staying quiet. Quite an achievement!

It was a proud occasion. Fifth generation copper, now with wife ready to hit the streets to start her *own* police journey. This is the first time in my family a copper's wife has also joined the job, which is indicative of the times we live in. We got some lovely photos, including some taken by the Force photographer. The Force flag was at half mast, a sad reminder that whilst this was a happy occasion, a serving officer had passed away the day before, from a heart attack. It left me thinking about the state of the job at present. The extreme stress and pressure everyone is under. It is not sustainable. What will come of us both?

I had a bad case of the blues the following day. Can't explain why. Sometimes I have these down days. Feel depressed for no apparent reason. My wife picks up on it very quickly. She got home from her last day of initial training and sensed something was wrong, as I was a bit despondent, staring into space. This set has been relentless and my anxiety has kicked in full force. My chest is painful and feels tight and each breath feels inadequate. My heart feels like it's constantly pounding away. I cannot switch off from work. Being issued a work mobile hasn't helped. It stays at home and I check my emails periodically, as there's nothing I hate more than trying to clear a backlog at the start of a shift, especially in custody as there's rarely a chance.

I picked up an email from duties, telling me that in just over three months time, they have cancelled a last rest day and made it a training day. Whilst this sounds reasonable in theory, I'm actually working an extra night the set before, meaning I will now be working a seven day set, have two days off (realistically 1.5 after sleep coming off nights) and then work another seven day set. I'm not as clued up on working time regs as I should be, but this sounds wrong. I genuinely feel like the job is working me to death and am convinced they genuinely don't give a shit.

Trouble is, who is *they*? I've often thought this about the police. It's like there's this faceless enemy constantly screwing you over. In this case, the Chief Inspector of custody has directed the rest day be cancelled for a training day. But I doubt he'd have known my predicament. He just needed to ensure everyone received this training. I can't blame him. Must be duties then. They should see the situation they've put me in, yet they still went through with it. But then they were told they had to cancel it as the training was mandatory. Couldn't they therefore have reallocated my rest day to the extra night shift just before, meaning I'd have a six day set, 2.5 days off, and then a seven day set. That would be better. But then I expect there's insufficient cover that night shift. I expect one of the other numerous sergeants affected will have already had theirs reallocated to that date.

As much as we moan about them, duties themselves are under an enormous amount of pressure to find cover that's barely, if at all, available. So I can't really blame *them*. The Chief Constable, perhaps? They're Head Honcho. But then is it *their* fault we have so few resources? Doubtful. More likely, this all stems from the government and budget cuts. So the source of the problem stems from outside the organisation, but what is the *Force* doing about it? What *can* they do? I don't know. If I had any real answers, I'd make them known. But I'm a custody sergeant. I do my job, to the best of my ability and crack on. But in the meantime, I can feel the strain it's having on my health. I'm genuinely left wondering how long I will last, before my body caves in. Will I make it to retirement? I've got twenty-something years left. I love my job and cannot imagine doing anything else. So I feel trapped, like I've got no choice but to carry on and risk my health.

My parents had the kids that night, as my wife was out celebrating the end of training with friends. As I arrived at work, my wrist gadget vibrated and lit up, revealing a message from a mate from response. "3 on route", it said. Brilliant. Though I expected nothing else from a Friday night, this pre-warning didn't help my anxiety.

As handover started, I caught sight of a DP being carried into the holding cell by officers on CCTV. They were in limb restraints (the DP, not the officers thankfully) and were quickly placed in a spit hood. I joked that I keep a carrier bag in my pocket for such occasions, then remembered everywhere in custody is audio recorded and apologised for the benefit of anyone listening in.

I checked my DPs were alive and before I put logs on their custody records to that effect, I decided to book the violent guy in, as officers had already been restraining him for quite a while.

I went out into the holding cell and the limb restraints had been removed, however, he began struggling again and these were reapplied. The arresting officer clarified he'd been nicked D&D but further arrested assault police x 2 for kicking officers on arrest. As he was still aggressive, I decided to authorise detention there and then and Route One him. A DO whisked off to get the cell mattress on the floor ready. We lifted him up, and carried him through to the cell.

He was still struggling, so was placed on the ground face down. We searched him, removed his handcuffs, keeping wrist locks on for compliance and removed his corded jumper, one arm at a time. One by one, officers left the cell, until it was just myself holding his legs and another officer on both wrist locks. The DP stopped resisting. I left and then the last officer quickly followed, however, the DP unexpectedly reacted and managed to dart forward, sticking his upper half through the door before it could be closed. I have no idea how he physically managed this from the position we left him in but felt stupid either way for having let it happen.

He latched on to the arresting officer's legs and his face was right up against them. To me, it looked like he was trying to bite the officer's legs. Either way, he was refusing to let go and I gave him several hard fist strikes to his upper right back demanding he let go, which he eventually did. I have no doubt this will have left him badly bruised, as they were full force thumps.

He was re-cuffed and the process repeated, this time successfully.

I started to complete a detention log, explaining the use of force. Halfway through, an affray alarm went. It was a different sound to the usual one, which confused me. Everyone quickly appeared in the main corridor and someone shouted it was the interview rooms, so we rushed down there. A DP had kicked off, having been further arrested in interview. As I understand it, he'd picked up a chair, throwing it about and had flipped the table and moved it up against the door, trapping everyone inside with him.

There were two female investigators, a solicitor, and an AA in there with him. The AA is a lovely lady, getting on a bit bless her and was left badly shaken. I cleared the corridor, ready to get her out first. She was taken straight into the nurse's office for examination. She was followed by the investigators and I followed one of them out of custody to check their welfare, aware there were already several others ahead of me in the room itself dealing with the DP. She was extremely tearful and in shock herself. We de-briefed what had occurred and when she had calmed sufficiently, we returned to custody so she could liaise with the lates skipper, who was overseeing the incident whilst we cracked on with running the block.

I finished my logs for the previous DP and set about releasing a few. My DO for the night was a skipper, covering DO MSL. The other charge room sergeant was on an extra night. As I had quite a few disposal reviews and releases to sort, my DO/Sgt disappeared to another charge room to start clearing the queue of arriving DPs. Due to this, they ended up booking in more than me, a fact they kept reminding me about, rather unhelpfully, given I hadn't just been sat on my arse doing nothing.

They returned when I booked in my next DP, who'd damaged the front of a police station by ramming a trolley into it. He was demanding a piss in the holding cell, so was brought through to use a toilet. He had yet to be searched and was obnoxious. He was demanding his cuffs be removed so he could get his cock out but these were left on much to his annoyance. Everyone else manages. He then complained he couldn't go, as the door wasn't fully shut and he was nervous. He was shouting abuse at my colleague the whole time, calling him a "CANCER CUNT". He ended up returning to the holding cell, only to then demand a piss again. He came back through, couldn't go and disappeared again.

Once I had loaded up the record, he came through and was booked in. I was surprised I managed to get through the process, rather than the predicted Route One.

The next guy was equally obnoxious. He'd assaulted a taxi driver and damaged his car. Once again, I somehow managed to get through the whole process. This is always beneficial, as no matter how horrible these people are, we need to know their associated risks. As he was escorted to his cell, he left me with a brain teaser, asking me "In a block of 99 flats, how many 9s are there?" I had no time that night to consider this but saved in my head for later.

Next up was a first timer. She was a middle aged lady, accused of biting her husband. She was extremely quiet and withdrawn. Otherwise, she had no risks identified.

Last up was a Russian man, accused of running round a Holiday Inn butt naked. Upon being challenged by staff, he assaulted them, went outside, and damaged a car. He was located by police and arrested.

He only spoke basic English, so required a Russian interpreter. He was very obstructive, repeating the same question over and over again, asking about his friend. I kept assuring him the officer would return to the hotel to check on him but despite this, the same question kept coming over and over… In the end, I ignored him and whenever the interpreter said he was asking the same question again, I would ask something about his health. I would get the answer but the question repeated again. I would then ignore it, and ask another risk assessment question. I think he cottoned on that I was now ignoring him and so when it came to his rights, he decided an ideal notification request would be for us to inform his friend he'd been arrested. You have to hand it to the guy. As annoying as he was, this was clever. Even though officers were going to check on his friend anyway, I now had an obligation under PACE to ensure this was done.

My dealings with the Russian were not over. He'd been searched by the escorting officer, and I wanted to check whether he had a cord in his trousers. I'd already hung up the interpreter, so did my best to explain what I needed to check by pretending to fold over the waistline of my trousers, saying "Do you have a cord in your trousers?" The Russian's response was to show me his penis. Not sure how that one would stand up under scrutiny (my attempt at checking for cord – not his bellend).

I got home and before bed, I considered the 99-flat teaser. How many 9s in 99 flats? I make it nineteen total, being 9, 19, 29, 39, 49, 59, 69, 79, 89, 90, 91, 92, 93, 94, 95, 96, 97, 98, and 99. There are several answers on Google, with one even going as far as to suggest that every '6' is in fact a '9' in disguise. I don't buy into that. A '6' is a '6' plain and simple. I'm going with 19.

I woke up around 1300hrs which was not good. I need to sleep through to at least 1500hrs between nights to feel I've had sufficient rest. My mind was too active.

I did very little that afternoon, to try and de-stress but felt anxious. We went to my father-in-law's that evening for a Chinese take-away. It was delicious, however, immediately afterwards I regretted the two platefuls I had and felt sick. This worsened as the evening progressed. I had an upset stomach for much of the set and this reared its ugly head, quite literally, before work.

We were a DO under strength due to sickness, with no pre-arranged cover, despite this having been previously raised. Running a busy custody block under staffed is dangerous. The PACE Inspector resourced an officer from response to cover the shortfall.

It was me and my former mentor in the charge rooms. Whenever this is the case, especially on nights, I always seem to get the DPs that require the most disposal reviews and releases. This meant that whilst I was giving that the attention it required, he was booking in prisoners. He would go on to book in about five more than me throughout the night, and boy did he keep reminding me of it. Rather unhelpfully, I might add. I was constantly busy the whole night, with, no word of a lie, not a minute to relax. And half the prisoners I *did* book in were a nightmare.

I cracked on with the disposal reviews. I typed these up as the officers updated me, knowing I'd not get a chance to later, having learned from experience.

I reviewed a shoplifting, where a guy from London had stolen items from a toy shop on two occasions, only to return a third time, be recognised and detained. However, he kicked off, assaulted the manager, committed a public order offence and damaged property.

The thefts were up together, but the assault on staff had outstanding CCTV. I decided to keep the whole lot together and released him under investigation so we could sort CCTV. I was too busy to look at the guy's previous. He offered to clear out his cell, stating he'd urinated in most of his cups. I've no idea whether he'd been trying to get our attention for the toilet or whether, from experience, he knew this was the easier option. Either way, I accepted his offer and let him dispose of his own piss.

I reviewed a high risk domestic, whereby the DP had assaulted his partner in a prolonged attack the night before, causing ABH injuries. Historic assaults were also disclosed but only the recent assault, I felt, was at the FCT. I wrote it up for CPS at about 0020hrs and the officer started work on this. I booked in a guy for a domestic assault. He was alleged to have punched his partner. He was on life licence for murder and was aggressive, rude and abrupt. I went through the whole risk assessment, despite him making it crystal clear he only wanted a doctor and solicitor, by karate chopping along the top of my desk saying "DOCTOR" and then "SOLICITOR" in turn with every other chop. Going through the questions anyway seemed to annoy him, so his chops became more forceful and I ended up getting a bit angry and found myself karate chopping my desk too, saying, "I" (chop), "WILL" (chop), "BE" (chop), "GOING" (chop), "THROUGH" (chop), "ALL" (chop), "THE" (chop), "QUESTIONS" (chop), "ANYWAY" (chop). He was a chopper alright.

Next was a guy concerned in the supply of class A. He'd been the passenger in a car, seen by officers engaged in a suspected drug deal occurring at the driver's window. The person outside the car ran off and was found in possession of suspected Class A. The two occupants of the car were therefore arrested. No further drugs had been located and given they were suspected of supplying, I authorised a strip search, concerned they may be concealing drugs on their person. Nil were found. He seemed a genuinely nice chap. Very polite, no risks identified. He requested a bible, pencil and paper, all of which I was quite happy to provide.

I'd reviewed a couple of other shopliftings earlier but hadn't had chance to action them. I knew I'd be charging and remanding the bloke, and was fairly sure he knew it coming, so decided due to other pressures I'd leave this for later. I saw an opportunity and nipped down to his cell, read the charges, explained my decision for refusing bail and he made no representations.

I had another one to do too. A breach of restraining order had come back from CPS, authorising charge and supported a remand. I decided to save that and book another DP in, aware of the "subtle" criticism I was getting from the adjacent charge room.

On paper, this DP looked straight forward. Criminal damage to council offices. DP stated he'd continue unless arrested, so was arrested.

I authorised his detention and asked the question I always do before I let officers resume. I asked whether they'd need any medication from home whilst in custody. I do this as the officer is still present. Trying to contact them later to retrieve meds can be difficult.

The DP declared he'd already taken all of his medication. I asked him to clarify what he meant, hoping he'd say he only took what was due. However, he stated he'd taken the remainder of the month's worth. It was the 5th. I asked him what he was on. The list was endless. Hospital it was then...

He explained he was a cancer patient, was supposed to be in remission but several recent lumps found. He was also an alcoholic. He woke up that morning, and decided his plan for the day - he would take all his medication and get arrested that evening. My decision making in the mornings usually consists of trying to work out whether to use the last of the milk and stitch the kids or be kind and have toast. I usually use up the milk.

The nurse examined him mid booking in and was concerned about his blood pressure, pulse and oxygen saturation. She recommended we call an ambulance, rather than convey in a van, as should he take a turn for the worse, at least she was available to help.

Sadly, I think the ambulance control realised this and there was a significant delay for this priority patient of around two hours. Halfway through that time, his condition worsened and they were updated but it still took that additional hour to arrive. The nurse was great – she regularly popped back to check him. Needless to say, I placed him on close proximity constants until the ambulance arrived.

Once that DP was booked in, I charged and remanded the restraining order guy. He made no reps and went back to sleep.

It was clearly a night for medical attention. Only, the next DP was more of an award-craving actress. Officers said she was walking, talking and smiling from the van to holding cell, only to then "faint". Sure enough, she was not responding to anyone and I requested the nurse see her. The nurse was satisfied she was faking it. I gave her the option of waking immediately from her "faint", or being carried straight through to her cell. She opted to continue the performance, so was lifted through and placed on the pre-prepared mattress on her cell floor.

I kept an officer on close proximity constants with her for half an hour, so I could be satisfied her condition didn't worsen. After that time, I got the nurse to check her again, and satisfied nothing had changed, I resumed the officer.

It was nearing the end of shift when charging advice finally came back for the earlier domestic I'd reviewed. There'd been technical issues with sending evidence to CPS, so the actual advice hadn't taken as long as it seemed.

They wanted the DP bailed for further enquiries. I agreed there was further work to be done on historic matters but was disappointed they'd not made a decision on the most recent assault. Bailed for further enquiries...that was something we don't do often anymore. Certainly, it was something I'd *never* done yet. Under new bail legislation, this would require authorisation by an Inspector, if they believed it was *proportionate* and *necessary* to do so. The training we had on this subject indicated pre-charge bail would now be extremely rare. Rather, we'd now release the majority under investigation and deal with any substantive offences that may then occur.

Having recently encountered this and been challenged by the Superintendant on my "mentality", I ran it past the Inspector and he decided to authorise bail. I ensured the bail date was the mandatory, set-in-legislation 28 days and got rid. I'd stuck conditions of non-contact and not to attend the partner's address, unless pre-arranged with police present. He'd negotiated the latter condition with the Inspector when making reps, stating he'd need work uniform etc. That seemed fair enough.

As I binned him, the overdose guy left for hospital with ambulance.

We handed over a full cell block to the two days sergeants, explaining they'd be an interview room down due to the previous night's antics. Live wires were still exposed from a wall plug that'd been ripped off the wall whilst furniture was thrown about. We handed over the full, just about still standing cell block of mid twenty-something prisoners to the bare bones days team and went home.

This set has been another relentless one. The 9 to 5 slog of the first four days didn't help but was hardly to blame. The sheer volume of work is. I've been left feeling exhausted, frustrated, bruised, aching, nauseous, and extremely anxious. Of course, I will battle through. I shall not moan. I will continue to do my best. The job will get 110% from me, as usual. I am now three months into my custody experience to the day, including training. They expect a minimum of two years. So, twenty-one months to go...

<u>Chapter Seven – Impending Nuclear War</u>

I did not spend my rest days contemplating the Trump v North Korea dick measuring contest. Though things *are* starting to get rather concerning. I think now would be a great time to make Team America 2, though I doubt even the South Park guys have got the balls after the Rogan/Franco *The Interview* fallout.

Instead, I made the mistake of seeing Cars 3 at the cinema. It was *alright* but definitely one of Disney Pixar's weaker efforts. I went for the kids really. I should clarify, I went for the benefit of my own kids, I didn't go *for* kids in general. Why am I typing this shit instead of just deleting?! Have I become *so* lazy that I'd rather continue my flow of typing than extend the fingers of my right hand up an inch and right to hit backspace?! Apparently so...

Nothing much more to report from rest days. The weather was fairly shite for the most part. Heavy rain for two days solid. Meaning my kids were starting to feel like Jack Torrance. Hell, my son even started mumbling "Redrum...redrum...", which was in no part influenced by me. Honest. Although, naturally, it was Snapchatted to concerned family members.

As is often the case, the weather turned gorgeous for my first day back in custody. We were blessed with a faulty affray alarm, meaning they'd decided to close eight cells, limiting the amount of prisoners left for us. Sadly, this alarm was fixed later that morning.

I booked in three people all shift. One a warrant, two for breach of court bail. The warrant was straight forward. I'd done plenty of those now. I had to double check a few things before I got the first BOB (breach of bail) in, not having done one before. My colleague recommended I lay the information during the booking in process, provided I was happy a breach had occurred. Laying the information is basically the equivalent of charging the DP. The breach was fairly clear cut. Officers had responded to a possible domestic in progress and one of the parties present had court bail conditions not to be there. He was put before the next available court.

The next BOB was slightly more complicated. That chap had a curfew overnight he had to observe, which was monitored via electronic tag. The company responsible had sent a statement through advising of the breach. I booked him in and only then did the officer decide to tell me there may be issues with it. They went away and phoned the tagging company, whilst I took a call out of nowhere from the OIC of the original job, for which the DP had those conditions. As if by magic, they'd been informed (pretty much instantaneously) their guy had been arrested and explained the mix up. They'd gone to court with him a few days earlier, where he'd applied to have his bail address changed. They'd agreed but hadn't explained the following steps well to him, prompting him to remove the tagging equipment himself when he got home and move it to his other address himself. Sure enough, the tagging equipment did not like being moved by non-approved personnel and sent a distress message to it's owner, prompting them to respond to check their kit was ok. Having not been granted entry to check it was okay (the chap had moved address as per the court's say-so) they recorded this as a breach. They only got the court's bail address memo *after* they sent us the statement but did not think to contact us urgently so we could disregard.

I released him NFA, telling him he probably shouldn't have moved the kit himself.

Having a third sergeant on makes all the difference and we had just that today. They'd sent one of mine to CPS and the decision came through just before handover. It was a young lady with several mental health issues, who'd entered a shop with a knife, made threats and demanded money. She'd not seen through her threats but rather waited patiently (in the queue, I believe!) for police to arrive. She felt safer in custody. That appeared to be why she got herself arrested. She'd disclosed recent self harm on arrival and stated to custody staff she intended on harming herself if released. Bail was denied.

The next morning, I had the DP handed back over to me. The Russian roulette on who'd get this potential death after police contact fell on me. I completed the pre-release risk assessment with her in my charge room, ensuring it was on CCTV. She made it quite clear she had intentions on harming herself but wanted to go back to the prison she'd previously been to, as knows the staff there. She is already under mental health services and declined any support I offered, albeit, was extremely pleasant and polite. What more can you do?! The PER form contained all the relevant risks. I heard the DO explain these to the court escort in the detail they deserved. Yet, once again, if she decides to kill herself within the next week or so, no doubt this will be attributed to *my* failings. At least, that's the picture the custody course painted for me. I'm fast running out of fingers to cross!

One guy was in for death by dangerous driving. He seemed surprisingly chilled, given the offence. He was adamant it was his mate driving, but he wasn't a grass. He told me his mate would be handing himself in. Given how chilled he was, this is entirely possible. Perhaps knowing he'd not done anything, he knew he had nothing to worry about. But I found it unsettling nonetheless.

The nurse was umming and arring over a DP that had a bad back and chest pains. She was in two minds as to whether he should be checked out at hospital. I said if it made her decision any easier, it was a minor criminal damage and I would be seeking to release him under investigation as opposed to sitting two officers at hospital with him for his entire visit. She opted for hospital and I got an officer to transport him there. Another DP down. I got rid of a couple other easy wins too.

As is often the case, I got wind of a CPS decision coming through just before handover to lates. This put the onus on me to start looking at the DP's previous convictions (precons) and work out whether to remand or grant bail.

The DP in question was one of two in for PWITS (possession with intent to supply). They'd been seen by plain clothed officers dealing from a vehicle. Upon being challenged, one made off on foot and the other tried swallowing drugs but CS spray and police baton foiled his attempt. The one that made off was caught and found in possession of a lock knife. Officers recovered around sixty wraps of heroin and crack. Good little job, that.

One DP was a clear remand candidate, with several previous for robberies. A custodial sentence was likely and they had previous for failing to appear at court and offending on bail. My colleague wrote up their remand decision.

I checked my chap's after handover itself, wanting to give it some consideration. He had no previous since 2015 and that was only simple possession of cannabis. Then, nothing prior to that since 2011 and only a few things from there going back a further four years. No fail to appear markers. No offends on bail.

I read the CPS advice and noticed they supported a remand on *both*, saying any application for bail was not appropriate.

Don't get me wrong, I'm all *for* remanding people. On response, as a PC, it was frustrating seeing so many get bail and I considered some skippers too lenient. But now I have a custody head on and just couldn't see the grounds here.

I considered doing it for his own safety. He was likely to owe people higher up the supply chain a great deal of money, given the quantity of drugs seized. People would be angry. Serious violence can occur. But I didn't believe he would be any safer in prison. Who goes to prison anyway? Baddies! Who would be after him? Baddies!

I left work having asked the OIC to make enquiries as to what police station in London would be ideal for him to report to, as part of his bail conditions. I suggested another not to enter our county at all, given he has no links here other than dealing drugs.

This was an area where I was a little uncertain and had to seek advice. Remanding people is sometimes clear cut but this was a case where I felt I was having to try and make it fit, where really it didn't. I think I've therefore made the correct decision. I shall check tomorrow and see whether the lates skipper thought otherwise.

That evening, we had my brother and sister-in-law over for some cards. Very civilised, I know! To start, my brother was the only one drinking, as I prefer to avoid drinking during the working set, leaving it for rest days. However, after watching him down a couple of Strongbows, I couldn't help but get the Captain out.

After finishing what must have been about ten Strongbows, my brother kindly informed us all of his strange bedtime routine of performing a 'safety wipe'. I'll leave that one to your imaginations.

I also felt the need to try and whip the tablecloth off, without the coasters going anywhere. I've done this many times before with great success. However, the coasters went flying off into the next room. My brother, keen to challenge me, repeated the trick, only this time with his mobile phone instead of coasters (I'm still not sure where they all went). He confidently placed his phone on the tablecloth and I started filming on my mobile. Just before performing the trick, he said "Watch this!" in the same fateful way people say "I'll be right back!" in horror movies.

Sure enough, his phone went flying, hitting the table, a chair and finally the tiled floor. Alcohol makes people stupid.

I crammed in a viewing of The Spy Who Loved Me, with the kids the following morning before work. For me, it's up there among the best 007s. Excellent score, gadgets and henchman. I reminded my daughter she'd met the producer once when she was with my folks on a sailing trip. Their club had ventured down a river and stopped at a pub for lunch. She'd polished off her grub before everyone else and in true child fashion, moaned they were still hungry and he'd given her one of his chips. Gutted I'd not been there myself, as the geek in me would've asked so many questions about the experiences of working on not one, but *two* Bonds (he produced Moonraker too).

Handover at work was slightly later than normal, as one of the two days skippers binned three simultaneously. I therefore took over five myself from an anticipated eight, which I was happy with. I then released four over the next couple hours!

On handover, I had heard the other skipper get told about an incident that morning where a DP had been found smoking in their cell. To my surprise, there'd been no mention of them being strip searched. As I completed my initial checks, I smelt cigarette smoke along a certain section of the corridor. I pinpointed it down to outside a particular cell and checked which DP the morning incident related to and sure enough, it was that one. I therefore went in with a DO and completed a strip search.

The chap removed one sock and it was like winning the fruity, only with matches. He also produced a blue plastic wrap from the same sock, containing tobacco and further matches. I explained we'd be completing the full strip search anyway, and was glad I did, as literally every item he took off had matches raining from them. Even his boxers!

The DO went through books he had in there and literally every other page had matches in.

Once we were satisfied all matches were accounted for, we left him to it and I placed a marker on PNC for 'conceals', so this would be a consideration for his next visit.

It was a really pleasant shift after the four I binned. I booked in another DP but then charged a shoplifter, keeping my count at one. You really do need shifts like that to recharge and manage stress.

I got some E-learning done, which is unheard of in custody! I got round to printing some duties sheets off for myself and the wife.

About an hour before handover, a warrant turned up. He had a recent 'conceals' marker, having been found smoking in his cell. With the last cell-smoker fresh in memory, I was keen to ensure this DP wouldn't be too. They shouldn't be routinely carried out, so I was keen to ensure grounds were justified. As the circs of the arrest were explained, it became clear officers had attended a report of a male in a public toilet suspected to be using drugs. They attended and knocked the door, identifying themselves as police and the DP came out shortly after. Clearly there would've been an opportunity to conceal and given the suspected use of drugs, I was therefore happy to authorise. Nothing was found but at least I knew there would be no secret smoking or fire risks to the block over the weekend of their stay.

I handed over my two DPs to a very pleasantly surprised nights team and then held a PDR meeting with one of the two DOs I supervise. Then, it was home time.

The next afternoon I was picked up by a DO to travel to another station, which had opened specially to cater for a local Op. As I was literally walking out the door, the wife answered the house phone and passed it to me, thinking it was the person picking me up. It wasn't. I was stood down from the lovely jolly I'd been anticipating and diverted elsewhere, still for the Op but somewhere busier. Having arrived there, we realised we were spare parts. Our usual station was clearly run ragged, with only two sergeants on lates and an almost full cell block. The Inspectors agreed it made sense for me to return to my usual station but said they couldn't make that decision, as it had to be made by the Inspector in charge of the Op. Someone I was struggling to get hold of! I did eventually manage to get hold of her and once I'd explained things, we resumed back to our home station.

The two sergeants there were booking in and I took disposals. Pretty much straight away as I landed, as people were loitering with no sergeants available to speak to.

There was a breach of non-molestation order, whereby a man had sent his ex partner numerous text messages since the order was granted recently. This was the first breach and I didn't anticipate the courts would likely give a custodial sentence and he had little previous. I was umming and arring whether to propose a remand, given he'd already breached an order of the court and therefore what bail conditions would he likely adhere to? I briefly discussed with another sergeant, who stated we wouldn't necessarily remand on first breach. I sent the job to CPS proposing bail with conditions.

I then reviewed a domestic assault, whereby the female DP had lamped her partner. I actually mean this as it sounds – she twatted him over the head with a ceramic lamp. This caused a small cut to his head. There was no complaint from him, but the attending officer had documented disclosure in their statement. In addition, they'd captured this disclosure on body worn video camera. There were photographs of the injury, the broken lamp and fragments of what appeared to be ceramic lamp in the victim's hair and on his clothing. The DP had provided a 'no comment' interview. It seemed pretty clear to me from the evidence available that the victim had been hit over the head with the lamp. I was satisfied the FCT was met and directed the OIC to seek CPS advice.

They clearly disagreed, having already added a log saying they didn't believe the job would ever be at the THT. The THT was irrelevant. The job was at the FCT as far as I was concerned.

I received an email from that officer's sergeant, stating they didn't believe the case was at the FCT and that they've been criticized by CPS recently for sending such cases for pre-charge advice, when really they should've been NFA'd by police.

I disagreed and stood by my decision. For me, the fact we had a visible injury (albeit, fairly minor) and photos of the lamp and fragments of it on the victim, this was clear cut for CPS. Of all the domestics we review in custody, ones with this type of evidence should, in my view, be pushed for victimless prosecution. In addition, this domestic involved persons with chaotic lifestyles, both being heroin addicts and the DP also being an alcoholic. This to me, raises risk. There was also mention of historic incidents involving the DP lunging at the victim with a knife. If I had NFA'd this and a murder occurred, I'd expect to be pulled up for not sending it. Don't get me wrong – if there was no injury and little other corroborating evidence, I'd have quite happily NFA'd it. But that wasn't the case here. I explained my rationale and directed the OIC to continue.

Shortly before handover, a DP arrived. I booked them in whilst the other skippers got ready for handover. They'd been nicked by armed officers, and transported by locals, who clearly knew little about the job. The booking in sheet stated 'Possession of a firearm', with the circumstances being 'DP seen in his address holding a firearm'.

I had to dig deeper myself by reading the initial call log - it was clear a witness walking past the address had seen the DP holding a gun, pointing it at another. A containment had been placed on and the DP arrested, having matched the description of the offender. A search was under way and persons were being spoken to now the DP had been removed and couldn't collude with witnesses. I was then happy to authorise detention. Especially given the DP had markers for mental health, firearms and checks also revealed he'd previously kidnapped a police officer. Basically, this was someone you did not want to be in possession of a firearm. I booked him in for the offence of possession of firearm with intent to cause fear of violence.

After handover, one of the other sergeants caught me and explained they'd decided to remand the breach of non-mol chap, the advice having come back from CPS to charge. They explained their rationale, keen to try and smooth things over to ensure I didn't feel put out. This had been a bit of a grey area for me and I was leaning towards remand for a bit. Ultimately, being reminded that nine out of ten murders are domestic related does put things into perspective. You can never be *too* careful. The fact he'd breached an order of the court did make bail conditions a bit of a mockery. To be fair to the sergeant I'd briefly discussed it with earlier, they were busy and didn't have full facts of the case. I'm still learning and was receptive to the feedback, reassuring them I was fine with their decision to go against mine and expect I'll be more confident remanding in future.

When I got home, my wife asked how work was and, as you do, I got off my chest I felt a little annoyed for not having realised he should've been remanded myself. That was the correct decision the more I thought about it. She recommended I watch a program 'Catching a killer' about a high risk missing person investigation in TVP that turned into a murder enquiry.

It was an absolutely brilliant program. Extremely upsetting, especially as young children were involved. The partner had basically found out his wife had an affair and killed her overnight, disposing of the body whilst the kids slept. One child had heard the commotion and explained during his video interview that Daddy had taken the rug into work the next day to have it cleaned. That poor kid. With no idea what that meant at the time, he'll grow up starting to put things together and begin to understand, a lot younger than most, just how cruel the world can be.

This program put things into perspective for me and is a chilling reminder of how important decisions are we make in custody. With it being relentless, if you need time to make a decision, you'll have to inconvenience people and turn them away so you can concentrate on things, rather than make quick decisions. The fact custody is busy and doesn't have enough staff won't save my job when things go wrong, I'm sure of that.

The following day was my wife's first shift at her new station, having now finished initial training. It was a training day, with no training planned. The shift were catching up with E-learning and she used the opportunity to do the same and sort her locker out.

That night, I checked what decision CPS made on that no complaint, lamp-over-the-head domestic. NFA. I forwarded the result to someone collating such examples to raise with CPS, disappointed they didn't run it.

I released two Lithuanian's, one of which I charged drink/driving, no insurance and driving otherwise than in accordance with a licence, and NFA'd for TWOC. The other was NFA'd for TWOC. This procedure was slowed down by the fact both required an interpreter. The charge wording for the traffic related offences was rather long winded.

I then charged another PBT (positive breath test – lazy police talk for drink/driver).

I booked in a guy who'd assaulted police by throwing items out a window at a domestic they were attending. One item, a bottle of perfume, smashed at the ground beside the officer, with fragments of the glass hitting their leg. It was really a means to an end but having said that, it's still unacceptable to be throwing things anywhere near an officer, so I had no issue accepting.

The rest of the night was blissfully Q. I got the PDR for my DO typed up and sent off.

I went home and had an awesome sleep, through to around 1600hrs.

I started my last night shift slightly earlier than normal. Whilst the wife is not independent, she isn't allowed a flexible working pattern. This will be the case for around twelve weeks, whilst she's assessed by her tutor. We work opposite one another, for childcare reasons. I'd been denied a permanent flexible working pattern but they *did* allow me to work varied nights for the temporary period. This was reflected on my duties, with a clear note from the DCI I was not to be varied on what are in reality, only about eight or so problematic duties.

In classic police-fashion, things didn't quite go to plan. Clearly I cannot be counted towards MSL on those nights, as otherwise it leaves a single sergeant in charge of up to a full cell block of twenty-something prisoners. But they did just that. One sergeant was varied at short notice due to an exigency (yay, go me!) of duty, leaving just myself and another. They noticed the day before they'd messed up and couldn't plug the gap. I wasn't approached by them at all to vary back – the note from the DCI was clear. Sadly, this meant the other skipper had to pick up the slack for the last three quarters of an hour, until days arrived.

Would we get fortunate and have a quiet shift, to make things not only easier but *safer* for that last period? Yeah right.

It started off manic.

Before handover, I wrote up a couple of DPs ready to RUI. The jobs were linked. *She* was a late-50s drug addict, very vulnerable and *he* was a seventeen year old from London suspected of cuckooing her address. Cuckooing is when a dealer takes over the address of a vulnerable person to use it as a base for their dealing activities. I'm no ornithologist, but I gather cuckoos do this. Well, cuckoos don't go into other bird's nests and deal drugs. But they do apparently invade other bird's nests. Now I've bloody got this mental image as I type of a stoned bird sat in a nest with their feet up and I've totally lost track of where I was going.

There was an issue with the seventeen year old, in that they were believed to be from a foster home in London but we couldn't determine where. I directed the OIC to make enquiries whilst we were on handover. Likewise, I couldn't release the woman until the OIC had booked their flat keys out of seized property. Why they were in *there* as opposed to her custody property locker, I don't know.

After handover, whilst I sorted my detention logs on DPs I'd taken over, my DO went and booked in a warrant elsewhere. It was then busy busy busy. A queue of DPs arrived, including some returning from hospital having already been booked in but with little done in way of risk assessments.

I was trying to update a custody record as my DO accepted back a chap from hospital. They'd had a catheter fitted whilst away and reeked of urine and shit. It was *very* off-putting and it took a while for the smell to dissipate. As soon as they left, it dawned on me the next person to enter would likely assume that was me. Great. Luckily, we keep a can of Glade handy for such occasions.

I became aware there was a van waiting outside for an ambulance to check over a DP before they came into custody. I went outside to investigate. I was informed the guy lived in some form of assisted accommodation and staff had phoned police due to his behaviour. He'd assaulted one of the attending officers by kicking them in the leg.

He was checked over and deemed not to require hospital treatment. He was then further arrested for assaulting and racially abusing staff at his residence, before being presented to me in custody.

He was hard work. He didn't become aggressive or violent, which was actually unfortunate, as it would've been a great excuse to Route One. As it was, he just took ages answering every question, being tearful. I was half-minded to abandon the risk assessment and take to cell anyway, as a queue had developed but thought the powers that be would disapprove should something happen. I stuck it out and eventually got the process more or less completed. Meanwhile, the other sergeant booked in a couple drink drivers, both blowing around 39/40Ugs at the roadside and having to queue to get into custody! The legal limit is 35. Fortunately both blew just over in custody – 40 and 43 I believe. Lucky indeed. Not for them, clearly.

In next was a schizophrenic who'd damaged five cars. Upon officers entering his address to retrieve medication for custody, they smelt cannabis and followed their noses to a box containing a large quantity of herbal and resin cannabis, deal bags, deal lists etc. He was further nicked for PWITS. Shockingly, during the risk assessment, it appeared he had a cannabis habit. No doubt this will be one of those PWITS where they claim to buy in bulk for personal use to save money and happen to be an avid collector of little plastic bags. This was quickly followed by a cheeky chappy who recognised me instantly, as I did him. I couldn't recall his name by heart but knew I'd booked him in recently. He was definitely someone you wouldn't fancy fighting with – well built and bulging biceps. Fortunately, he was in the mood for joking about and having a laugh. Which I'm all up for provided you can get through what you need to. And we did. He was by far the easiest customer of the night, yet arrested for probably the most serious offence – a knife point robbery.

Last up was a female for domestic assault on her partner and eighteen year old son. Aware my colleague was busy, I volunteered to take her. Then I heard her crying and regretted my kindness. She'd apparently returned home, grabbed her partner by his throat as he lay in bed and the son had then got assaulted as he tried getting her off dad.

She was brought in front of me and wouldn't shut up. She shouldn't be there, she kept telling me. Sadly, given her drunken behaviour, that was *exactly* where she needed to be. I got one question of the risk assessment completed, before she turned to the arresting officer and started lashing out. Route One it was. As we popped her in a cell, I realised she had a belt sewn into her dress. There were no female officers available and it would've involved taking the whole dress off. She settled straight away, lying on the bench. I decided to manage the risk via CCTV, not wishing to fight a drunk woman and strip her naked. That's often why people are brought *into* custody.

I handed over all my DPs to my colleague around half five, leaving him with responsibility for around twenty total. It got worse – when we did the handover, we both realised he'd have to wake them all up and check they were alive and well. That is what *has* to happen when you take responsibility for them at the start of your shift, so we decided that *must* be done taking over responsibility at *any* time. Hardly fair on the prisoners at half five but then duties left us in that position. I couldn't let the wife be late for her first proper shift.

My first rest day involved the usual bare minimum sleep, followed by a couple hours peace before collecting the kids from holiday club and taking them to swimming lessons. My son had his first lesson the week before and taking them both is tiring but rewarding nonetheless.

The following day I stuck Moonraker on for them. My lad seemed to love that one – it's an enjoyable but profoundly silly Bond film. It was clearly an attempt (succeeding too) to cash in after the success of Star Wars – the ending of the previous 007 film stated Bond would be back in For Your Eyes Only but producers clearly saw their opportunity to capitalize on space-fever. "I think he's attempting re-entry, Sir!" – got to be the best line in the franchise.

I worked overtime that night on response. This was another shift I'd effectively made for myself a couple weeks back by putting the offer out there to duties. It was a fairly boring shift. I had to review around four or five mispers, something I certainly do not miss! But it was easy enough and therefore easy money.

We met my folks for lunch the next day, just about cramming it in before my son's doctor appointment. For a couple years now he's been moaning about his knees. We assumed it was his 'go-to' excuse for not wanting to walk and preferring to be carried instead. A couple of years on and we now feel like awful parents and were worried perhaps he had something seriously wrong. It turns out they're both fine and he'll live. For Your Eyes Only followed, with Octopussy seeing out the final evening before my shifts started again.

Things appear to have calmed down somewhat in the dick measuring contest. I just read Trump believes the North Korean threats could be good for Guam's tourism industry. There's a police phrase reserved for such people – "Four-Zero".

Episode Eight – The Last Jedi

My mind started wondering off to the world of movies, as it often does. You may have guessed I'm somewhat a fan. Star Wars soon came to mind and I instantly forgot I was supposed to be writing a book and started searching trailers online. Then, something in my mind twigged and I realised I was off track.

I suppose you could view custody as having a light and dark side. The light side being, of course, the Jedi master sergeants. And the dark side being the scrotes. Or perhaps the solicitors? One things for certain...Jabba seems to have a season pass.

First day back and I reckon I've already managed to upset someone. No-one likes their prisoners being NFA'd for D&Ds, but I had to do it. There was *no* evidence of the chap being drunk or disorderly. Circs were, the DP had been restrained on the ground by doorstaff at a club. Police were called and the first officer on scene cuffs the guy whilst he's still on the floor. Doorstaff explained he was extremely drunk and had refused to leave. In their statement, the officer then states he stood the guy up and realised he was intoxicated. They then arrested D&D.

Now, I fully expect the guy was shouting and swearing, being generally obscene with his language, all with slurred speech, stinking of booze and almost falling over he was so drunk. But none of that was in the statement. I pinged an email off to the officer afterwards, copying their skipper in, recognizing they were a student officer and this probably should've been picked up by someone observing their work. I kept the email polite and made it clear I was keen to ensure they understood where they went wrong, so their next D&D gets a more positive outcome.

A drink driver came in soon after. He was a polite, young guy who'd clearly had a skin-full the night before and didn't think about the potential consequences of getting behind the wheel come morning. He blew around 58Ugs in custody. I gave it a couple hours before charging him. He got really upset when I explained he'd have to wait in a cell for that time, so I let him use the exercise yard and he stayed there the whole time. He seemed genuinely nice and it was clear he wasn't a bad person. He'd just made a very bad decision.

One officer was determined to confuse me that morning. A twenty-one year old was brought in for around seven or eight offences. These included sexual assault, two GBHs, three ABHs and a concerned in the supply of cannabis. I think there was another sexual assault offence he'd been nicked for too. It wasn't really the officer's fault. They'd spotted this guy and knew he was outstanding. Whoever was collating the jobs hadn't thought about doing one overall arrest strategy and so there were about three or four separate ones, all for different offences, with different references numbers on. The officer had written the wrong references against the wrong offences and it became a bit of a muddle. One thing was clear – this guy was clearly on a destructive path. You'd never have guessed it though, dealing with him. He looked like a bit of a dweeb.

I took minimal disposal updates that morning, as we were blessed with a third skipper, who took the majority of those. Custody seemed a bit more relaxed and things were running efficiently.

The next morning was a different affair. Once I'd booked in a warrant, we had a full cell block. We had three sergeants on again. One of the others contacted the control room and told them we were closed for business.

A short while later, the duty Inspector contacted me and asked why we were closed. Who had made that decision and on what grounds?! They sounded genuinely angry. I found this bizarre and explained I'd made the decision we were closed on the grounds we were full and couldn't fit any more prisoners in custody! I felt like breaking it down further...this is the number of cells we have...this is the number of prisoners we have. This leaves no spaces. I felt this was not a good career move.

I reviewed a job whereby damage had been caused to a bicycle and the victim verbally abused. The DP had stated the bike was in fact theirs and had been able to describe it in remarkable detail. It seemed clear it must have at one time been their bike. Whether it still was needed further investigation. There were also CCTV enquiries outstanding and I decided to release them under investigation, as this was hardly the sort of job requiring full use of the PACE clock.

I also reviewed a job whereby a male was seen rifling through charity bins. These turned out to be landfill bins as opposed to donation ones. He'd been detained for a search and admitted having a knife in his pocket. A lock knife. He was therefore arrested but was quick to say he'd found it in the bins. In interview, he again stated he'd found it in the bins, didn't realise it was a lock knife and said he intended on handing it to staff at his hostel. Clearly a load of bull. Surely, if you found a knife in a bin, you'd leave it there. Not take it out to hand it in to someone, who'd probably only put it in a bin anyway. The fact he'd previously been charged with a similar offence didn't help his defence. It was clear he'd be contesting this and I therefore sent to CPS. They, however, wanted a statement from the charity confirming they would never put a knife in their bins. Again, I was not looking to remand this chap and released him so that enquiry could be completed, as ridiculous as it seemed.

One DP was on the charmingly titled 'poo watch'. They were a sixteen year old suspected transient drug dealer. Officers had nicked an older guy for PWITS and searched his address. There, they found a drug user and this sixteen year old. The drug user confided in officers, revealing the young lad had plugged drugs. This is another charming term for when someone has shoved drugs up their jacksie to hide them. The officers searched the lad and found drug paraphernalia, a large quantity of cash, mobile phones and a tub of Vaseline. Hmm…what could that be for?! Dry hands, perhaps.
Having a sixteen year old on poo watch is far from ideal. He'd been strip searched the night before, but nothing found. I doubt he'd have consented to an intimate search, as he'd already refused hospital. Two officers had to remain on close proximity with him, so should he need to shit, one would observe, whilst the other would have the (crap) job of sifting through the product. Not really worth the bonus pay, that. His mother arrived and was polite enough but a bit demanding. She wasn't happy the room we'd set aside for her to chat with her son was a camera cell. We had no other rooms available that had CCTV and clearly there was a need to continue observing. I had no issues with him going in a non-camera room with his solicitor, as I'd like to think even a solicitor would be good enough to alert officers if their client suddenly shat out a kinder egg.
Ultimately, investigating officers needed to decide what the long term plan was with this chap. He'd never been arrested before and was, after all, a child. If there was no significant intelligence he was a major player (doubtful if never arrested), it'd be unlikely we'd seek to charge him and gain authority from the court to keep on poo watch for the next week. I directed officers to make these enquiries, which were still ongoing as I handed over to lates.

I started the first late realising I had the second late and first night off. I saw this leave a couple months ago and couldn't work out why I'd booked them. I saw my last night had been declined, so can only assume I'd put in for the whole set at one point and only been granted a couple useless days in the middle and forgot to cancel. As it was, with the kids off, I decided to keep them but simply forgot about them. After the shift I was about to experience, they couldn't have come at a better time...

There were two sergeants on. A queue of three developed whilst we were getting handover from days. I got my DO to start loading the custody record for the first during handover and afterwards, I authorised detention and left them booking in whilst I checked my DPs were alive and well. I then added my detention logs formally taking them over whilst the DP was being booked in. He was hard work. An arrogant, knew-it-all man. Mr Twat if you will. Had to be in and out quickly as he was the boss and needed to collect his employees from various sites. I explained that wasn't going to happen but that we'd permit him a phone call. He disliked having to take off his watch and was very keen to tell us it cost £9000. The DO held the watch as carefully as you would a newborn baby, gently wrapping it in an evidence bag, then into another for added padding. He explained it'd be placed in the safe for additional security. It was very hard for Mr Twat to keep arguing the toss when we were being this accommodating.

Once he was in his cell, in came the next. She'd been arrested for assaulting her partner. I genuinely felt sorry for her. She was an alcoholic, who disclosed during the risk assessment she'd been raped a few days ago. It turned out, she'd left a voicemail on a friend's phone, saying what'd happened. The friend clearly misunderstood and thought husband had raped her. The friend reported this and police attended. The incident had *already* been reported by her. Yet, whilst police were there, the husband happened to disclose that morning they'd had an argument, during which she hit him on the arm. Much to his protest, she got arrested.

She was anxious about being placed in a cell, having previously been kept in custody for quite some time. When asked the 'self harm' question during her risk assessment, she stated she wanted to kill herself. She was coherent and perfectly polite. I thought that was an understandable state of mind to be in, so soon after such a traumatic experience. Fortunately, she made it clear this was more out of fear of staying in custody, as opposed to genuine intention. She accepted help in custody from our mental health liaison. We gave her a book to help keep her distracted.

Throughout booking in these two, a DO had kept updating me a DP was becoming more and more agitated, demanding an Inspector or they'd tie clothing round their neck and do a 'dirty protest'. On handover, I'd been warned about that guy and that he did this last time he was in. There'd been no CCTV cells available, so he was placed in a non camera cell that had a toilet, as he'd stated on arrival his main gripe last time was a lack of facilities. He made it clear he'd no wish to speak with a sergeant but wouldn't disclose *why* they required an Inspector.

I instructed the DO to see if the Inspector was free to humour them, keen to avoid a dirty protest. They were unable to locate them and sure enough, the DP started wrapping clothing round his neck. I therefore started reviewing risks of other DPs and made a decision to move one from a camera cell to elsewhere, as they'd been calm during their stay to that point. The problem DP was then moved to this camera cell. Fortunately, on route, he removed all clothing of his own accord, except socks and boxers.

Unfortunately, it was not long before he started his dirty protest. Shit was smeared over the camera, meaning CCTV had become useless. He then started to tie his socks together and threatened to place them round his neck. I went to the cell and could smell shit from the other side of the door. The DP showed me his socks tied together and told me what he was going to do with them.

I left a student officer (there on attachment, lucky him) watching him, whilst I spoke to the other sergeant. We decided to put on scenes of crime overalls and go into the cell to remove remaining clothing. Just as we kitted up, looking like a couple of cheap imitation ghostbusters (or sandwich factory workers, for that matter), some ICVs turned up. These are Independent Custody Visitors. I'd learnt about them during training and was told they generally pop into custody unannounced about once a week. This was the first time I'd seen them. What a time to choose! They're volunteers from the local community who check how DPs are treated and report back with suggestions for improvement. This serves as another way of improving public confidence in police and allows us to be more transparent in how we work.

We brought them into the charge room so they could be present whilst we discussed what we were about to do and how we would achieve it. I'd not expected such a formal briefing and expect my colleague put it on for their benefit. I was prepared to just get on and do it but couldn't mock the professionalism of my colleague's approach.

I felt like a right tit – stood there with a blue plastic shoe covering on my head, as my overalls were lacking the built-in hood my colleague's had. But I'd rather that than get shit in my hair.

This was not how I expected my day to go.

In we went. The DP jumped up off the bench and backed himself against the far wall. He became aggressive and threatened violence. He was a weedy looking chap and I had no concerns about getting him under control, but was more wary of shit being flung. As it was, I couldn't see much shit, other than on the camera and some on the rear of the cell door. I knew he must have some on his hands and when he pointed them aggressively at my colleague, I grabbed hold of the arm nearest me to keep it under control. He'd actually put his socks back on by that point but we still wanted them removed. We made it clear if he didn't do it himself, we would. He eventually did and threw them one by one out the door. Fortunately, the officer stood there caught them before they landed in his face.

We decided to leave the boxers on him and afford him the opportunity of maintaining some thin slice of dignity. He said he'd wash the shit off the camera if we brought him some water but then stood up and started wiping it off with his bare hands. The water supply had been cut off from his sink, fearing a cell flooding. He declined our offer to turn it on for long enough for him to wash his hands. Dirty bastard. Mr Shitsmear, I decided.

I kept the suit on for the next quarter of an hour, anticipating a quick return that fortunately never happened. I took it off carefully, and stored it under my desk for reuse if required.

I then completed a use of force form and decided a 'near-miss' report appropriate, due to what we'd been exposed to and the potential for it to have gone differently. In good old police fashion, these forms are lengthy and time consuming. I kept minimising them to deal with other matters, only to find when I maximised them they'd timed out and needed restarting. This became somewhat tedious.

Once caught up, we booked in a domestic criminal damage. I was beyond caring it was a couple days old and minor damage to kitchen drawer. It was a domestic after all. The officers had been waiting the best part of two hours, whilst we dealt with Mr Shitsmear and other issues. Once the circs had been given, I got the officers on their way.

Another sergeant on restricted duties then appeared from nowhere and explained they'd taken a disposal review of mine on, as the officer had been loitering for ages. They wanted to discuss a point of law. The job was a shoplifting, whereby a female had stolen items whilst the male waited outside the shop. The male then popped his head briefly inside the store as the female came running out and handed the items to him. Her view was this was a handling on the male's part, rather than theft, as *she* had appropriated the property and *he* played no active part in the removal of the goods, only took them from her as she left. I had my mind on other things and to be honest, was prepared to go along with this. To be fair, it sounded logical. I think it could be argued either way. With the DP contesting he was even there, a handling offence would require CPS advice, whereas a shoplifting could've been charged by a sergeant. I was pretty sure what CPS would say but off it went regardless.

I prepared a remand rationale for the DP in question, knowing they'd be charged with at least one other shoplifting admitted anyway. They'd previously been sentenced to a month in prison, suspended for six months. We were still within that period and I therefore believed it highly likely they'd receive a custodial sentence for this latest matter. In addition, they were heroin and crack dependant, unemployed, with no way of funding this habit. To top things off, they'd failed to appear at court only a couple months ago.

At the start of the shift, my DO had expressed a wish to be trained in disposals, should the opportunity arise. We received word CPS had authorised a charge on a DP in for domestic assault.

I talked them through the process, and off they went. It was all going so well. The DO read the charge and explained their bail conditions. He was clearly worried about how he'd see his children and I explained I'd get the OIC to contact the victim to discuss this and keep him updated. The DO started the pre-release risk assessment. Then came the "Do you have any thoughts of suicide or self harm?" question. "I'm going to slice the fuck out of myself" was the reply. This coming from a chap with markers for self harm by cutting.

The guy wanted out there and then. Wasn't going to happen. He started pacing about, getting more and more worked up. I explained I wasn't prepared to let him go straight away having just made that comment. I said he'd need to calm and talk to me, or I'd remand him for his own safety.

I asked my DO to get the mental health liaison to come talk with him. She was great and the chap did calm. She established his previous self harm was a form of release and he also suffers with anger management and has a tendency to say things before thinking of their consequences. Her records showed he'd never cut deep but rather superficially. He started focusing more on his children, saying he just wanted to leave and go to work, otherwise his family wouldn't be able to afford to continue living in their home. The more he started talking about providing for his children and focusing on the future, the more satisfied I became his threat was another outburst as opposed to a genuine intention to kill himself. He assured me he'd book an appointment the following morning to see his doctor, to get his meds reviewed. He was handed details of support agencies. He phoned his mother to collect him. I felt more confident letting him go was the right decision.

But no-one has a crystal ball. This chap may still go and kill himself.

A queue of people waiting to speak to me had formed. I no doubt pissed them off by shutting the door and allowing myself twenty minutes to write a damn good NDM documenting my decision. I could hear moaning from the other side of the door. People getting frustrated with me. The door served as a symbol I was not available, as opposed to shutting out any noise. I could hear people just as well as if it were open. They either didn't know this or didn't care. But, in the nicest way possible, sod them. This was my job on the line. *Potentially.* I'd like to think not. More likely stress, worry, upset, guilt, a long drawn out PSD investigation, followed by coroner's court etc. If the worst happened, the least I could've done was a bloody NDM explaining my thought process. They would have to wait.

I think only one remained outside by the time I finished. Clearly they'd found someone else to sort whatever problem they had or found someone else to review their job. I like to think I'm generally approachable. I needed that time to focus and felt better for doing so. Not entirely better, mind. My anxiety was kicking in. Tightness in the chest. As usual, I tried ignoring it. After all, I was too busy to really pay it much attention.

Updates started coming in for DPs I'd booked in earlier. I got my DO to action all of them, once I'd written them up. Mr Twat would sadly be NFA'd. A passerby had seen him banging on his wife's car window, demanding to be let inside. Upon being let inside, he was heard to verbally abuse her and as she drove off, he was seen to hit her. Normally, this would be pretty good evidence. Sadly, the call taker had only taken the witness' first name and mobile number. They hadn't stuck around to speak to officers. The OIC had tried several times but was unable to contact them. There was no trace of them on our system. The victim had actually provided a statement confirming *no* assault had occurred! The DP provided a no comment interview. He looked rather smug as he left. We carefully unwrapped his watch for him, ensuring this vital bit of extortionate wrist equipment was returned in pristine order.

The pleasant alcoholic lady would be NFA'd. Her husband refused to provide any statement. There were no visible injuries. This pleased me greatly. He collected her from the station, much to her relief. She was signposted to alcohol support services.

I hadn't heard *anything* from the OIC for the CPS handling job. I contacted them and they were only just beginning the paperwork! It'd been over two hours since the other sergeant reviewed it! I chased them along a bit.

The OIC dealing with Mr Shitsmear came and saw me. I explained we'd have to provide him an opportunity to be interviewed and to also get dressed for it! She explained there were other jobs he'd previously been released under investigation for that needed further questioning. This job was starting to get more and more griefy. I made her aware of the dirty protest and she explained she needed to get him charged for one he staged last time. Sounded like a plan to me. Here's hoping the courts recognise the sheer disgustingness of it and go for a suitably horrible sentence. Doubtful.

The criminal damage to kitchen drawer guy was NFA'd too. There was no complaint. He'd gone no comment. We had photographs of the damage. But then, I can't count the amount of times I've accidentally pulled a drawer out too far and the bloody thing has dropped to the floor. Maybe I'm just clumsy. She wanted him back. It was clearly a day for poor domestic detection rates.

Just before handover, word came from the handling job that CPS viewed it as more of a theft and that therefore a custody sergeant should be able to make the charging decision. This didn't surprise me in the slightest. I said I supported the review of my colleague and we should stick to our guns and keep it as a handling. There was clearly a double conversation going on, as I then heard the OIC speak to the prosecutor on another phone and they said if we wanted to get the handling authorised, they'd need a much better statement than the pro-forma one that had been taken. I'd not read it myself, but from what was described the criticism sounded fair. I said if the statement was too poor for a handling, it would be too poor for any offence. Poor is poor regardless! CPS said a promat would be required. I hadn't reviewed the job earlier but that sounded fair enough – the DP had denied even being there and the witness' explanation for knowing them was vague.

I handed over the remaining crap to nights, as the holding cell started filling up. They had two skippers on and as guilty as I felt for doing so, I abandoned them to go home, away from the madness and stress. I had two days leave. Much needed as it turned out. Time to chill away from people covering cells with their own excrement.

On that note, as I left, I remembered my dinner was still in the fridge. Hadn't had time to eat it. I went to turn the corner leading to the staff kitchen and as I did so, almost bumped into Mr Shitsmear, as he was escorted back from interview. That was close. Inches away from literally coming face to face with the vile creature. He looked at me, clearly disgusted at what he saw. The level of disgust on his face matched my own. I was unable to hide the expression of hatred on my face. How can someone in society be *that* horrendous?

So, that leave that couldn't have come at a better time...

I took the kids swimming for their weekly lesson. No issues there, other than I noticed my daughter was being made to do six lengths at a time - a big step up from the one / occasionally two she'd been doing before moving up a stage. Her breaststroke looked way more professional than anything I do but her breaths when popping above the surface looked far too short. I reckoned she was swallowing quite a bit of water and she confirmed this afterwards, stating she found it hard going.

We enjoyed a movie evening, watching The Living Daylights. The kids loved the Gibraltar opening, having both been there. My daughter was then sick pretty much all night long.

We'd run to her room and help with one wretching session, only to put her back to bed and hear another start twenty minutes later. That pattern continued through the night, even when there was nothing further to sick-up. I ended up sleeping on her floor, as I couldn't be arsed to keep moving between rooms. She finally settled around four in the morning, so I returned to my own bed, having only dozed at best on the floor.

This lack of sleep made me ratty the following day. I tried retreating to bed that morning, but failed to get sleep. I became stressed and bored, frustrated my leave was being spent confined to the house. Very selfish, I know. But I'd been desperate for these rest days and they felt wasted.

I spent much of the following day getting harassed by duties, sending me texts asking if I'd work a late, instead of a night. I ignored the text. They sent another that afternoon asking if I could start my night slightly earlier. I ignored it. My wife was at work on a day shift. There was no way I could do a late and I wanted to spend time with her in the evening before I disappeared to work. I don't think that's unreasonable. You have to have work/life balance. Sadly, being harassed by work is stressful. That's your home time. *Away* from work. It wasn't appreciated. I certainly wasn't going to respond. Why should I? We watched Licence to Kill that afternoon and I pointed out all the bits I reckon accounted for its 15 certificate. That's some good parenting there.

I started that night by booking in a warrant. However, this was a *bail* warrant. Shouldn't have even come to custody. I had avoided them like the plague on response, as did everyone. They were griefy, as no-one *really* knew what to do with them! Plus you got no credit for them, given it was not an arrest brought into custody. Therefore, the proactive officers saw no reason to go hunting, as they weren't seen as prey.

But this had arrived and so a custody record would be created. I had mixed advice on whether to turn away and not authorise detention, or whether to authorise and simply bail on the custody record. I did the latter. Problem was, when it came to bailing, there was no facility to print paperwork, due to warrants usually going straight to court. I had to phone the other force, whose warrant it was, and ask what court, date and time to bail them to. Once I established that, I wrote down these details and handed them to the DP on a piece of paper. There were no other skippers to consult with at that point and the DO with me was just as clueless.

The DP was pissed. They became aggressive to the point where at one stage, I thought I was going to have to take them straight to cell. But this was a bail warrant! Could I stick them there for a few hours until sober? Possibly. But even if that *was* legal, it was far from ideal. They shouldn't have been there anyway! I decided to chance it that matey actually understood what the hell was going on and handed him this scrap piece of paper and instructed the arresting officer to get rid asap.

That one will probably come back to bite me, I thought...

I took on disposals that night.

One of the skippers told me they'd written up a breach of a S35 dispersal notice for NFA (without boring with relevant legislation and specific Act, this is in essence a power to require a person to leave a specified area if they are being anti-social).

I read their write up. From what I gathered, the DP had been inebriated on arrest to the point he urinated himself. From the officer statements, there was doubt as to whether DP was fit enough to actually understand the order he'd been issued. The log stated he'd now sobered up and should be NFA'd.

I retrieved him from his cell and he followed me to the charge room. He walked slowly and with a limp. He didn't seem to know how he'd injured his hip. When I got him in the light of the charge room, he appeared clammy and his forehead was wringing with sweat. I informed him he was being NFA'd and started the pre-release risk assessment. He looked drained of all energy and practically had his tongue stuck out, like a dog on a scorching day. He craved water. I got a DO to bring him a couple cups. He needed more. He said he needed to use the toilet. He followed me to the nearest toilet and started staggered all over the place. His jeans fell down and I told him to pull them up but he said he'd no strength to do so. He went into the toilet and I heard a crash-bang sound. Something wasn't right. He eventually managed to get himself out the toilet and looked pale and ill. I asked if he wanted to see a nurse. I was reluctant to release him in that state, concerned he may collapse and I'd have a death on my hands. He agreed a nurse would be a good idea. Trouble is, I'd already NFA'd him. I had to pop him somewhere awaiting the nurse. And from what DOs told me, the nurse would only see someone in custody, not someone who'd been released. It was one of those cases where I felt calling an ambulance would be a massive waste of time, especially on a busy Friday night. The DP agreed to go back to his cell and I'd hoped the nurse would be able to pop down and quickly see him.

Unfortunately, there is an admin process to follow. The nurse had to be called through, despite her being on site. She was also on her meal break. Bad timing or what?! I found her in the kitchen and she was just finishing up. She was perfectly nice about the whole bizarre situation I'd found myself in and agreed to see him, but was probably a further twenty minutes before doing so. The whole time I started sweating myself, worried about this breach of PACE, unlawfully detaining someone.

I was only too pleased to escort the nurse to his cell myself. As if on cue, he then started vomiting over the cell floor. The nurse checked his vitals, which were all fine. She seemed to think the DP would be allowed some rest to recover from what was probably just a killer hangover. I explained I'd no power to keep him any longer, and as he was medically fine, I'd be releasing him. I saw the look of unease on her face, but this was on me, not her. I was just pleased that *medically* he was fine.

He just about managed to stagger out the rear yard, with a warm pasty I'd heated for him. Five minutes later, I realised he'd left his cash in the charge room. I was about to place it in the safe, when I suddenly thought I bet I could find him. Sure enough, I found him metres down the road, sat at a bus stop still awake, much to my relief. I returned his cash and went back to custody.

We hit a busy period and I helped by hanging a custody record, preparing myself to accept a DP into my charge room. The circumstances of the arrest were completely missing from the form, which I promptly returned to the officers to correct. One of the other skippers then took the form, saying they'd prefer me to stay available to take an upcoming post-interview update.

The update came soon after. It was a domestic assault. The victim had provided a statement and there was a photograph of bruising, which corroborated her statement. I wrote it up, directing the officer to seek CPS advice.

I used the remainder of my time that night to add court folders to incidents and complete pre-risk assessments as best I could, from risks already identified.

Then rest days finally came. Hopefully these would prove to be sick-free.

They were. But I did have a nasty case of the shits but more on that later...

I spent the first evening at a fundraiser concert for a member of one of the lesser known bands from the 80s. I'd never heard their music but was drawn to the event by the announcement that a well-known former world champion snooker player would be there. Indeed, I got to meet him, which was brilliant. Although, he was socially awkward, which made the encounter brief and frustrating. Frustrating, because I'd hoped to grab a selfie! And ask for a few memories from his snooker days. I left it at a handshake and brief chat about the gig.

After a few excellent (and reasonably priced) ciders, I gained the courage to ask for that selfie, and got it! I went back up to him between sets and explained I'd regret not asking and could I be *that annoying twat* for a few seconds. He was perfectly polite and accommodating and it was a great photo. The evening ended with a weird DJ set. I felt like I'd joined some form of cult. Everyone was moving in some form of trance, as if they were performing a ritual. It was entertaining though, for sure, and I thoroughly enjoyed it.

The next day was my twelfth wedding anniversary. I spent the day recovering from a hangover, whilst the wife was at work.

The kids had spent the previous night round my folks and would spend that night there too, as I'd made plans to take the wife away for the night.

I met them down the pub for lunch and spent some time with them, before returning home to get ready. I drove my wife to a B&B, where I'd booked what was advertised as the 'four-poster' room, which sounded a bit smutty to me. We then enjoyed a very posh dinner, which cost me around £215. It would've been far more, but they undercharged me. I like to think they spotted the special effort I'd put into looking rich and posh, but really knew I was a pauper, so reflected that with a little helping hand with the bill. Their cock-up paid for our wine.

It was a lovely romantic evening and on that note, I was pleased with how things were progressing...although the four-poster should be renamed the 'neighbour-disturbing squeakathon' but the sofa did the job very nicely instead.

But despite a satisfying end to the evening, I literally could not sleep. I blame the cheese-course. I've previously found eating plenty of cheese and drinking lots of wine has this effect.

To make matters worse, around three in the morning, I got the shits. Too soon for it to be the posh dinner. Perhaps the pub lunch? Either way, I found myself sitting on the loo for what seemed an eternity, making extremely loud fart sounds, which I'd no doubt the wife could hear, thereby un-romanticising the evening.

These bowel movements sadly continued throughout the following day. I was working overtime that night, and tried getting sleep during the day but failed miserably. I was knackered for my shift, which involved a hefty amount of travel. On a positive note, it was a bank holiday and involved working into my last rest day, so I'm fairly confident my B&B and posh dinner expenditure will have been mostly recouped. Perhaps before tax at least.

That afternoon, I let the kids watch GoldenEye. This now appears to be a 15 certificate too, and I'm not surprised, given how excited Miss Onatopp gets. I found myself skipping those scenes, to save having to explain her thrills!

Chapter Nine – Countdown to One Sixth

At the end of this set, I will have been a sergeant for four months. A month of that was the training but I'm certainly including that as part of my custody time. That will therefore be one sixth already done of what is generally accepted a minimum two year stint in custody.

I am enjoying it more than I thought I would. Enjoy is slightly misleading. It is relentless most of the time, but it's systematic and once you understand the processes, it's relatively easy; just stressful.

That's not to say I've mastered it all yet. Far from it. I still feel like I have a massive learning curve to climb. It's just that I'm a fair way up that slope already.

One thing I need to get good at fast is remembering names. I know everyone on my team, but names of investigators who speak to me every day...they all know my name. But then there are fewer of us and lots of them. I'm slowly getting there but it's still awkward. Especially when you've dealt with them several times already – you just can't ask someone their name when you've dealt with them that many times. It's embarrassing.

Being almost four months (or one sixth) into my (hopefully just) two year stint in custody is a relief. It's a decent chunk done. What worries me is that there are plenty still in custody past their two year mark, still waiting to get out. There's another course running soon, so I expect there'll be some changes ahead. Then I'll be one of the old sweats. And that's a scary thought...

I took a charge room my first day back. There were four of us. Two in charge rooms, one on disposals and one actually physically binning people. The system flowed quite nicely and I was left to book in without the need to also juggle reviews.

And there was a fair amount of booking in to do.

First up was a chap in his twenties, arrested on suspicion of possession of indecent images of children. These are often the first ones through the door. The OICs must be wisened to the ways of custody. Get in there early and it's all yours. Take your pick of the interview rooms. Get in there and nab the AA first if required. Most of the time, they're ready to interview.

Given the offence occurred in April, I did call the arresting officer through to discuss the necessity to detain over a voluntary interview. Although it had occurred four months prior, it'd only been brought to police attention recently and they needed to establish in interview what other access to children he may have, so any such children could be safeguarded whilst he was in custody. Seemed reasonable enough to me.

Next up was much the same thing, plus more sinister offences. A same-sex couple were both brought in for the same offence, plus sexual activity with a child and sexual activity with a person with a mental disorder.

Fortunately, the next job was a bit lighter. A non dwelling burglary from four months ago, whereby a fingerprint hit had since been received identifying the suspect. Attempts had been made to get him in over the past three months. He'd attended the station with his solicitor anticipating a voluntary interview. The thing is, it was about £4000 worth of jewellery stolen. There was no way he'd still have it but you can't *not* search his address. A Section 18 would be required.

I heard the solicitor was mighty pissed off...no doubt because she now knew she'd be sat around for ages waiting for interview.

Then there was a guy for concerned in the supply. A total of three were nicked during a section 8 warrant, after a large quantity of suspected class A drugs were found.

One of my DOs then told me they had another force on the line, wanting to know what paperwork was issued for that bail warrant I'd dealt with on the last night shift. Knew that'd come back to bite me! Embarrassingly, I explained the very official bit of paperwork I'd issued was a scrap bit of paper, with the court, date and time handwritten. I explained I'd since learned what paperwork *should* have been issued and they very kindly set about completing this on my behalf and emailed it over, plus sending the original in the post to the DP. Why I hadn't thought about doing this retrospectively, I have no idea.

Another DO also came and found me, advising I'd left my set of keys in a cell door. I thought things were going so well! I offered to bring in cakes for my faux pas but he explained he was on a diet and preferred an apple. An apple it was then! The usual band of DPs arrived bang on handover, so once I'd gone through my lot, I went and quickly booked one in to help lates. It was a PWITS job, whereby the officer had detained a male for a search and located a large bundle of drugs. The DP was good as gold. I authorised a strip search, as when the officer detained the male, drugs were on the floor of the car where the DP was sat, with his flies half open and he'd hesitated when the officer asked if he'd concealed any. Nothing further was found but it meant I could stick the DP on sixty minute checks, confident he wasn't going to have a custody drug binge.

I handed over the extra prisoner to lates and went home. There were four of us again on the second day turn. I took the role of booting people out, whilst the other 'spare' sat amongst the investigators, taking updates as and when they came. Trouble was, no updates came until lunch.

Before then, I took on the checks of DPs going to court and ensured their respective risks were documented in their PERs. As usual, there were some missing, which I had to add. Hence the importance of double (sometimes triple) checking work done by others. After all, we'd be the last ones to have touched the forms before they were passed to the courts and therefore ultimately, as I see it, it's our sign-off.

One of the updates that eventually came was for a guy to be charged with shoplifting and breach of a sexual offender registration order, along with a domestic assault that CPS had authorised. My colleague had recorded a remand rationale and emailed it to me. It covered the fact they had a horrendous offending history, including offending on bail. Part of their sex offender order was to update police with any change of address within seven days, which they'd failed to do. Clearly, there is the argument if they failed to comply with this condition, what bail conditions could be put in place that they *were* likely to comply with? In addition, it covered the fact an address couldn't be ascertained for them, as they'd point blank refused to provide this in interview.

I went to retrieve the AA and charge the chap. I'd checked with my colleague whether I should invite representations from the solicitor prior to charging. They suggested I crack on and if the DP wanted to make any, to *then* approach the solicitor. As I walked away with the AA, a colleague of that solicitor caught wind and said there would likely be reps made and would I wait until they were out of another interview before proceeding? I explained I was hoping to get their client into court that afternoon and did not wish to delay the process, in case that meant their client would have to wait until morning court. They didn't appear happy and requested I note the custody record that they'd asked for that to happen, which I said I would. I did say I'd come and speak to their colleague afterwards as soon as they'd emerged from interview.

I charged the DP and informed him of my remand decision. I invited any reps from them and they said "I'm better off in jail". I updated the custody record and was then updated the solicitor had finished interview.

The solicitor was mighty pissed off. I can only describe the way he spoke to me as angry. He didn't shout but was quite clearly worked up – I guess he'd already decided he was going to lay into me and his adrenaline was taking over. First of all, once I'd introduced myself, he sarcastically thanked me for not waiting. I explained my reasons why. He said not having an address was not grounds to remand the DP. I tried explaining that committing further offences was our main concern but he kept talking over me and it was impossible to hold a civilised conversation with him. He clarified with me I intended on getting his client into court that afternoon. I said that was certainly my intention and I'd do my utmost to achieve that. Clearly a fan of sarcasm, he stood up and as he left the room, sarcastically said "Well, good luck with that!" to which I thanked him, much to his annoyance.

I stuck a log on the custody record - a very polite but accurate one, basically detailing how much of a douche the guy was. After handover, we had a meeting with the boss, during which he explained some upcoming process changes, which were rather unpopular to the more established members of custody but didn't bother me a great deal, having not been there long.

I was then set to disappear but caught wind two of my DPs were to be NFA'd. I stayed on and booted them out, to assist lates.

The first late was pretty busy.

One of the first reviews was a harassment. God it was messy. The days sergeant had reviewed it after interview and directed further enquiries be completed, including a section 18 search for mobile phones.

Once those enquiries had been completed, I had to try and get my head round it for CPS advice. I was reliant on the verbal update I'd had from the OIC but everytime I spoke to them, they slipped in more information about the incident I knew nothing about. Ideally, I'd have read the job from start to finish but I simply didn't have time. Far from ideal, I know. But that's how it often is. I effectively blagged a review I felt covered the key points and directed them to get pre-charge advice.

Another domestic incident involved an assault the evening before, where a female had been pushed to the ground and on falling, knocked into an ornament, damaging it. I was told the DP admitted pushing her. Officers found a small amount of cannabis on him, which he'd admitted. The catch was, the whole morning the OIC had been working on the job, they'd failed to notice an outstanding assault the DP was wanted for, involving the same victim. I was pretty annoyed this had been missed and politely explained they should've picked that up upon first reviewing the job.

It was passed to a lates investigator to pick up the pieces. They eventually arrived, further arrested the guy and re-interviewed. He made admissions to the earlier assault too and the officer's own sergeant reviewed for CPS, as I was engrossed in other things by that time. I kept myself occupied releasing several DPs in a row. Some under investigation, others NFA.

I eventually got round to being in a position to book a prisoner in. The first was a fail to appear warrant. He was no trouble at all.

Next up was one of two youths nicked for shoplifting and theft of pedal cycle. Mine was a fourteen year old and the other, booked in next door, was eleven years old. Mine was calm and compliant. The younger one was Route One!

Third in was a female arrested for breaching a restraining order. Officers found her at an address she was prohibited from attending, following a tip-off.

She had to be assisted walking into the charge room – never a good sign. She could barely talk. I got my DO to fetch a chair for her to sit on. She stank of urine. She was drunk and incapable. Far too drunk for custody. We got the nurse to see her and after a quick glance, she'd already made her mind up hospital was the best place for her. Her blood pressure and blood glucose were also both too high. The DP just about managed to slur she was diabetic and hadn't taken her tablets in ages. Off she went to hospital with the officers.

Just before I booked her in, I was updated CPS had verbally authorised a charge of harassment for the earlier DP I'd reviewed. The paperwork hadn't been received, so I proceeded with booking the above lady in. That became a medical emergency of sorts and I was then anxiously clock watching, given the harassment dude had minutes left on his clock. As I dealt with drunk lady, I prepared the disposal, getting the bail conditions set up.

Once she'd left for hospital, I got the harassment dude in and charged him with seconds left.

In the rush, I forgot to give him his charge sheet, with bail conditions. Bollocks.

I found it on the printer later and realised. I contacted a colleague I used to work with, knowing they'd help and they delivered it for me. Phew!

Before handover, I booked in a female arrested for child abduction. She'd been issued a couple of CAWN notices – child abduction warning notice, due to harbouring regular missing youths. That evening, police had found those youths at her address. There was evidence she'd been allowing them to smoke cannabis and one female youth present had to be taken to hospital for taking unknown pills. The DP's own fourteen year old daughter was taken into police protection.

The DO drew my attention to the holding cell CCTV. The DP was rifling through her handbag, whilst the officer had their back turned. She then produced a mobile phone, tapped away on it and then placed it to her ear. Cheeky woman was making a phone call! Worse than that, the arresting officer was completely oblivious. I went out and made her hand over the phone.

The lady was in custody for the first time and seemed weirdly calm. I'd got the information about her daughter from speaking to the officer in private. During the risk assessment, I asked the DP if she had any care issues that would cause concern. She said her daughter would no doubt be at home waiting for her. She clearly hadn't been told her daughter was taken into police protection. I couldn't believe that. I told her this and expected floods of tears. Nothing.

On handover, the DS from investigations joined us. I've not seen this before and it was good to see him joining in and providing updates from their side on jobs. However, when I handed over the domestic assault, saying it was with CPS, he informed me they'd had a result back for the assault and he'd suggested a penalty notice for the cannabis.

I explained I'd already checked PNC and it showed at least three previous for cannabis over the years and I'd intended on charging that, as we are supposed to deal with cannabis in an escalatory fashion, ie, warning on first offence, penalty notice, then court. If the chap's been to court three times already, he's clearly not learning and therefore not likely to benefit from any drug awareness course as part of a conditional caution either.

I told nights I'd boot the guy out, so they needn't worry about it.

There were four sergeants on the second late, but one covered DO MSL. Another covered disposals, leaving two for the charge rooms.

On arrival, I noticed the drunk and incapable woman had spent five hours at hospital the previous night. She was destined for remand. The child abduction lady was also still in but was released not long into our shift – I never did find out the result.

I booked in a chap who'd breached his post charge police bail conditions. I kept the officers in the holding cell long enough to satisfy myself the breach was sufficiently evidenced and laid the information on him as soon as detention was authorised.

If there's one thing I'm starting to learn in custody, it's when there's a dodgy prisoner arriving. The officers will generally want to come and explain the circs to you before you get the sheet slipped under the door, to save you having to call them in and ask "WTF"?

The next guy was a pre-emptive "WTF?" kind of circs, although actually, upon being explained, I saw the officer's predicament.

The chap had come into the station to report a domestic assault. He told the officers the previous night, his partner had come into their bedroom and grabbed him by the balls, waking him up. He admitted to slapping her and for some reason showed officers texts on his phone, some of which were from her. So far, fairly normal. Here's where it got complicated...

The texts from her were along the lines of "I think you've broken my jaw".

They decided at that point to arrest him sus GBH. I gather there were no officers free at the time to call at her address and verify what she may allege. They had to make a decision there and then how to deal and given her injuries sounded a lot more serious than some tender testicles, they opted to nick him.

It was unusual, but I was happy to book him in and the officers set about tracking her down. I was updated later they'd done so and took her to hospital for her suspected broken jaw to be examined.

The DP made all sorts of significant statements, that I noted down and got him to sign. These included him admitting slapping her. We also found a lock knife in his backpack, which he said he'd forgotten was in there from a camping trip.

A short while later, two youths were brought in. One had been arrested for possession of cannabis, whose details were doubted and the other detained for a strip search for drugs. The one under arrest was strip searched first and found to be in possession of more cannabis and cash, which, oddly, he'd opted to store between his butt cheeks instead of a wallet. I personally find a wallet *far* more convenient and less embarrassing when paying for groceries.

When this discovery was made, the officer decided to nick the other straight away sus concerned in the supply. I authorised their strip search but nothing further was found.

I booted out 3 of 4 youths arrested for PWITS. From what I gathered, they were all first-timers. Hell of a first offence to commit. I didn't know the job well and was just grateful someone else had reviewed it whilst I sorted incoming DPs. They were all released under investigation (RUI) for further enquiries.

I binned another DP RUI before handover to nights.

The following shift should've been a first night but was in fact a third late. These oddities occur now and again to provide extra cover on busy weekend shifts.

However, this particular late shift was far from busy and was actually rather leisurely, for our custody centre was closing for a week of refurbishments, meaning we were no longer accepting new DPs that Sunday afternoon. Well, we would've accepted warrants or breach of bail but none came. We were simply binning what we already had and keeping a few in on remand to court the next morning, which would empty the block ready for the works.

It's amazing what difference it made, not having any incoming. I was able to spend time on making quality decisions and write ups. Ones with fewer spelling mistakes! On my 'alive-and-well-checks', the drunk and incapable lady (yes, still there, awaiting court!) said she'd been unable to keep anything down and had thrown up all food and drink offered. I arranged the nurse to see her but realised that had been a pattern of behaviour throughout her stay and she'd regularly been seen sticking fingers down her throat. Having explained how ill she was to me, she then asked for a cup of coffee. I suggested that perhaps it would be wise to await the nurse's visit.

I took a domestic breach of restraining order update early on. The guy had been nicked for assaulting his ex and damaging her property a few months beforehand. He was charged and released with bail conditions. He broke those conditions over the next two days and was arrested and remanded to court, where he was found guilty. A post conviction restraining order was subsequently granted, which is what he'd now breached.

I directed the officer to seek CPS advice. The victim had supported by providing a statement and screenshots of his phone calls. The DP had admitted making the calls and attending her address, stating he needed property back and had explored all other avenues but felt he had no choice but to get it back himself. There was clearly a RPOC.

The officer gave me the heads-up that the solicitor would want to make reps against remand on the basis that 1) his client would lose his job if remanded and 2) his client had significant care issues, due to his current partner having recently had breast cancer surgery.

I didn't really care about the job issue (although would go on to tell the solicitor when taking reps that I was indeed sensitive to that issue, but that his constant breaching of conditions/orders meant I would still be remanding) but did wish to prepare for the possible need to concede to the care issues.

I directed the officer to contact the DP's current partner and ask about those issues. The OIC came back a short time later with a deservedly smug look on his face and informed me she'd kicked him out a few days beforehand for drinking too much and not helping her as he should. She confirmed she had other support from friends and family and as such, did not require him to care for her.

Naturally, I let the solicitor give me his reps and I addressed each in turn and he said he felt 'shot down'. This experience went much better than the one the other day where the solicitor got all sarcastic and angry. The solicitor effectively said "well played sergeant, well played". Brilliant. I've learnt from this – preparation is key. At the end of the day, your decision stands. But it makes it a lot easier to argue your case.

I received a CPS result for a DP who'd been sentenced to life for murder sixteen years ago and was released a few months ago. He'd been nicked the previous evening for domestic related damage and another sergeant had written it up for CPS. The offender management detective sergeant was keen for a remand, as an emergency recall would follow. He was keen to the point where he'd asked the other sergeant to try and get them remanded for anything we could, even drunk and disorderly.

The CPS result was NFA.

I read the arresting officer statement. I'd been told the DP had urinated in the back of the police van and there was the possible option of charging and remanding for damage to the van. Trouble was, we were beginning to treat this DP different to how we would others. I totally got the reason why. But it didn't seem right, even given his previous. It felt like we were trying to find something that just wasn't there. The arresting officer statement detailed how the DP had kicked out when the rear cage door was shut. There was no assault police. No immediate violence anticipated. The urinating in the van was described as 'the DP went to the toilet'. I think it's clear what this implies but it's not specific enough. Did he or did he not urinate in the back of the van? Where was the photo of the urine? Was the van taken off the road for a while on a busy Saturday night so that it could be cleaned? Did we have to call out a professional cleaning service? What was the cost of this to the Constabulary? What was the inconvenience and knock-on effect of the van being out of action for so long?

None of this was in the statement. Nor was there any mention the DP was drunk.

I simply couldn't find anything else to charge the DP with. He was living in approved premises as part of his licence. I phoned the DS and updated them. They appreciated my position. I phoned the approved premises. They confirmed they'd held the bed for him. I phoned the senior probation officer. They'd been getting more and more concerned about his increased drinking and poor behaviour over recent weeks but there was insufficient for an emergency recall without charge. They'd probably still pursue a slow-time recall but that would be decided the following day.

I organised a lift home, courtesy of the Constabulary, to ensure he went straight back there. It was the least I felt we could do, to minimise the risk of him going straight back to his partner's. It was the only thing I felt we could really do. Fortunately, he jumped at the offer.

Once I sorted that, there was a big lull. My colleague had a few live prisoners still, but all mine were sorted and I was only left with those on remand.

Just before handover, I walked past my colleague who was escorting a prisoner back to their cell. I instantly recognised the DP as someone I used to get on with really well from my days on response. He was a nice enough lad who used to cause issues down town on a Friday night but would never cause me problems when nicked. He then got into the wrong crowd and being the sheep that he is, followed them into heroin and crack hell and got himself hopelessly addicted. Family and friends deserted him. Cravings for that next hit clouded his judgment, as he stole from those close to him.

I think I bemused my colleague as I walked past them – he instantly recognised me and we casually fist-pumped. He'd just been charged and remanded for about eight offences, including shopliftings and non dwelling burglaries. Think he was just glad he had a bed for the night.

My last job before handover was RUI-ing a fourteen year old first timer for PWITS. Clearly the first offence of choice locally as the last couple days had shown.

There was naff all for nights to really do after that, let alone me, so I made my escape.

The last night consisted of prisoner transport! Two of us were crewed in a van, to alleviate additional pressure placed on response in transporting DPs to a temporary custody suite further afield. Only, no-one got nicked. Well, not quite true.

I heard one unit call up 'state nine' and asking which custody centre they'd be off to ('state nine' being the phrase used by officers over the radio, indicating they have made an arrest). I volunteered our services and started towards. They called up and disclosed their DP needed hospital treatment. They then called me directly, explaining their prisoner had overdosed and slit their wrists! It makes you wonder whether they'd have tried their luck at custody first. A couple of custody sergeants volunteering to come collect them and all of a sudden, hospital is the better option. I may be doing them a complete disservice...but reckon I was spot on.

We transported three people all night –people *released* from custody. Whilst not obliged to provide lifts home, overnight there's a lack of public transport, and with most DPs having a list of vulnerabilities the size of a vegan's grocery bill, it helps the pre-release risk assessment knowing they're getting home safely.

I knocked off an hour early, realising I'd cocked up childcare that morning and would have sole responsibility for the kids whilst my wife was on days. I got home to see she'd set up a picnic breakfast for them both in the lounge, with a film ready to go. I got into bed around five in the morning and I went down at ten, albeit, my five year old had misunderstood the definition of an emergency and had interrupted my sleep at various points to tell me about another spider on the ceiling he'd spotted.

Rest days, as usual, flew by. I finished the latest series of House of Cards, which I'm starting to get a bit fed up with and hope they out Kevin Spacey as the murderer he is and have done with it. But I expect they'll drag it out and I'll stick with it like the mug I am. Little did I know what was in store for the actual actor at that time!

I also managed to binge-watch the entire third season of Narcos, which is just fucking awesome. The wife and I caught up with Game of Minges (you'll know it as *Thrones* but given the content, I feel *Minges* is more apt).

I did work a night shift of plain clothes overtime as part of a TFMV (theft from motor vehicle) Op, but I was given such a vast area to cover, I could only spend minutes in each area before moving on to the next and as such, predictably missed all the crime that *did* occur that night. But it was an easy six hours of overtime I wasn't expecting to get as sergeant!

Chapter Ten – You'll Float Too!

I was desperate to get the first day back done and dusted, so I could head to the movies and see IT. I'm not a massive fan of the original 1990 made-for-tv effort. I remember kids at school saying it'd terrified them. Truth is, I was probably around fourteen when I saw it, so was a bit older than they'd been. I recall being a bit bored. Having recently seen clips of the original, there's a chance I'd enjoy it more these days, so may have to check it out again. But my VHS copy has long since gone.

First day back was something of an oddity. There were several prisoners in, almost a full block, but the interviewing teams seemed to get going a lot earlier. Perhaps it was a simple case of the jobs being up together for once. Perhaps it was that only one of mine needed an AA, which avoided the usual queue. I didn't care what the reason was; it simply meant the day was less stressful and I was able to achieve things at a manageable pace.

I received one update around half nine, which caught me off guard by how early it was. This was a heroin addicted shoplifter, who had swung a punch at the arresting officer. She'd only been released from prison on licence eight days earlier and had a horrendous offending history. The OIC told me they'd even said in interview they'd continue to offend and when would they be in court?! That was an easy charge and remand decision. No solicitor. No representations.

A Section 5 Public Order arrived – they'd refused all details on the street but had provided details in the holding cell and checks revealed they were no trace on PNC. With no previous convictions and their details now known, they were suitable for a fine. I explained to the officers I didn't believe there was a necessity to detain him at the station now we'd established all this and as such, wouldn't be authorising detention. They were fine with this, issued a ticket and dropped the chap home.

There was a slight pause before further updates came, the first of which I missed as I'd popped to the toilet. My DO told me and a few minutes later I saw the DS review recommending a charge. I checked the DP's previous convictions and, whilst wishing not to undermine their review, contacted both and suggested an adult conditional caution may be more appropriate, as there was a particular course available ideal for addressing the DP's behaviour in this instance. They agreed this was a great idea and word came through later the victim was supportive too. I issued and got rid.

There were other disposal reviews that occurred but nothing of any real interest. The day went by very quickly and off I went home. It was time for IT.

Spoiler alert for this paragraph only...I went with my brother. Within the opening five minutes, he turned to me in disgust when a young kid's arm got bitten off. The film had certainly set its tone. Things never quite got *that* nasty again but the damage had already been done and left people on edge wondering what horrific acts of violence would occur next. The film had an awesome *Stranger Things* vibe to it. Which is a weird comparison I know, as *Stranger Things* owes a huge debt to the original and indeed, therefore the book, in terms of the gang of kids teaming up against a monster. But the latter is fresh in the mind and so is a *relevant* comparison. The clown was creepy as fuck, as was the red balloon floating across the screen periodically, signalling something bad was about to happen. I was really impressed with the young cast and the film certainly didn't hold back on subject matter, covering an awful lot of adult themes. Fortunately, it didn't include *that* scene from the book – if you've read it, you'll know. The less said about that the better – it's *wrong*. After the film, my brother popped back to mine for some classic, slightly lighter-viewing A-Team over dinner and as he headed home, naturally I left some voicemails on his phone in my best creepy voice, "You'll float too...you'll float too...YOU'LL FLOAT TOO!"

It's his birthday in a week. I'll be sure to buy a couple of helium-filled red balloons and tie them to the drain outside his house.

I was greeted with a full cell block the following morning. On handover, I was informed two of my prisoners were on constants. Just as handover finished, they slipped in the revelation that DOs were covering this, as response had been unable to source anyone. Or rather, it appeared the nights Inspector had basically said it wasn't *their* problem and it was for *custody* to sort. That was certainly my viewpoint prior to joining custody, but when you realise quite how busy it is and how few staff you have, you soon realise. On the face of it, I'm quite certain that response see our typical five DOs and think to themselves we're flush – why can't they do it? But it's not as simple as that.

One DO covers admin work. They take on everything from scanning on nurse/doctor forms, completion of PER forms, emailing embassies, taking calls from solicitors, AAs, enquiries from elsewhere, buzzing people in and out of the block, contacting Immigration, courts...the list is virtually endless. It is a non-stop role.

Two DOs are on DP checks. DPs are usually on either thirty or sixty minute checks, but custody sergeants can pretty much make them what they want, dependant on risks involved. As you might expect, DPs tend to be rather demanding – requesting food, drink, trips to the toilet (if without one in their cell), a period in the exercise yard...by the time a DO has done one round of checks, it can be time to start the next. But they need to add a log on each custody record before they do to ensure they are compliant with PACE and to document that checks are being completed in accordance with the individual's care plan. It is not uncommon for checks to be overdue. Quite often they have actually been completed, but the DO has not had chance to update them on the system.

Two DOs are on booking-in. They support the custody sergeant in the charge room to varying degrees based on need - by either simply searching the incoming DP and logging their property, to virtually completing the whole process, including PNC checks, loading the custody record and completing the risk assessments, rights, etc. A sergeant would have to be on hand to authorise detention in such instances, and would also be responsible for finalising the risk assessment and setting a care plan based on risk. The booking in DOs would then potentially take the DP photograph, fingerprints, DNA and escort them to their cell, ensuring the cell is clean, a mattress is present, they are provided with blankets, offered food or drink, shown the location of the intercom buzzer in case they require assistance...

Sometimes DPs want showers. For some, a custody block is the first time in ages they get a bed for the night. They like to take advantage of the facilities. Especially those being remanded to court. They like to smell nice for the court. I guess it creates a better impression than forcing magistrates to hold their breath.

It will come as no surprise that cells don't have showers. Therefore, a DO has to escort them to a shower and stand guard whilst they wash. Some DPs are quick, others take their time. Time we simply don't have. Booking-in DOs tend to get this job, otherwise those on checks wouldn't get them done on time, breaching PACE. The knock-on effect is the custody sergeant has no support, meaning the booking-in process takes longer, fingerprints/DNA don't get taken straight away causing issues later, OICs have to wait longer before a skipper becomes available...

You may think a full cell block won't need two booking-in DOs. With no spaces free, there'll be no incoming prisoners to book in. However, there are usually a ton of fingerprints/DNA outstanding from the night before and these DOs are constantly playing catch-up. Without them doing this, DPs can be released without being properly processed.

So there is far more to the picture than response appreciate. And I can confidently say that having recently been on response.

So I contacted the control room and requested two officers attend to cover these, which they did. Both DPs had stated during their risk assessment they had current thoughts of self harm and may do so in custody. There had been no CCTV cells available, so they had officers sat with them. You could consider putting people on ten or fifteen minute checks, but as above, this causes so many issues for the DOs on checks.

I liaised with the other charge room skipper and discussed what DPs we had in CCTV cells that could be moved. My colleague found one of theirs they were prepared to move elsewhere, so we swapped the DPs round, and I got the officer to stay on constants but via CCTV for an hour whilst I satisfied myself they were going to settle and not take the opportunity to self harm as soon as they thought they weren't being watched. After that hour, I stood the officer down and was prepared to manage the risk via CCTV, which is displayed in the DO office.

Unfortunately, all other DPs in CCTV cells needed them due to their risks (most had previously self harmed in custody). It was quite some time before another camera cell became available but when it did, I repeated the above.

I saw an email that had been sent late the day before, from the OIC for the conditional caution job. They requested I scan the signed caution form on to the job, otherwise they'd struggle to get it filed. I hadn't done this. I'd assumed once the DP had digitally signed the form, it would remain on the computer. Apparently not. I sent an email apologising. Every day is a learning day.

A DO brought me a suspicious looking blue pill they'd found by a DP in their cell. I was fairly confident the sixty-one year old gent with walking stick who found it had not been pill-popping, and that it'd been simply missed from a previous detainee. We'd never prove who and even if they *were* in a CCTV cell (which they weren't), we couldn't spare the hours and hours it would take to view the footage, all for one stray pill. I passed it to the nurse for destruction. The DO organised a near-miss entry on the accident management system to document what had occurred.

As we were full first thing, with DPs only starting to trickle out the door from mid morning, I only booked in two DPs the whole shift. These were connected. They'd both been arrested for a Section 4 Public Order offence – essentially causing fear or provocation of violence. The first of these instantly recognised me. I'd been the last person to arrest him, about a year beforehand. I'd spotted him near to an address where there was recent intelligence he'd been dealing on behalf of transient dealers. I'd stopped him and detained him for a search. I found a small amount of cannabis on him, along with pills. Not enough for supply but simple possession. As such, I'd taken him to a nearby police station for voluntary interview, but reconsidered my options upon realising how much intelligence there was on the address (also where he resided) and decided to arrest him and so I could search the address. Sadly, nothing further was found and no transients.

He was extremely chirpy and proud of the fact he'd been off heroin and all substitutes for six months, explaining he'd moved out the area into his mum's whilst he got clean. He was now working at a local pizza delivery chain. I was genuinely pleased for him but will be getting my pizza elsewhere from now on.

My booking in DO was constantly being called away to take nurses to cells, take outstanding prints etc, so I found myself being bothered non-stop to also take people to cells. This meant I wasn't able to review jobs and come handover to lates, I had no idea what each job really involved, only able to pass the bare minimum information. Let's face it, the risks are the important bits to handover and I knew those very well.

I collected the kids from my parents after work, where they'd been whilst my wife got sleep after her night shift. My mum told me my brother had been round to see the kids and he'd mentioned he had a bad dream about a killer clown! Bless him! That evening, I proceeded to leave further voicemails and sent him a picture of Pennywise via pretty much every social media app.

I was on disposals the first late turn. I was pretty much non-stop the first few hours.

Two youths had been arrested overnight as one was found in possession of a bag containing a lock knife, sharpened bicycle spoke and homemade taser. The one that hadn't been in possession of it and denied all knowledge was an easy NFA! The other admitted the lock knife, and making the homemade taser but went no comment to the bicycle spoke. Apparently that is the current ad hoc weapon of choice on the streets. As if the lock knife or homemade taser weren't good enough... The taser needed sending off for testing, to ensure it was as thought and claimed; much in the same way we'd still get heroin tested even if a DP admitted what it was. He was RUI.

An OIC updated me their CPS advice had come back to charge with harassment. Their DP had also been found in possession of cannabis. They'd previously had a warning but nothing else drug-related, so I considered an out of court disposal, such as fine or drug awareness course, however, to be completely honest, decided it was easier to simply charge for both. They didn't seem the sort of person who would benefit from a course or likely pay a fine.

Another CPS result came through from a job days had reviewed. This chap had been arrested for domestic assault. It turns out he and the missus had experienced difficulties in their relationship, and so decided to go on holiday as a kind of 'make or break' scenario. It broke, big time. She ended up reporting him to Spanish police and fled back home a day early, reporting him to local police so he was arrested on his return. Trouble was, the assaults from Spain weren't our jurisdiction. The historic assaults from this country were summary only from ages ago, meaning the six months from offence date within which they had to be prosecuted had expired long ago. CPS *were* willing to consider a coercive and controlling behaviour charge, but once lots of further work was completed. The DP was therefore RUI for these enquiries to be completed. The Inspector gave me the heads-up he'd been told there may be a case to consider for bailing under new legislation, however, I felt that as they lived separately, he had no right to her address through any ownership/tenancy and she supported police action, this was not necessary, as should he contact her or attend her address, there would likely be substantive offences committed anyway.

There was a lull early evening and I took advantage by sorting one of the most important jobs in policing – arranging my annual leave. I'd emailed duties requesting a set off in two months time but had heard nothing. They'd sent an email recently advising of a massive backlog they're struggling to work through. I'd phoned them and was told it was somewhere in the region of 250 emails. Ridiculous.

The direction we'd had was that if an email related to that same week and needed action, to send an email titled 'URGENT THIS WEEK' and it'd be looked at. I needed to book flights and wasn't prepared to wait until the backlog was sorted, fearing that'd be weeks to come and render the whole thing pointless. I sent the email, marking as urgent. Unfortunately, within an hour of sending, I discovered my folks were actually unable to assist with childcare that week anyway, meaning the holiday wasn't meant to be. I decided against sending yet another email to duties and will let them apply the leave and then email requesting it be cancelled!

I was asked to review a breach of non-molestation order. An eager-eyed copper had spotted a driver seatbeltless and stopped the car. The officer described how the guy appeared really nervous and upon checking PNC, discovered the non-mol. His colleague checked details of a female in the backseat and found her to be the applicant of that order. She didn't support police action, stating she'd been marched to the courts by CSD (Children's Services Department) and didn't want it in place. She refused to provide a statement.

However, there was domestic history between the two, with her making an allegation of assault a couple months prior.

The OIC argued the case for it not being in the public interest, with her not supporting. However, I felt the order had clearly been granted for a reason and at the end of the day, he knew it was there and had chosen to breach an order of the court. Police officers could evidence the breach, even without her support.

She said it was raining, so she contacted him for a lift. He said he'd gone to get cash out and upon returning to his car, his ex and child were sat in the back! Not finding this account in the least bit plausible, I sent the job to CPS. They NFA'd it, saying we couldn't disprove his account. I felt it needed to go to CPS but wasn't passionate enough to argue the toss over this one.

I was back in one of the main charge rooms the following day. I took over five prisoners but was told to disregard two as they were going straight away. It was a pleasantly Q shift! A shoplifter had been arrested for four such offences. Only one arrest record had been set. I discussed with the OIC, who informed me the arresting officer had failed to crime two of the four offences, or pass on any information at all about them so she could record them. As far as I was concerned, we therefore had two.

The OIC explained they needed time to review CCTV prior to interview and when they finally came down, the nurse had just ruled the DP was withdrawing and was unfit, requiring a rest period. That meant a medical review at midnight, when the investigating teams were off duty and response unlikely to be able to provide through the usual strapped resources. The DP had been arrested at eleven that morning! Bedding down for interview the following morning would leave things too tight on the PACE clock. Fortunately, the OIC offered to stay on and deal once fit.

The DP was wanted on warrant, so wasn't going anywhere, however, it was an out of force warrant and they had little in the way of convictions. I therefore proposed we didn't refuse bail for the thefts but rather bail those and simply keep him in on the warrant. Otherwise, he'd go to local court for the thefts, no doubt be refused by the out of force court afterwards and return to our station on 'lockout', spending yet another night with us! It didn't seem proportionate. Nights would later agree with this plan.

Around five, I was offered an out of date tuna and sweetcorn sandwich. I accepted.

In came a rape. This was a historic one from 1998 to 2000. There were scant details on the booking in sheet provided by the arresting officer, so I read the job myself and saw it'd been geared towards a voluntary interview the following day. Trouble was, they'd been unable to contact the suspect. His mum had informed him police were looking for him and he handed himself in. There was no reason I could see why they couldn't still interview him as a voluntary out of custody. The arresting officer had no idea about the necessity (?!) so they phoned the DS, who told me they wanted to control the interview. I mentioned the voluntary interview that had been planned and he said what if the DP decided to up and leave? I explained if that happened and the OIC had further questions they needed answering, it would then be necessary to arrest and I'd gladly accept. They said there was some suggestion the DP was autistic and required an AA. I explained that, like solicitors, these could be called through and arranged by the OIC out of custody. I did not authorise detention.

In came a domestic related breach of non-mol order, assault and damage. The order didn't prevent him from attending his ex partner's address, as she liked him to have dinner with their kids on occasion. However, it prohibited him from threatening her with violence, damaging her property, pestering her and so on. She realised he'd left cat food in her bed and ripped up her clothes. He'd also pushed her.

He was anxious about the possibility of missing work the next day, but otherwise calm and cooperative.

The last DP that evening had breached court bail conditions. I kept the officers in the holding cell whilst I checked the evidence and prepared the information so it was ready to lay upon the DP. He too was anxious about work and *was* definitely going to miss his. I permitted him a phone call, which calmed him down.

I stayed up late that night watching Fear The Walking Dead to try and make myself as tired as possible to sleep well into the next morning in preparation for nights.

That night, I managed to embarrass myself fairly quickly. I was frantically trying to add all my handover logs to confirm I'd taken on responsibility for and had checked my DPs. Whilst doing this, I became aware of a person in a suit standing by my desk and told them if they wanted to provide a post-interview update, they'd have to wait. I took a second glance and realised it was the DS and they'd actually come to offer assistance in reviewing a job. I accepted their kind offer, explaining I had two officers already queuing to see me, one of which involved ten shopliftings.

The other was a youth nicked for two shopliftings, breaching a dispersal order and a public order offence against a PCSO. He'd admitted one of the thefts, denied the other, sort of admitted the public order and to be honest, I can't recall what he said about the dispersal matter.

NFA-ing the un-admitted theft was an easy decision, as officers had since viewed CCTV and decided it was NOT him. I reviewed the dispersal order job, deciding it had been issued within the correct area, however, there was no evidence in the PCSO statement that any documentation had been provided, nor was there evidence the prohibited area had been explained. Further, they were found a short while later *outside* the area, advised they were breaching it and were directed back *into* the area itself! We had therefore caused a breach of the order ourselves! NFA.

In relation to the public order, he admitted telling the PCSO to "FUCK OFF" several times but denied calling him a "NONSE".

I released him under investigation for the two offences, so YOT could advise whether there was any intervention work they could do with him, as opposed to prosecution. I doubted that.

The one with ten shopliftings was all over the place. Some had evidence, others next to nothing. A no comment interview had been provided. I ended up NFA-ing three, RUI-ing four and charging three, refusing bail as there were two warrants outstanding. The DP made no reps, neither did the solicitor when I phoned them, blatantly waking them up. The nurse then updated me an immigration prisoner (who'd already been in two days, awaiting collection), had disclosed an overdose of amitriptyline just prior to arrest. His obs were fine but she set about contacting doctors for advice and determined the alleged amount should've already shown its likely fatal effects and that a medical review later that night would suffice. Comforting. As it was, immigration came to collect him prior to then, so I made sure they were suitably briefed.

My first DP of the night arrived in a dressing gown and was taken straight to cell. Oddly, he calmed like the flick of a switch once in his cell and I was able to complete his risk assessment and rights there. I took the belt from him but allowed him to retain the gown, much to his amusement. He was alleged to have literally forked his wife in her face. That's right, a *facial forking*.

He'd heated it up in a frying pan and held it against her cheek, causing a red mark which was indeed, cutlery consistent.

Next up was another DV assault; this time just a shove. He was perfectly pleasant. No issues there.

My third and final prisoner of the night was a juvenile for theft from motor vehicle and bladed article. He was found near to a recent theft and found in possession of the stolen items. He also had three knives on him. Why anyone would need three knives is beyond me. Even two is a bit excessive but I suppose one per hand if you feel so inclined. But *three*?

We only had seven in that night, which meant when CPS advice finally came back around four in the morning for the job the DS had kindly reviewed, I was able to give it my full attention. Sadly, I realised he'd sent it to CPS on the threshold test, which meant we'd be looking to remand. He hadn't discussed that with me and remand is *my* decision. CPS certainly supported one but the fact PNC was down for maintenance wasn't helpful. Fortunately, the DS had completed a detailed MG7 (remand application), detailing the extensive previous the guy had, albeit, none for about a year. I just got on and remanded the bloke and fortunately, he made no reps! Didn't phone the solicitor and invite any from him! Besides, it happened to be the same one from earlier and I didn't want to disturb him *twice* in one night!

Once that was sorted, I had free time on my hands. That doesn't happen often. I took full advantage, getting a PDR done and tidying up jobs for days.

Three of the DPs I took over the following night were already remanded, so I completely their reviews when I did my initial checks. I was constantly bothered as I did my initial logs however, so I forgot to record the reviews until several hours later. This creates the impression I've breached PACE, whereas I hadn't.

I had a poo watch debacle to sort out. A drugs warrant had been executed at an address earlier that day by the local neighbourhood team. They found a guy in the bathroom squatting, with lube next to him and his trousers down. He was either having some form of 'pleasuring session' or, more likely, had seen the coppers coming and decided to plug their drugs.

An x-ray at hospital had been inconclusive and he'd also managed to leg it from officers there, meaning he was out of sight for about half a minute before officers kept eyes on during a foot chase and he was detained half a mile or so down the road. I was told he'd been handcuffed, but clearly there was the chance he'd been able to, well, guff them out I suppose and perhaps shake them down his leg?! God only knows what these people do in situations like that.

As if that wasn't enough, there was a further cock-up when he arrived at the nick. He'd been placed on close proximity, 'poo watch' constant obs. I was told the DO took him to the cell and the DP then asked for a sandwich. The DO went to the kitchen to fetch said sandwich and then panicked, realising they'd fucked up. They ran back to the cell about three minutes later, by which time there was evidence the cell toilet had been flushed and the DP had used several tissues from within the cell. The toilet's blocking mechanism for 'poo watch' scenarios had not been activated and so it seemed likely any drugs had been flushed away. But they couldn't rule out the possibility they hadn't been, so he was kept on 'poo watch' for the entirety of his stay.

The DS leading that investigation contacted me and explained they didn't have enough to charge DP with any of the drugs offences that night and could we use the clock to see if he produced anything by morning? I said what enquiries did we have left for which we could drag out the clock. There were none. Clearly that wasn't going to happen then. I'd not dealt with this type of situation before and it certainly didn't come up in training. I gather that where there is sufficient evidence, we often look to apply a holding charge, to get the DP before court and then we apply for a certain amount of time to keep DP at the nick to continue 'poo watch'. Trouble was, I was being told there was insufficient evidence at that point. We considered the escaping unlawful custody matter. Again, I have no knowledge that could assist me in making this type of decision, but even if charging and remanding for that was an option, to enable the 'poo watch' to continue, I was mindful of the fuck-ups that had already occurred and was it really worth continuing with it? I thought not. The DS agreed. I RUI'd him for all matters, much to the relief of the two response officers waiting for a bowel movement.

I was sorting that out when an officer found me to discuss three arrests that had been made and would I mind them coming into custody at that hour given their ages? Two were fifteen and one fourteen. All were accused of beating up a homeless man and producing a knife at some point during the assault. I had no issue with them being there at all. Another DP in custody was there for GBH after a school stabbing and they further sold the matter by explaining the father of the victim for the GBH job was said to be looking for these three youths, having somehow heard *they* may be responsible for his son's stabbing. There was some suggestion the knife produced during the homeless man assault was the same one used in that incident. They needn't have bothered further selling it – a homeless man had been assaulted by three youths. Custody was the right place for them, as far as I was concerned.

I authorised detention of all three, leaving the DOs to complete the majority of the booking in procedures, which I then reviewed, completing risk assessments and setting care plans.

I then booked in a drink driver. He'd blown 38Ugs at the roadside, meaning he was just over the limit. He'd been nicked for no insurance and driving otherwise than in accordance with a licence. 37Ugs was the lowest he provided in custody, but 40Ugs is the minimum we actually charge. Lucky day for him in that respect but he still got charged with the other traffic offences.

It was ten past midnight and I'd already booked in more DPs than I had the whole of the previous night!

Next was a domestic ABH. The guy was a real twat. I saw him appear on the holding cell camera. Officers placed him in the cage but didn't close the door and he walked out! He then sat down on the bench and gave them little cause to then justify standing him back up and placing in the cage. They'd missed their opportunity.

He then needed the toilet. Officers asked if he could be brought through and I asked if he'd been searched. They didn't know! How you cannot know if someone you're bringing into custody has been searched is beyond me. That's your responsibility in escorting them. They searched him and I showed him through to the toilet. He complained he couldn't go whilst still cuffed. Now, I've not tried this before, but he was cuffed to the front and I reckon I'd be able to manage that. But it's still not an unreasonable request I suppose. Trouble was, with drunk argumentative people, it's often one thing after the other. Once the urination was complete, he refused to leave the toilet, demanding a cigarette. I could sense the DO and the DP were about to tussle and, keen to avoid it, I entered the loo in a last attempt to resolve the situation. This chap had markers for assaulting police in custody and was extremely aggressive at times. The toilet was cramped and not an ideal spot for having a bundle. Fortunately I managed to talk him round to leaving the loo and, much to the annoyance of the officers, I told him he'd have to wait back out in the holding cell until I was ready to accept him.

He came through a few minutes later and started crying. He apologised for his behaviour. I managed to get everything completed I needed to. He said he'd had ten stellas. It was clear he was expecting to be dealt with overnight. There was no way that was going to happen, even if the evidence was up together. He was pissed. However, I managed to avoid the subject, meaning he stayed compliant and enabling us to even get his fingerprints taken; something I was convinced when I first saw him arrive would not happen.

A university student was the following DP to arrive. They were no trace on PNC and appeared to have had a moment of madness, smashing up flowerpots and other garden furniture with a pole. He reckoned he'd had half a bottle of vodka and gin too. He stank of booze but was surprisingly coherent. His main concern was whether his antics would affect his studies.

I received a text from a mate on response I used to work with, saying two were on route for a theft from motor vehicle. I got their names in advance, meaning I saved time by doing their PNC checks and previous custody record checks prior to arrival.

The first one in had clearly smoked heroin recently but was able to answer questions.

The second one in was drowsy as hell, falling asleep at the charge desk.

Concerningly, the second one had a screwdriver and screws still in his outer jacket pocket. It's amazing what gets missed on the street and custody is a real eye-opener to stuff like that. We bagged that up separately, reckoning someone would probably want to seize that, given the offence!

Eight prisoners booked in by me; seven by my colleague. Fifteen total all night. And a Thursday too. Not even the weekend. Barely a moment's pause.

And to make things worse, the block stank of puke. The cell nearest the main office was a puke minefield and the smell had drifted far. I'd attempted to mask it by spraying Febreze along the corridors, however, it seemed to amplify the smell and make it worse. It made us all feel like vomming ourselves.

I handed over to days and got out as quickly as I could.

I slept in slightly longer than normal for a first rest day, knowing I'd be out late for my brother's birthday. We gathered at his house for some pre-town tins, pizza and drinking games. We played one called 'twenty-one'. You have to go round in a circle, each saying the next number in sequence, although if someone says two in a row, it reverses the direction round the circle and if three numbers are said in a row it skips a person. If you get your number wrong or hesitate too long, you have a two finger forfeit. That sounds painful but it actually relates to your drink. The person who ends up having to say the number 'twenty-one' has to down some drink too.

Once we'd mastered the basics, alternative words were chosen each time a person reached twenty-one. Ours happened to go, one, two, penis, testicles, five, six, seven, ten, ten, nine, ten, twelve...Needless to say, when it got to what should've been 'eight', I was fucked every time.

We walked to the train station, carrying the remainder of the Strongbow crate with us for our journey. I think we were supposed to get a lift there off my bro's pregnant missus, however, I'd apparently blocked her in. I hadn't – but believe she was probably concerned about the parallel park she'd need to do upon returning!

We got on the train and I realised I was half wankered already.

Upon arriving in town, we still had four cans left. This is when I was taught about 'burying beers'. This is a dog-like routine, whereby you hide your beers somewhere in town, so you can come back to them later, much in the same way a dog would a bone. The idea being so door-staff do not confiscate them. We choose the hanging flowerpots at the train station. In they went, one by one, when nobody was looking. We all checked the flowerpots from various angles, to satisfy ourselves they were well hidden.

I ordered some cheesy chips at the first pub, desperate for more food already. Ciders and, for some reason, Jack Daniels too.

The next pub was where he'd planned on us staying the remainder of our evening, as there was a good atmosphere and live music. On route, my brother had a run in with a homeless man. He didn't like the way my bro declined to give him change. His insult to my bro was rather amusing though, "David Bowie wants his jacket back". That's become an instant favourite of mine.

On the walk back to the train station, I decided I needed a burger. I was told we didn't have much time and was at that point where I couldn't even work out the time or comprehend that the last train would not wait for us. All I knew was the kebab shop dude told me my burger would only take four minutes, which sounded good to me.

I finished it off just as we arrived at the station. We located our ciders, dusted off the earth from them and waited on the platform. A train started approaching just as I'd noticed some vending machines on the opposite platform. I was assured it was *not* our train, however, sadly, they were taking the piss. I only realised this as I was purchasing my Twix bar and had to leg it back over the bridge and only just made it on to the train. Bastards.

It was probably a good thing we walked back from the station. I think a car ride would've finished me off. We all crashed round his that night. My head spun as I got into bed and I had to keep opening my eyes to focus on things, before closing them and trying again. I must have passed out rather quickly and woke around six in the morning after only a few hours sleep with a banging headache and never really got back to sleep after that, with the usual problem of getting up for a piss and my heart then starting to pound. Get that pretty much every time after a heavy night of drinking.

I was supposed to be on the piss that night too. It was my father-in-law's birthday, and he'd hired out a hall and was supplying all booze himself. I decided taxiing the family there and back would be too expensive, and that, as opposed to being hung-over, was my main reason for driving.

The kids did remarkably well considering it only started *at* their bedtime. There were the predictable tears as the evening drew to a close, with the slightest disagreement setting them off.

That was followed by a nice lazy day, where I did very little, other than having a meal with the family that evening, again for my bro's birthday.

Chapter Eleven – Pension Roulette

I'll come to that in a minute.

Things looked good on first glance Tuesday morning. But they weren't quite as they seemed. Five sergeants?! Surely not?! Not, indeed...

Two were on a course. Stress management, at that. How ironic. I heard they basically said two things. One, it is better to take a few days off sick when you start to feel stressed, than throw a wobbly and get signed off for long periods of time. Two, have a wank at work. Trouble is, you do one and you're seen as the other.

Another has currently got no access to the custody computer system. I.e. it's as if they're not there.

So two sergeants it was. And it was *manic*.

I took over about nine DPs from nights. My colleague a few less. Four were due in court, four were live prisoners and one was a right fuck up by the arresting officer. They'd gone for ABH and harassment but, realising the DP had breached court bail conditions, also nicked him for breaching those. Whilst this may sound right, it causes problems.

It means the DP has to be put before court within 24 hours of the arrest (for breach of bail). If they are nicked overnight, then morning court would be the ideal (and safest) option, as if the courts don't accept in the afternoon (through being too busy) then we'd lose the breach of bail job altogether.

If we opt to send them to the next possible court for the breach, you have the option of either marking the DP as 'not for release', RUI-ing the substantive offences, or NFA-ing the breach. 'Not for release' means you request the courts return the DP to the police station once they've dealt with the breach matter, so they can then be dealt with for the substantive offences. The PACE clock keeps ticking in such cases, so the longer they're at court, the less time you have to interview them once they're back. However, there's no guarantee they'll come back, as they may get 'potted' (sent to prison). Then you'd have to either go through the laborious process of a prison production or attend the prison and interview them there. A royal ball-ache, basically. RUI-ing the substantive offences is also a pain to investigators, as they'd much prefer to get on and interview them whilst they were at the station. NFA-ing the breach is never the preferred option, but if you're confident the substantive offences are likely to result in a charge, this wouldn't cause any harm, as you can use the breach of bail as justification for refusing them post charge bail.

It's therefore always better to 'save' the breach of bail as a card up your sleeve and play it when your investigation is complete in custody. Much the same way you would a warrant. Plus the look on someone's face when you NFA them for a job and arrest on warrant is priceless. They've got one over you, act all cocky and then you drop the bombshell. The knock on effect in this particular instance was we would effectively get two bites of the cherry in respect of the harassment. He'd be off to court to face consequences of breaching his bail conditions in contacting the victim. He would return to the station and then be investigated and potentially charged and remanded to court again for his repeated contacting the victim, ie, pretty much the exact same incident only dressed up different. At least there was the assault to fall back on.

I knew from the outset one DP in particular would cause me issues later on. Their relevant time (arrival time in custody from which the 24 hour PACE clock starts) was 1400hrs. They'd been nicked for robbery. With the majority of interviewing officers only appearing in custody late morning, all wanting the same solicitor, all wanting the same interviewing room, this would prove to be an arse. And it was. But more on that later...

It took me ages to get my initial handover logs written. I then started checking the PER forms for all my DPs off to court, to ensure they reflected the relevant risks. I did not, however, remember to complete the pre-release risk assessments before everyone disappeared. This completely slipped my mind, but it's worth noting they completely bypass you in the charge room and are whisked off to court as soon as their transport arrives. The only way to really get these completed is to pop to each individual's cell early on. I tend to take screen-prints of RAs to cells, scribble answers and invite them to sign by pen, scanning them on later. But on this occasion, I forgot. One of my DOs brought this to my attention, jokingly advising I'd let my standards slip. They were right. I was annoyed. But we live and learn.

Word reached us Immigration had three on route who already had IS91s served. These, as I understand them, are documents advising the DP they will be held in a detention centre, ultimately awaiting deportation. Sometimes DPs are arrested on suspicion of immigration offences and arrive at the police station as PACE prisoners, but when IS91s have been served, they arrive as non-PACE prisoners, with the cells used until they get housed elsewhere. I gather the police get paid for this. How much, I'm not sure.

The three on route morphed into four. Two per charge room.

I could hear officers in the corridor outside loitering; wondering when a skipper would become free to issue rights or review a job. I simply didn't become free. Straight after the immigration DPs, a rape arrived. They'd previously been arrested a couple months prior and released under investigation. They had been re-arrested following enquiries which revealed fresh evidence. Whilst I'd not booked such a prisoner in before, I recalled this scenario from training and it followed new bail legislation. New evidence gives you the ability to arrest again, if the necessity exists, with a brand new PACE clock. This chap was a RSO who they were looking to charge and remand. I was happy to authorise.

That was followed by a chap who'd been nicked on two 'fail to appear' warrants. Trouble was, one was a Crown court and the other, Magistrates. I was told he'd have to go to Crown first and they'd accept him that afternoon. He was anticipating being sent down. I can only assume he'd then get passed straight to Magistrates and if, as the case would likely be, there was insufficient time left that afternoon for that to happen, he'd be either returned to the police station as a 'lockout' or go to prison and get taken to Magistrates the following day. I never did find out what happened sadly, as it would've been good to know.

It was about half one in the afternoon. I then received update from the robbery interviewing officer. Half hour remaining on their PACE clock. I *knew* it would come to this. People kept entering the charge room to speak to me about things and I told them I simply couldn't and they'd have to wait for lates. Again, rights needed to be issued. No sergeant free to assist. A skipper elsewhere had reviewed a job to assist and emailed me saying to charge and remand. I sent a brief email back saying it would have to wait for lates as I was snowed under. This had to have my complete concentration or the DP would walk.

The robbery was not a robbery. Matey was a drug user and alcoholic. A prolific shoplifter, who often verbally abuses or threatens staff, sometimes assaults them. This time, he'd gone armed with a hammer. His behaviour in the shop had been somewhat erratic to say the least. He'd selected the usual shoplifter items, but rather than leave with them, he approached the till and threw them at the manager. He then produced the hammer, waved it about and made threats of violence. Once he left, he was approached by a PCSO who attempted to detain them. However, he threatened them and was arrested by police shortly after.

In interview, he'd been further nicked for two other jobs too (just what I needed!). One was a shoplifting, which he fully admitted and the other, a public order, which he denied. The shoplifting would be charged, the latter NFA'd.

Regarding the non-robbery, the DP had stated he'd been in hospital the day before and given medication that meant he went funny and couldn't recall anything, but clearly accepted it was him and was sorry for what was alleged.

There was simply no time to send this to CPS, nor was there time left to ask an Inspector to review and consider an emergency charge that could be later ratified by CPS. I decided to charge him with two Section 4 Public Order offences (causing fear or provocation of violence) against staff, one of the same against the PCSO and one possession of an offensive weapon, being the hammer. The first three were summary only offences, for which I could make the charging decision. The offensive weapon is either-way and under CPS charging guidance, I could make the decision in cases where a guilty plea was anticipated.

This chap had not made an admission. He simply had not *denied* the offence but CCTV was overwhelmingly clear, showing him with a hammer and he had shown remorse. I blagged the guilty plea anticipated on this basis, prepared to lose that charge at court if CPS decided to drop it.

I'd finished typing my review at about ten to the hour and the OIC went off to put charges on the box. Realising that would never happen in ten minutes, I got on and charged the DP for the shoplifting, so I could get him charged with *something* within the PACE clock. I refused bail due to his horrendous offending history, which he didn't argue. I returned to his cell and charged him with the remainder of offences, when they'd been prepared. It's fair to say I was feeling rather stressed by the end of all that, but decided to ignore current expertise advice by not nipping off to choke the chicken.

In retrospect, whilst typing this, I reckon I should've charged that shoplifting and sent the OIC to CPS, as once they'd been charged and remanded for *something* we had all afternoon and night to play with. I'd also failed to consider the involvement of a weapon would likely result in Crown court, which also meant CPS advice should've been sought. What do they say about benefit of hindsight?

One of the people who'd been harassing me whilst I was desperately trying to get all that sorted was the Inspector. So we chatted in a side office and then came news no custody sergeant wants to hear.

A DEATH.

Someone I'd had responsibility for on my last night shift the set before had hung themselves in prison. Apart from visiting them at the start of my duty, I'd had no other dealings and handed them over to days. They were alive and well at the start of my shift and evidently, also alive as they were handed to the courts that morning. The sergeant before me booked them in. The sergeant after me booked them out. But I'd had responsibility in-between, so naturally my name goes on the shit list.

I was told not to worry. But also advised the Force had voluntarily referred to the IOPC but that they may decide to allow local PSD investigate. What was there to investigate? None of *us* were in that cell with him in prison.

Naturally, the main focus will undoubtedly be on whether relevant risks were passed to the courts and, in turn, passed on to the prison. The importance of the PER form shows its weight in gold here.

Did I check his PER form on nights? I seriously doubt it. It was manic and I barely paused for breath. Two sergeants. Fifteen prisoners to book in all night, eight by myself. I usually do my best to check them on nights but would *always* do so when on days releasing them to the courts. The Inspector assures me the PER looked good. Phew.

He ended that discussion by assuring me this was all just procedure and I needn't throw a wobbly. Should I, as those on the stress awareness course discovered, take a few days off? No, I shall not. I've genuinely not been *that* affected by this news. At least I don't think I have. Yet. I know his death is nothing to do with me and it's extremely unlikely *I'd* be faulted for anything *I've* done. However, this is another thing that will get stored in my subconscious. I'm worried these things will gradually build up over time and one day, topple. Welcome to pension roulette. Participation mandatory. Comes with the territory. Deal with it.

Fuck.

The second day shift was a definite non-event, in the morning at least. There were four skippers on, so I sat with investigators, awaiting their updates. Problem was, as usual, no interviews took place until late morning.

As there were four sergeants on, we decided to set allocated meal breaks. Mine was midday. I went to custody and ate mine in the kitchen. I'd been set half an hour, but was conscious that updates may start coming soon. I left the kitchen after about ten minutes and walked past the charge rooms. I'd clearly missed an update. Officers were stood talking to one of the sergeants, who was reviewing their job. They made a snide remark and I reminded them it had been *they* who set my break at that time!

I went back to the investigators and there was still nothing for an hour or so, then, of course, they all hit at once shortly before handover, resulting in a rather stressful end to an otherwise boringly Q shift.

I watched one of those *'so awful you have to see it'* films that night, namely 'Killing Hasselhoff'. Bizarrely, it featured a cameo from Michael Winslow playing himself, who is better known as Larvell "Motor Mouth" Jones from the Police Academy movies.

For the first late, there were three skippers, but one was still without full computer access. They would take disposals, writing the reviews and email them across to us for actioning. On handover, I was told one of my DPs had a gammy leg. I'd dealt with them several times before out on the streets and tended to get on well with them. They were a heroin addict, who had a penchant for rifling through bins on nights. Whenever they were wanted, all you had to do was tour the local charity shops and recycle points and you'd usually find him.

The leg in question was the result of years of drug abuse, injecting into the same spot over and over. He'd usually bring this up out on the street and show off the dirty bandage. But out on the street you're blessed with fresh air. Custody was a different matter.

If I'd forgotten to write down his cell number for my initial checks, my sense of smell would definitely have honed in on him. The corridor outside his cell reeked.

Reluctantly, I dropped the hatch to speak with him. He looked clammy, gaunt, ashen and mumbled to me he was okay. The stench of rotting flesh was unbearable. This was, essentially, a talking corpse. There was no way I could hold a conversation with him. A second was long enough. I wanted to puke.

His prints were outstanding, so a few minutes later, my DO got him out the cell and took him for processing. I could tell this was underway as the unpleasantness had spread to the charge room and beyond. Out came the Febreze.

The OIC for a criminal damage job came to see me, once I'd had chance to read the job. A female DP was alleged to have gone to a pub where her ex partner worked, armed with a hammer, and caused damage to property. All because she'd learnt he'd stopped paying her mobile phone. Shortly beforehand, she'd text her mum (also works there), saying she was on route to smash the place up and kill him. She took her baby along for good measure. Presumably as a witness, albeit, not independent and incapable of producing anything other than dirty nappies.

Upon entering, she went behind the bar, with her hammer, stood with it up to her shoulder in an 'armed and ready' pose facing her ex, and then began damaging items.

I was talking the job over to the officers. I suggested that for CDI purposes (crime data integrity), they'd need to consider whether to record the crime of aggravated burglary. This may sound far fetched for what was really a simple damage job, but under crime recording standards, they pick the bones out of such incidents. She'd indicated she was going there to kill him. Fair enough to therefore say at least with intent to cause GBH? She'd entered the pub with her WIFE (no, cease *those* thoughts now – this means weapon of offence, imitation firearm, firearm, explosive – clearly the first one in this instance) and entered part of the building as a trespasser (staff only area behind bar), with intent to cause GBH and damage. The victim was the landlord. He also disclosed historic assaults. So the officers further arrested her for aggravated burglary and ABH. Funnily enough, at that point, she decided a solicitor may be useful.

My first prisoner of the day was a twelve year old shoplifter, who'd resisted arrest. There'd been an email about him recently and I recalled reading he was becoming more prolific of late and it served as a 'heads-up' should he be presented to any of us in custody – i.e. please authorise his detention.
I did and blimey was he stroppy. He disclosed ADHD but little else on the risk assessment. He was crying throughout, demanding we let him phone his mum. Whilst I would not normally entertain such demands, I was conscious of the fact this was, after all, a young child and speaking to a parent was a fair request. I afforded him this opportunity and she told him she would not be attending, as had nobody to look after her baby. This made his paddy worse. The duty AA assisted so he could be booked in as full rights given and he continued sobbing in a cell. There was recent police intelligence this young chap was using and dealing crack cocaine. At twelve years of age! What has the world come to?
Next, was a guy who'd been nicked for domestic ABH. The circumstances were slightly unusual, in that the victim suffered mental health issues and had disclosed to her MH worker and to a facility she'd been admitted to, that he regularly beat her. The MH worker reported this to police and upon attending, officers witnessed bruising to her arms. In he came. With statements booked for the following morning from those professionals, he'd be bedded down for the night.
A female shoplifter followed, having been identified from CCTV for a theft from Iceland that occurred a few months ago. She'd been evasive and was also wanted on warrant for failing to appear at court. She made no reps when I informed her I was refusing bail for the shoplifting, as it made sense to me for all matters to be dealt with the following day at court.

Residents on an estate had made several calls to police about a guy driving his vehicle whilst drunk. Police located the car smashed up with him in his flat nearby. It transpired he'd made threats to residents who called police, saying he'd burn their houses down. He was presented to me on suspicion of driving whilst unfit through drink and threats to cause damage.

He blew 107Ugs on the Intox machine. Apart from being a bit gobby, he was generally compliant and caused no real issues. He would also be bedded down for the night, with several victim statements to be obtained.

About an hour before handover, a sixty year old woman was brought in for domestic assault. She had a bleeding toe, which left red blobs across my charge room floor. My DO got her a chair and mopped up the trail she'd left from the holding cell, also providing first aid in the form of a plaster. A neighbour had witnessed her lumping her partner over the head. Going through the risk assessment, I asked if she was drug or alcohol dependant. It was as if we were in a support group session, in that she suddenly realised she had a problem needing addressing. Several Bacardis meant she too would be bedded down for days.

Just before handover, word came that the twelve year old's jobs were far from up together. I added a rationale to the custody log as to why I'd be bedding him down for the morning. His solicitor made reps and I explained my reasons. Unfortunately, I then became aware there was a backlog of disposals awaiting actioning. The sergeant on these had taken several updates but not typed any up as she took them, meaning they all hit the charge rooms at once just before handover – far from ideal. I was half an hour late for handover, keen to get rid of them straight away. Unfortunately, one of these was Gammy Leg Man.

His solicitor popped his head in, explaining he had an unusual request. He said he'd known his client for many years and he was clearly in such a bad way. He produced a tenner and went to pass it to me, explaining he'd like it given to him on release so he could get himself home.

Whilst a nice gesture, I wasn't going to explain to the solicitor that this heroin addicted burglar would most likely spend this nice gesture on his next fix, making the gammy leg slightly more gammy in the process. I advised we'd sort him a taxi home. He said he'd still like to give us the tenner to contribute towards it. I politely explained I could not accept money from him.

I booked the taxi, realising I could get both DPs in it to save money, as they were going back to the same place. Not ideal, sending two burglars off together, as they'd most likely go straight out burgling again. But then, I decided they'd only likely meet up later anyway, so we might as well save a few quid. Poor taxi driver though...out came the Febreze again, making the room slightly more acceptable for nights to use.

I got home and realised I hadn't eaten in twelve hours, so ate dinner whilst catching up with season two of Sense8.

In typical job fashion, my second late was in fact a night elsewhere. Thus, creating three nights in a row, with a hefty amount of travelling for good measure.

The station I was covering was renowned for having minimal footfall. This was the second shift I'd worked there, both times taking over four and handing over the same number. Two were live prisoners and two had been remanded. The two remanded were high risk of suicide on release. One of the two live prisoners came back pretty much on handover with four charges for breach of non-molestation order authorised by CPS. I told the OIC to expect a remand and that I would look at it in due course once I'd settled.

I NFA'd a domestic assault early on. She'd been accused of trying to smother her partner with a pillow and throwing a metal clothing bin at him. He hadn't reported this at the time, but rather two days later. Therefore, there was no *res gestae* evidence in the form of body worn video showing the victim's demeanour at the time, or showing pillow or clothing bin out of place. He'd received a small cut to a finger, although she claimed he'd done that working on his car a few days prior. Usually, I'd send jobs with photographic evidence of an assault to CPS, however, I wasn't convinced this extremely minor cut would make or break this particular case.

I received a call from a mental health practitioner who explained they were not able to attend overnight to assess one of the two suicidal chaps on remand. They explained someone on days may be able to attend that morning but I stressed my concerns the guy would be off to court before they'd arrive. I wasn't getting anywhere and would later just ensure the PERs for both troubled individuals had their respectively risks clearly identified.

I was then about to review the non-mol job when a DP arrived. This only prisoner of the night came in the form of a prolific offender, who'd been ejected from a pub, only to punch the doorman on his way out, causing loose teeth. He was aggressive in the holding cell and continued to be when presented. He refused to engage with the risk assessment, so was taken to his cell Route One.

I then charged and remanded the breach of non-mol DP. He wasn't happy, but didn't cause me too much grief. He had a meal and settled for the night after a brief strop.

An hour or so after the Route One, the DO asked me to join them for the next check, as they'd been difficult to rouse on the first. They weren't rousing easily on the second at all and, worse still, a large lump had formed on their forehead that definitely wasn't there on arrival. He'd been on CCTV and I was confident this must've been caused prior to arrival. However, alcohol plus head injury equals hospital. Two response cops arrived and took him away.

Some time later, I received a call from the officers, saying matey had calmed down and would need a CT scan in due course. They asked whether we could release him under investigation so save officers having to sit up the hospital with him. Around that same time, the patrol skipper came in, so they'd clearly all had a convo prior to calling me. He too was asking the same. I was extremely reluctant to release him. He was clearly a violent individual, marked up as a prolific offender. Should he discharge himself from hospital and die, that would come back on me. Likewise, should he become violent at hospital once police resumed and end up getting nicked again, that would just be plain embarrassing.

I got their issue – not enough resources. But then that's an organisational problem, not mine. If this chap was released and died, not enough coppers on the street wouldn't save my arse.

I thoroughly checked the PERs for all three on remand and much to the clear annoyance of the DO sat next to me who'd already either completed or checked them himself, I added bits that I considered needing adding. The risks were all there, it's just I hate it when there are sections of forms that aren't filled out purely due to repetition. If a box is there, it should be completed. If there's too much repetition, this needs feeding back as opposed to ignoring the boxes. After my recent death incident, I was keen to dot all i's and cross all t's! Otherwise you just know that one missed box will be *THE* reason that person ended up dead and not that they were, in fact, going to kill themselves anyway.

Route One guy returned much sooner than expected, with a head injury advice sheet and instructions for us that he should be returned if he vomits more than twice or his condition worsened. He was so sleepy that any hostility he still had towards us was suppressed. I therefore managed to get through his risk assessment and rights, before returning him to cell.

The last couple hours were Q, so I managed to get some admin done and submit my mileage claims etc. The days skipper arrived in good time, enabling me to slope off and start the trek home.

I had a fairly poor sleep between shifts, meaning I arrived tired at work that night. I'd only been expecting two sergeants, but two more appeared!

It was strangely Q for a Saturday night. The two extra sergeants realised they pretty much had nothing to do, both opting to take leave. I took over four prisoners. Yes, four! Unheard of. One of those was a BTP job.

I booked in four overnight.

First was a drink driver, who blew 64Ugs in custody and was charged after being bedded down for a few hours.

Second was a guy who'd failed to stop for police, failed to provide a specimen of breath at the roadside and was said to have driven dangerously, though I wasn't convinced from the circs provided. A call had come in reporting he was leaving a golf club and headed for a nearby hotel. A traffic unit picked the car up as it entered the hotel but upon the blue lights being illuminated, the car turned around and sped off. Unfortunately for the driver, he clearly didn't know the area and went down the dead end road of an industrial estate. He mounted a kerb and called it a day. I knew exactly where this was...just down the road from my house! (I wish to clarify, he was unwanted riffraff in an otherwise very pleasant estate, I'll have you know).

He had markers for being concerned in the supply of cocaine and during the risk assessment, showed me two scars on his abdomen from where he'd once been stabbed.

He went on to refuse any specimen in custody too and was bedded down for the night.

Third was a domestic assault, although from the look of the DP, I think they nicked the victim.

He limped into the charge room, unable to put any weight on his right foot. Instantly, I knew he'd be off to hospital. There was no point in the nurse seeing him. In addition, his left ear had been bleeding, as there was blood inside where it had pooled and dried. Behind his ear was swelling and bruising, along with bruising on his neck just below. More concerning still, my DO noticed his left pupil was smaller than his right. I didn't see him again that night.

I received word from BTP around half four that their evidence review officer had authorised a charge of obstruct a carriage by an unlawful act. New one on me.

He was nineteen years old, has aspergers, and dislikes his current supported accommodation. He was seen by the mental health liaison and deemed to be at high risk of suicide or accidental death. Adult Services had already confirmed there was nowhere else he could go. The DP had already said that if released, he would do the same thing again.

The DP had been in custody around three times in forty-eight hours, returning to train tracks each time upon release. That wasn't going to happen again. I remanded him. Although I fully expect that when he pleads guilty at court, he'll be handed a community order and when he realises he's back off to the same accommodation again, he'll return once more, to the tracks. We'd essentially put a plaster on a wound that once removed, would continue bleeding. We're reliant on another agency (the ones actually suited to deal with such individuals) actually stitching the wound.

Fourth and last DP arrived just before handover to days. Very annoying, that.

They claimed to be Moldovan, and were alleged to have drink driven into the side of an elderly couple's house, causing substantial structural damage and some debris to fall on one of them resulting in minor injury. They'd also been nicked sus TWOC. He had reddening to his face but officers stated he'd been seen by ambulance at the roadside and deemed not to require medical attention. However, officers had no paperwork from them and as per our policy in such situations, I requested the nurse be called through to check he was fit to detain.

I got through the risk assessment with him without issue but when the Intox procedure was commenced, officers updated me he had suddenly required a Russian or Romanian interpreter. I provided them with the details of the telephone service we use.

The last night was very busy. I immediately found myself booking in a DP – before I'd even started work! They were very compliant and pleasant. We shared similar tastes in music, a conversation that came from me booking in his property and noticing he had a plectrum with him.

He was alleged to have pulled his ex partner off her sofa, causing lasting pain and also causing damage to her front door. He was completely sober and the job appeared up together, but given the time of day, I knew it was likely response wouldn't have resources to deal, so was confident he'd be there until morning.

On handover, I took over an additional seven prisoners. My only other sergeant colleague that night took over far more. Another prisoner arrived. They were one half of two in for criminal damage. He too was sober and pleasant, albeit, he had markers for violence. There were outstanding enquiries on that job, so I informed him he'd be in overnight.

I then booked in a drink drive. They blew fifty something at the roadside and I think 46Ugs in custody. I marked them down for charging an hour later, although would later revise that to three hours following advice from the nurse, who considered him still intoxicated around the time I'd hoped to bin him.

Two response officers updated me regarding a DP they'd interviewed. He was the Moldovan man from the night before. Turns out he'd spent much of that day up the hospital with a fractured jaw! So much for the attending ambulance crew that'd deemed him okay. In addition, they'd not been able to get hold of a Russian or Romanian interpreter for hours, delaying his interview. If only he'd been able to manage without...that was his own fault.

Despite admitting being the driver at the scene, he'd provided a no comment interview. Nobody had actually seen him driving. I was of the belief that if all enquiries were complete, CPS would charge him aggravated TWOC but there were still enquiries outstanding, the most important being the seized car with blood on the airbag. This would prove beyond all reasonable doubt he was the driver.

The officers were expecting to have to get CPS advice. I thought about it, but given the lack of admission in interview, I considered the FCT not met due to this outstanding key enquiry. I considered sending it to CPS on the THT but didn't believe a remand necessary. After all, his immigration status had been cleared up and he'd provided an address. I decided to release him under investigation.

I booked in one of three that arrived for a TWOC of a Porsche. I recognised my one – I've definitely either booked him in or released him recently.

He had markers for violence towards police, in particular, for spitting and head butting officers. He appeared chirpy on arrival, and I completed the whole risk assessment process with him, taking his photo. However, I started to cover his rights and he requested a phone call to his partner. There was a queue at the back door and we were extremely busy, so I declined but said we'd try to facilitate it in due course.
He went quiet and the cheeky smirk disappeared. "Take me to my cell now" he shouted. He went to leave but the officer blocked his path. I could see this going wrong. I hadn't yet worked out what cell he was going to and desperately started clicking away to see what was available. I found one and selected it but as I escorted him down the corridor, I realised I'd only just released the Romanian from there and was unsure whether it'd been cleared out. As I walked past the DO office I asked a DO covering that cell's checks and my question was met with a blank stare. I repeated my question with more urgency and still a blank stare. She panic-answered 'yes' but as I arrived and the DP entered it was clear the previous chaps blankets and rubbish was still there. The DO arrived, realising they'd panic-answered incorrectly. The DP started to get *really* worked up. I think he'd been building himself up to shout and swear and kick the cell door the moment he was put there, but hadn't accounted for the spring-clean. Sure enough, after those few awkward moments, upon closing the door, he started kicking the hell out of it and shouted and swore. I had said "no" to someone who doesn't take "no" well. He clearly needed to be taught this lesson. When you've done wrong and you're in police custody, you don't get to run things.
I remembered to take my kit home, having arranged more overtime on rest days and with PST my first day back.
I got home and the wife shot off to work. I sorted the kids for school, dropped them at their bus and went to bed, going out like a light, knackered.

Having not yet really found anything productive to do with my rest days, such as exercise or getting out the house full stop, I once again caught up with various TV series.

This was pretty much the theme for the following day too, although I did manage to cram in an hour of Die Another Day with the kids before putting them to bed and getting ready for an overtime shift consisting of plain clothes proactive patrol looking for baddies breaking into cars.

It was myself and a mate from shift, same one as before, going round on the hunt. It was very Q. We had someone cycle off from us around one in the morning. I was driving and pre-empted where he was heading and parked up to cut him off, but sadly my crewmate was a little slow and naive on the actual stopping front. Rather than standing in his path and getting hands on, he identified himself as a police officer, requested he stop, and matey simply cycled around him! By the time I'd turned the car round he'd cycled back to talk to us, having clearly already dumped whatever he had on him. He claimed he'd been smoking a joint and didn't want to get nicked for a pathetic amount of weed. I searched him anyway but, funnily enough, he was clean. Well, he was actually a filthy homeless heroin addict but I mean to say he had nothing illegal on him.

Around an hour later we were in a different part of the patch and saw a guy walk from our right to left at a junction we approached. We decided we'd stop and have a word. Only as we turned left, he'd disappeared. I got out on foot whilst my colleague drove around the estate in what he called 'stealth mode', which was in fact simply without headlights and with the diesel engine still giving the game away a mile off.

I checked front gardens, under cars but couldn't find him. I found an alleyway to hide in and remained there for best part of half an hour, feeling like a criminal myself, hoping he'd resume his walk and fall into my hands. It didn't happen.

I went for another walk and heard shouting. I walked towards and became aware of someone loitering round the corner. I crept up to the corner but they heard me and said "Is that you ***?" I identified myself, instantly recognising the female as a local heroin addict, with a reputation for selling herself for pocket change.

I knew exactly who she thought I was – I said that person's name and she confirmed. They were known for theft from vehicles – exactly what I was after. I suspect she'd been waiting for him to return, only he hadn't – no doubt because he was still hiding from *us*! I also reckon she was looking to pimp herself to occupants of the mental health accommodation she was directly outside of, as again, she has previous for preying on vulnerable people.

I gave her outer jacket and handbag a token search, not wishing to stab myself in what was a minefield of syringes. Clearly nothing stolen in there, so left it at that.

She explained she'd been waiting for him to return so they could go up an alleyway together to locate some food she'd stashed. Would we kindly help her retrieve it, as it was dark and she was scared?

We agreed to assist, really out of curiosity. As she led us up the dark alleyway, I started to realise this was not the best idea, having no body worn video on and with *her* reputation!

We responded to a burglary in progress which turned out to be sus circs only. I mean, what kind of burglar takes advantage of an unlocked door, only to go inside, put the lights and television on and not bother stealing anything?! She had a cat. I reckon it'd stood on her remote. No burglar. Cat burglar, anyone?

We blagged an extra hour of overtime, in a last ditch effort to find a crim. Sadly, nothing.

I only grabbed a few hours kip, keen to not waste most of my final day off. Took the kids swimming that afternoon, finished the Bond movie and had a few drinks. Probably more than I should have given PST was the following morning.

Chapter Twelve – The Copper Diet

Now, I'm sure there's plenty of coppers that have a diet that ranges from half-decent to extremely healthy. I like to think I'm at the half-decent point.

There are some shifts that make lates plus 'kebab night'. Or 'chinese night'.

My shift on response was never like that. Gone are the days when the whole shift eats a meal together. Some shifts do seem to manage it but whilst they're all sat in there, jobs are being neglected and overlapping shifts get stitched. Like most things, it tends to come down to who the skipper is and how in control they have things.

In custody, you can't leave to grab grub. It's whatever you took in with you. You often go hungry even with food only metres from you, depending on how manic the shift is.

I've now started leaving supplies at work, so I don't have to take a meal in every day. I try and eat as healthily as I can in custody, as I know that whilst the majority of the meals my wife cooks at home are healthy, I still snack on chocolate. That's my weakness. Choooooocooolaaaaaaate!

First day back should've been a fourth and final rest day. But this was PST day. Personal Safety Training.

It wasn't too bad. The instructors kept it shorter than scheduled. I got my annual exercise in. Passed the bleep test. Whilst hung-over I might add. I blag that every year and could keep going if I wanted but they always stop at the required pass mark.

But the thing I love most about PST is the location. Our location provides a very nice village bakery a five minute walk away, where they do the best minted lamb pasties I've ever had.

So, first day back was a day of exercise, with a pasty and cinnamon whirl for lunch. All the hard work effectively undone by meal choice. But fuck it.

One of my DOs had developed a severe limp by lunch and I suggested they have a word with the trainers and drop out, knowing first hand how a knee injury requires rest.
I had a beer and Jack Daniels before bed. I tend to save the drinking for days off but this should've been one of those really. So it counted.
First proper day back was business as normal. Two sergeants and five DOs – one covering from elsewhere as our DO's knee hadn't recovered.
I took over eight DPs, whereas my colleague took seven. Mine were all live prisoners, whereas he had some due in court.
The first incoming DP arrived around nine. My DO loaded the record, whilst I researched the last three CRs for risks and warning markers.
Then the DP was presented to me. Face to face. About a metre away. We instantly recognised one another. I saw him gulp. He probably saw me staring back at him for a second longer than social etiquette generally deems acceptable, whilst I double checked what I had come to realise. I was definitely right. Bollocks. This was my next door neighbour.
He'd been arrested on a fail to appear warrant. Original offence of drug driving, among others. This didn't surprise me. I'd often smelt weed being smoked in their garden. I'd seen the police round there once after a massive argument between him and what was quite clearly an ex partner.
I say hi to him in passing but this has only been a handful of times. We own. He rents. Fortunately this means one day soon there will no longer be an issue. In the meantime, things are going to be awkward as hell.
"We know each other don't we?" I asked. "Yep" was his reply. "We're neighbours aren't we?" I said. "Yep" was his response.

He indicated it was fine and he didn't mind and I could continue. I asked the officers to explain why he'd been arrested and then authorised his detention. However, this didn't feel right and was far too awkward. So I got the other skipper to swap with me, explaining to the DP we'd need to ask all sorts of health and welfare type questions and it would only be fair to him having someone he didn't know go through those. Otherwise of course, the risk is he won't disclose important stuff through embarrassment.

We made a priority call to the courts requesting they take him ASAP! However, he spent the next three hours sat in a cell. He complained about crumbs on his cell floor and that he'd been bitten whilst in there. I can certainly believe the latter; I get bitten all the time. Fleas, mosquitos...custody has it all. It's such a delightful place to work.

I took a post interview update around half ten, which caught me by surprise, as I don't usually see people start arriving for interview until around then. This was a domestic related TTK (threats to kill). The DP was alleged to have sent a message to the victim requesting back fifty pounds she owed him. When she refused, he said he'd go round her dads. She then called him a "fucking cunt" and sent other abusive messages to him. At some point during this 'conversation', he sent a message stating she better pay up, as he's already being done for attempted murder again. I think we can all guess what he was implying here, but it's certainly far from a direct threat to kill someone. You could argue it's an offence of malicious communications, however, she'd clearly been sending abuse to him too, so I could hardly get him done and not her!

I was surprised to see a job like this had made it as far as custody and strongly suspect people find it far easier these days to make an arrest than justify why one was not made for a domestic related matter.

The next review came straight after. A drink driver had failed to stop for police and decamped. A hungry police dog found him hiding in a bush. He matched the description of the driver. He had no insurance and no driving licence. Officers seized the car but I couldn't see them doing forensics on it. Perhaps they may have done. The chap had gone 'no comment' in interview and I decided as he'd not *denied* the offence, or given any reasonable excuse for being in a bush near the scene, there was a realistic prospect of conviction and I charged him with all four offences. He didn't seem surprised.

I booked in a TTK / Section 4 Public Order DP who'd been arrested following a to-do where she used to work. She was a bit scatty but otherwise caused no issues. She'd not eaten in four days, and declined our grub, so I asked the nurse to pop down and check she was fit to detain.

A further review came, but it involved a job the OIC's DS was already well aware of. It concerned a DP who'd been entrapped by one of these paedophile hunter groups. He'd admitted around six offences in interview. The OIC was hoping I'd be looking to remand the chap, as they wanted to send to CPS on the THT. We can only do this when looking to remand. I had a quick look at the guy's previous. I considered the potential for vigilante action as a result of him being "outted" on Facebook. I agreed that if the DS reviewed the job itself, given they already had knowledge, I'd stick a rationale on for remand. I was later told even the solicitor had told the OIC the defence would not be opposing any remand at court. Clearly they too had concerns.

My colleague was tucked up from about one, with a (very rare these days) bail return.

Around quarter past one a Sergeant from investigations came down and advised me they'd reviewed a job and written it up for RUI. I went to release them soon after but saw no review had been added to the custody record. I pinged them an email but got nothing back. A DP had been waiting for ages in the holding cell. I decided to get on with booking them in. This took way longer than anticipated, as they were Romanian and spoke no English.

She'd been nicked on suspicion of assaulting both her children. Her husband then arrived soon after. He'd have to wait for lates.

I was half an hour late for handover. I hadn't eaten. After handover, lunch was my priority – not the RUI that'd been written up by that point. Lates would sort that. I went home and ate. Was wondering whether my neighbour would be disqual already. Doubtful. I expect he either pleaded not guilty, given his stated employment was removals (ie, dependant on being able to drive) or, more likely, the case was adjourned. He'd probably return home in his car and smoke a massive spliff in the garden. Or he may think twice about this now. Who knows. Only time will tell.

As it was, I was sat on the shitter later that evening and heard part of a conversation next door. I only heard key words but they were enough. "Neighbour", "so awkward", "probably thinks I'm a right cunt".

Yes, sir. I do.

I took disposals the next day. The first of these came around half ten. A DP had been arrested for a racially aggravated public order offence. They were further arrested in interview for a similar offence.

The OIC explained the DP had been on his own and the victims were in a group of three and were all well known little shits. They'd been stood at opposite sides of a railway barrier and when it lifted, they started walking towards one another. The DP was alleged to have shouted racist abuse at the black member of the group and tried to kick out at him as they all passed one another. One of the group had called police, who attended and made the arrest. Statements had been taken by response from the victim of the racial abuse and one friend but not the other friend who also claimed to have had threats directed at him.

The OIC updated me that in interview, the DP stated he was too drunk to recall but did most likely make some racial comments but he wouldn't have meant these, as members of his own family are from ethnic minority backgrounds. He said he wouldn't have made threats of violence, as there was one of him, and three of them.

I directed the OIC to obtain a statement from the outstanding victim. Firstly, she couldn't understand why I felt this necessary, stating they were all from the same group and therefore not independent. I explained the outstanding statement was from someone purporting to be a victim and that before I could consider any charge on the offence against them, I'd need a statement from them. Astoundingly, she couldn't get her head round this! She said they were all well known shits and would all say the same thing. I can't NFA a job because the OIC thinks they're local shits. Ok, they may have convictions for dishonesty offences, which would likely sway your decision. These lads did not. They were all eighteen/nineteen years old, with limited previous. The statements we had corroborated one another. I explained if we were able to get the outstanding statement, we could put to CPS that day, otherwise I would be looking to RUI. She felt we had enough to take it to CPS already. Once again, I explained there was a victim who had not yet been statemented. We needed their evidence! I was seriously considering banging my head against a wall at this point. I gave it such serious consideration that I examined the wall for suitable space, but alas, there was none.

She went away and obtained a statement. As it was, having got the statement, it was clear from reading it that no additional offence was made out. This guy didn't fear any violence against him. In fact, he undermined the case to an extent, by calling the DP a "cunt" on occasions. The OIC was then saying how she felt a conditional caution was most appropriate. It didn't fit the bill for this at all. The offence had not been fully admitted. It would be rare such a disposal would be considered for a hate crime anyway, let alone with a DP who had previous convictions for public order, albeit, from some time ago.

I wrote it up for CPS, recommending a single charge of racially aggravated S4A POA. Word came through later this had been authorised. I felt reassured in my decision making.

Next to review was a domestic related false imprisonment. The victim said her husband returned home and she told him she wanted a break. He went mad, locking her in the house, refusing to let her leave. However, he did permit her a phone call to her mother. The victim took the call in their bedroom and he barged in halfway through, taking the phone from her and started damaging items. There was a statement from the victim, however, no photos of any damage had been taken to corroborate her account. The greatest undermining issue was the arresting officer's statement, which showed on arrest, the DP did have keys for the patio and garage doors, but that the front door keys were hanging up. Ok, he could've placed them there quickly when they arrived but it didn't help evidentially. Plus, the OIC spoke to both sets of parents – her mother was angry and concerned for her daughter, however, his mother confirmed her son had called her during the incident and asked her whether she could attend and give the victim a lift to her own mothers. Not the sort of behaviour of someone who wanted to keep her at the address. I NFA'd him.

There was little else for me to do, as, typically, the remainder of the interviews happened around handover itself. I did book in a prisoner around that time, allowing the others to hand over to lates.

It was a domestic related matter, whereby five ABH assaults had been disclosed over a three year period. It was one of those where officers had failed to locate the suspect and, having phoned them to arrange their arrest, they'd clearly been in contact with their solicitor and organised it so they would turn up at the station with them. This is a typical strategy to try and secure a VA (voluntary attendance) interview, as opposed to being arrested. However, I was satisfied the arrest necessity reasons given were legit and authorised their detention. I was mid rights and the solicitor walked in the charge room and made reps about the arrest necessity. I politely asked them to leave, explaining I had already authorised detention and would finish the booking in process before speaking to them. However, afterwards, they disappeared into an interview and I never saw them again. Before I went, I issued a conditional caution on behalf of a colleague. For some reason, I couldn't link the offence to the disposal within the custody record. It's times like this that you wish things were paper based. How much simpler is it to write on a bit of paper the offence?! Nothing stops you from being able to do this, unless, perhaps, you run out of ink. But there's already another pen to hand. Here, it was a classic case of 'computer says no'. I was ready to put my fist through the screen.

It appeared to be the fault of the OIC. I since discovered they'd tried following the out of custody conditional caution process, which cocks up things for us. I had to manually type out the caution form and get our IT support to sort the computer record out. I had to get the custody record reassigned to a special dummy IT custody block, so that they were no longer shown as on our site! Otherwise, that cell would've been out of action all weekend, just because I couldn't close down the record!

I took a charge room the following late shift. The cell block was full on my arrival, though a couple were binned whilst we took handover. We were a DO down and the spare skipper 'floated', assisting where they could, whether it be searching DPs, logging property, or booking in.

The majority of my DPs were all custody officer reviews, meaning they'd either been charged and remanded, or were warrants etc. There were three DPs in for a double stabbing, which I was told, was GBH but borderline attempt murder. One DP had been remanded for around twenty shopliftings. I expect he'll get a couple of weeks custodial for that. We need the American justice system over here. No messing about. Not saying it's entirely ethical but it certainly keeps the crims where they need to be.

I booked in four people that shift.

The first was a breach of post-charge police bail conditions, meaning they'd been charged with an offence (this one a domestic assault) and were due in court soon. The officer had clearly not pre-warned the DP he'd be off to court in the morning, so as soon as I explained why I was authorising detention (to place before next available court), he kicked off. Fortunately, he decided against becoming violent, and opted instead for shouting and swearing. He did eventually calm and I managed to get the whole booking in process completed before taking him to his cell.

Second in was a fail to appear warrant. The DP's vehicle had been flagged on ANPR and a traffic unit had stopped him on the motorway, following an activation on their in car computer. He would not stop talking. He was desperate to let me know his partner was at home and he cares for her twenty-four seven. He explained she has a heart condition and the stress of him being in custody would likely send her over the edge and result in her blood pressure skyrocketing. I asked why his stated address was different to hers, if he provided twenty-four seven care. My colleague asked why he was out at work if that were the case? When asked, he said there were no family or friends that could care for her. She was no longer speaking to her mother, etc etc. He was clearly over embellishing. I sent the arresting officer to her address to clarify and word came back that she was absolutely fine. She said her mother lived round the corner and could help if required. #BullshitArtist.

Third in was a breach of non-mol order. I'd booked in him at least once before, for exactly the same thing. Officers found him at his mother's address, which was the breach. He would later kick off in interview, upsetting the same AA that had been present in another interview-gone-wrong recently. He was marched back to his cell, charged and remanded.

Last in was a Polish lady on suspicion of domestic assault and damage. She was alleged to have pushed her partner and taken a hammer to his four-hundred pound watch. She requested an interpreter, which took about half an hour to arrange, but it was one of those classic scenarios where they end up answering the questions before they got translated, so her English was clearly adequate enough. But there were occasional words she *didn't* get and so one would be required for interview, to ensure the defence didn't have it easy. It was quite late on in the shift and officers were still progressing enquiries, so I was fairly confident no interpreter would be available for interview until at least the following morning.

Before handover, I RUI'd two out of the three GBHs. First one was easy. The second, not so much.

The problem occurred as they'd been on 'supervise-all' the majority of their stay. This meant dry cell conditions, ie, supervised toilet visits, no washing of hands, supervised meal/drinks and no fingerprinting.

Forensics were only completed at the close of play, so fingerprints were literally the last thing done before they left. I was seconds away from releasing number two (not *that* you anally-minded cretin) when my DO signalled for me to drag it out and keep him there (I'm now editing this and realise how strange this sounds, so naturally I'll keep it in). I dragged out the process as much as I could before there was literally nothing else for me to do or talk to him about. I explained we needed to ensure his prints confirmed his identity. He started pacing about nervously. He headed towards the door and gave the handle a not-so-subtle test to see if it was unlocked. He had clearly provided false details – *that* much was clear by his demeanour.

Sure enough, another sergeant then asked to swap with me. The DO explained he'd come back as a different person on the fingerprint machine. A prolific offender from London. Not shown wanted but clearly either thought they were or didn't want this crime attributed to them.

I popped upstairs and discussed with the DS. They weren't anywhere near ready to send to CPS on the THT, so came downstairs and basically confronted the guy, who admitted he'd given his cousin's details. I added a warning to PNC. The DS explained to the chap he may end up having an obstruct police or similar tagged on the end whenever a charging decision was made.

I shot off home straight after handover.

After another crap sleep, I watched some tv and had lunch, before leaving for work. As I walked to my car, I heard a voice saying "alright mate". I could hear them but not see them. I walked round to the other side of my neighbour's car and saw them crouched down, working on it. Yep, it was the neighbour I'd had into custody.

It was actually a bit of a relief. A 'clear the air' kind of conversation. He appreciated I was just doing a job. We agreed it had been awkward as hell. I asked if he'd known what I did for a living beforehand. He hadn't. He said they'd had suspicions my wife was job. Goes to show her gob is louder than mine. She's clearly more likely to get beheaded on route to work than I am.

He told me he'd gone 'not guilty' at court and was there until three that afternoon. Apparently one magistrate in particular had already decided he was guilty and treated him as such. He'd argued the police had sent the summons to his DVLA address and not his home address. I wanted to suggest perhaps he should change this and that he was probably lucky not to have received a hefty fine from them, but decided against it. He said even the court officer had warned him during his rant to shut up, as the magistrate was renowned for holding people in contempt.

I wanted to say, "You're clearly guilty. Neck tatt = twat. Plus you're always smoking cannabis in your garden, which is obviously why you've been *drug driving*". However, in an effort to maintain good neighbour relations, I opted for something similar to "I just wanted to make it clear there is no ill-feeling".

I went to work, more hopeful things won't be as bad as first feared.

There were four skippers on duty and six DOs (one restricted). I took over eight DPs, though two of them disappeared on recall to prison before I even had chance to pop logs on saying I'd taken them over.

Only two were live prisoners. One a breach of non-mol and the other being the Polish lady from the evening before! The earliest they could secure a Polish interpreter for interview was four that afternoon! Her clock was fast disappearing. The rest were warrants.

I had a quick look at the MG3 from CPS for the racial public order job I'd sent to them the day before. Whilst word had reached me they'd authorised a charge, I was curious to check exactly *what* charge had been. They agreed with my decision to NFA the public order on the friend. The offence simply wasn't made out. They'd authorised charges of racially aggravated S4A POA and a further S4A POA on the same victim. Whilst they were not prepared to accept a plea for just the latter, I reckon they wanted him charged with both, so they had one to fall back on should the racial not succeed. However, I then saw the charge wording completed by the OIC. The plain, non racial S4A offence stated it was against the friend. The OIC had clearly not read the MG3 in full and had skipped to the very end where listed charges are shown. They'd therefore clearly assumed the non racial one was for the friend. That was now their mess, I decided.

Once again, there'd be four prisoners to book in.

First was a breach of court order warrant. He was no issue at all. Straight forward. No risks. Boom.

My DO then disappeared for a meeting with the boss.

Second was an extremely emotional woman for D&D. I'd chosen poorly there. I asked the spare DO to search her and booking in property.

She claimed her father had died recently and that was why she was upset. If I left it at that, you'd probably get all sympathetic and wonder why we kept her in custody. Because she was vile, that's why.

Her behaviour was all over the place. One minute, she'd be calm and respond to questions, the next she'd be screaming abuse.

During her risk assessment, she disclosed cancer and Hep C, among other illnesses. During a previous risk assessment, she'd stated she suffers seizures and that failure to take her medication can result in comas. She was telling me she couldn't recall when she'd last taken her meds. Brilliant. I arranged for our HCP to see her and placed her on fifteen minute rousals until seen.

She was soon strip searched, as by the time they'd got her a hot chocolate and taken it to her cell, she was sat on the loo, smoking a cigarette! They confiscated the pack and lighter from her. The pack had blood on it and she'd told them she was on her period. It doesn't take a genius to work out where they'd been hidden.

Word then reached me that she was pressing the buzzer, claiming she had a knife in her pussy and would kill herself. I spoke to the sergeant and DO who had done the strip search. They explained the rather unusual method of strip, as chosen by the DP. Apparently, the DP opted against the dignity-preserving top half first, bottom half second approach and took all her clothes off at once. It didn't stop there. I was told how she then decided to squat (we don't use that word any more or make them do this – she chose to do so of her own accord) and did so a bit too far, losing her balance and performing a roly-poly, ending up with her arse in the air and feet pointing towards the ceiling, resting against the wall. Whilst maintaining this position, she'd reached her hands between her legs and spread her labia wide open, affording the officers an unexpectedly graphic view into her vagina. I was therefore confident she didn't have a knife lodged there as claimed, or that she'd have been able to perform such acrobatics comfortably had one been tucked up there.

I decided against constant supervision at that point, as she was in a CCTV cell and requested I be alerted to any further concerning behaviour so I could review that decision as the shift progressed.

Next in was a guy for concerned in the supply of class A. Officers had completed a routine check of an address suspected of being cuckooed. The co-accused had run off and so was strip searched in custody. Mine had been strip searched at the address. A quantity of cash had been recovered, along with drug paraphernalia. It was the usual sketchy circumstances for a concerned in the supply job, not that I minded authorising detention. They were blatantly bang at it but as always, proving it is another matter.

I was updated that Mrs Vile had covered the camera with a dirty sanitary towel and was threatening to kill herself. I went down to the cell and a DO was there, who showed me she'd also placed food and a further sanitary towel over the glass perspex of the hatch. We could not therefore get a view into the cell. The time had come for constant supervision to be necessary.

We entered the cell and removed items as best we could. There's always a balancing act in these situations. She was clearly on her period and required sanitary wear. To deny someone this would no doubt be interfering with their human rights. But clearly when they stopped using them for that purpose we needed to take them from her. When she calmed, further hygiene kits were provided. And so on.

I used the spare DO to cover close proximity constants.

Last in for me that night was an Iranian chap, who'd pretended to be Bulgarian to the officers on the street. He'd been arrested on suspicion of TWOC, obstruct police and traffic offences, the clear necessity being to ascertain who he was.

He required a Farsi interpreter and, once again, would answer some questions before they'd even been translated. The earliest they could arrange a Farsi interpreter was for ten the following morning. As usual, the interpreting took some time, so we missed the six or so lockouts that arrived around that time, requiring a bed for the night.

I read the arresting officer statement for Mrs Vile. I was satisfied the drunk and disorderly offence was made out and added a review authorising a charge. The HCP had written her up as likely to be fit to charge shortly after ten that evening. It was around half eight by this point and she was still causing problems and stating she wanted to kill herself. It had become necessary to have an officer on constants, due to the threat she posed. The custody sergeant who'd been on disposals covered this, assisted by the DO.

Our mental health liaison had already screened her on their system and confirmed the various mental health issues she'd disclosed. She would require an AA for any interview. They were concerned about the threats she'd been making to kill herself and agreed with my suggestion they needed to at the very least offer her some form of signposting towards bereavement services, if what she was saying about her father was true.

They would not see her whilst she was drunk and abusive, explaining they would be unable to conduct any meaningful assessment of her. They were happy to see her in the morning, should she still be in then and that if due to be released overnight and we had concerns she may harm herself on release, to contact the out of hours crisis team and request they attend.

I researched Mrs Vile on the system and saw an assault she was outstanding for from a few months prior. It was an assault on a paramedic and for some reason, the OIC had simply filed it having been unable to locate her current whereabouts. Since when do we do this?! Surely in such circumstances, we step up our efforts? The filing had not yet been approved by a supervisor and I'd like to think it would never have been anyway.

I liaised with the ERO and explained my plan was to have her further arrested for that assault. By the time she was deemed sober, the duty AA would have left and there would not be one available again till the morning. We would therefore have to bed her down for interview in the morning, by which time the relevant in-custody support she required would be available to see her in person. The plan may be scuppered overnight if she provides details of an alternative AA, although I noted there were a couple of statements outstanding on that job, so we could always use that reason to keep her until the morning, for those to be progressed. As well as having concerns about the risk she posed to herself, she was also under a suspended sentence.

I wrote up my rationale on the custody record, believing this to be in her best interests and also in the interests of that assault investigation. It was a cheeky work around to avoid her being released so soon after making threats to kill herself, as D&D is a non imprisonable offence, so remand was not really an option. Remanding for her own safety would only result in her attending court and being released, as they'd have no other option.

Someone from investigations popped down shortly before handover and made the arrest.

I handed over to nights, only to learn afterwards that whilst I was doing so, Mrs Vile had assaulted a DO in the vilest of circumstances.

The Inspector had entered the cell to complete their review of her detention. He left the cell. The door was closed. All good so far. But then, true to form, she placed a dirty sanitary towel over the perspex again.

They'd therefore re-entered the cell, by which point it'd magically disappeared. She was adamant she'd flushed it. On being told another strip search may be required, she whipped off all her clothes again. This was in front of the female sergeant, female DO, a male DO and male Inspector. The male DO had grabbed a blanket and held it in an attempt to cover her and afford her some dignity.
However, Mrs Vile then lunged forward and pushed the female DO backwards, causing them to hit their back on the corner of the wall behind them. Worse was still to come. Mrs Vile then reached between her legs, removed the bloodied sanitary towel and flicked it upwards, slapping the DO's bare arm. This is extremely unpleasant at the best of times; knowing she disclosed Hep C on booking in makes it even more so. She then threw the sanitary towel at both DOs, which fortunately missed them, landing on the floor outside. They all shot out the cell and closed the door.
I stayed on and took a statement from the DO who'd been assaulted. This was the first victim statement I'd taken since promotion. Had to be a good one!
They explained they'd been doing the job for nearly twenty years and in all that time, this was the most disgusting assault they'd ever been subjected to. Period...
I stayed up that night finishing the latest season of Homeland, trying to secure a late morning lie-in before my first night shift. Another crappy sleep sadly.
The next afternoon I'd intended on writing this book. But the bloody house alarm kept beeping loudly, indicating some form of fault in the system. It was a loud piercing sound, audible from anywhere in the house. Typing the code in would only give a minute's silence before it was required again. Nothing drowned out the sound. Not the tv, not music, not even heavy metal on full volume with earphones in. I was quite literally going insane.

Fortunately, the wife managed to get hold of someone who agreed to come out that afternoon and put an end to the madness. I dread to think what we'll get billed but it'll be worth every penny.
I worked elsewhere that night; somewhere I'd only worked once before.
I knew a couple of DOs but everyone else was new to me. The DOs did most of the booking in – I just had to be on hand to authorise detention and sign off the care plan.
I took over four DPs. Couldn't complain!
One was a career burglar, who'd been produced from prison to join officers on a TIC drive round. TIC stands for 'taken into consideration'…it's basically an opportunity for a crim to cough other offences and get naff all for them - otherwise they risk being linked to the crime later and having yet another court date, where yet another sentence could be imposed. He was basically out on a jolly, the idea being he'd point out houses he'd burgled.
One was a DV assault, who, on my initial check, was asking me how much longer it'd take, as he desperately needed to get home to feed his iguana and had work early in the morning, only to five minutes later break his wrist by punching his mattress repeatedly. Fortunately, the CPS advice came back soon after, so I was able to release him, advising him to take himself straight up the hospital.
The other two were assaults and needed AAs, so would be bedded down for the morning.
I went on to book in a further four that shift.
The first was a seventeen year old, who'd been wanted a few months for aggravated TWOC, but had also been arrested on a stolen bicycle. Officers had received intel he was going to screw over a shop that evening and upon checking that premises found it insecure, so further nicked him sus that, oddly enough finding a bunch of tools in his backpack too. The fail to appear warrant would be a nice little card up the sleeve for the next day.

A sixty-three year old man for DV assault followed. He had various medical issues, carrying with him a hospital grade cushion to sit on in his cell. His wife had disclosed a year's worth of abuse.

A Polish gent for assault was next. He was pissed – declaring ten pints but spoke English better than most locals. He'd have been a handful if he'd kicked off. He made me laugh…everytime the DO asked a question, he answered with the world's most sinister laugh, followed by (Polish accented) "Fuck, man. You are wasting my time" or "Why you ask question?".

In an effort to tick off as many European countries as possible that night, a Hungarian female decided to stab her boyfriend when he admitted cheating on her. Officers were called and he remained tight-lipped, however, she quite happily explained what she'd done, showing officers the knife.

He had a fairly respectable stab wound to one upper arm. She was calm and compliant, again spoke great English. No issues there. I stuck her on supervise all, dry cell conditions until the DS reviewed and decided forensics weren't required.

And that was my night. Relatively calm. A relaxing shift. Nice break away from the usual chaos.

I got a sub-standard sleep between nights.

The last night, I booked on in straight away. BTP officers had nicked one for D&D on a train. The guy had refused to leave, dropped his trousers, shouted and swore. And was an alcoholic, complete with catheter and bag attached to upper right leg. He sadly felt the need to drop his trousers again in the charge room, for my 'benefit'.

I'd spotted a criminal behaviour order (CBO) on his PNC record and directed the BTP chaps to further nick him for breaching it, having been found drunk on public transport – the second of many conditions on the order.

Then a DP whose name I knew very well came in. She was banging away in the holding cell for ages. When I was ready to accept her, I sent the DO to get her and moments later the affray alarm sounded. She'd placed a cord from her jumper round her neck and pretended to be unconscious on the holding cell floor. The nurse was already in there when I arrived, declaring it BS.

She was well known for mental health issues, having historically wasted an awful lot of police time by phoning in threats to take her own life. She had a CBO granted prohibiting her from making BS calls to emergency services – they had reduced but still happened. I thought she was probably in for such a breach but it turned out she'd instead racially abused a PCSO.

I'd have stuck her on constants regardless, as she *always* plays up in custody, placing anything and everything round her neck. She's just one of those you don't take a chance with. You *know* she'll do something. With no CCTV cells free, it was an easy sell to the officers. Constants it was.

She wouldn't comply with the risk assessment or any of the procedure, so was Route One'd down to cell.

And she gave me the biggest headache of that night. Shouting away down the corridor, urinating in the corner of her cell...horrid person.

I became aware of a drink driver kicking off in the holding cell. He appeared to have super strength and was being placed in limb restraints by officers. He was taken straight to cell – not ideal for a drink driver with whom you still have to go through the procedure with, or else risk losing the job, however, a necessity for officer safety. He was ridiculously strong and would not stop screaming his head off. I was concerned it may be excited delirium. None of us are medical experts, but this is often brought up in frontline training and first aid as a big no-no in custody.

Excited delirium is a medical emergency – without intervention, people may die of respiratory or cardiac arrest. Key signs include extreme agitation (yes), delirium (hallucinations, disorientation, confusion – he was certainly the latter), hyperthermia (stripping off to cool down – he hadn't stripped but appeared hot through his fighting – I didn't have a thermometer to hand mid struggle sadly), and superhuman strength (he was certainly difficult to restrain). This wasn't my DP and I wasn't booking him in, but I made the call he should be treated a medical emergency and instructed a DO to call 999 and get a crew there asap.
And to their credit, they arrived fucking fast.
In the couple of minutes it took them to get there, the skipper overseeing them requested we halt phoning it through, believing things to have calmed slightly. I said it'd already been made and we should keep them towards so the medical experts could make that call. I think I pissed them off. I may have stepped on their toes but I'd rather that than nobody make the call and the bloke dies.
As it turned out, paramedics didn't believe there was anything wrong. But I get to keep my pension. So it's all good as far as I'm concerned.
My colleagues were concerned the third person I booked in that night desperately needed help. She actually *did*, suffering PTSD from having been sexually abused by her father. However, what colleagues meant was because she found me attractive! There's nothing more gratifying that an attractive woman saying this to you. When you're booking in an absolute munter on the other hand…
Rest days flew by once again. I went out with colleagues one night. They all stopped drinking soon after the curry. I carried on, thinking they were all pussies. I questioned my decision making later that night when I woke up retching, making it to the toilet just in time. Most upsetting of all was the pukey splash-back I managed to get on my new Hot Fuzz tee.

Chapter Thirteen – Bang

New set, same old shit.
Took over five prisoners the first day back. Two went to court early on. I booked in a further two that shift.
The first was a chap I knew from my time on response. He was a local drunk, who would gob off in the street, recognised me on arrival, was always polite enough and fucked off on request.
It's not until you work custody you realise quite how bad these people's problems are. Type 2 diabetes, stomach ulcers, depression, alcohol dependant, can fit on withdrawal...
He was just a happy drunk to me before. But there's a lot more than that going on. You see a completely different side to people in custody. Don't get me wrong, he was still perfectly polite, but you view them differently when you know all their health stuff. It's more *real*. It all suddenly makes sense. You see what affect the long term drinking has had on them. I could smell the booze coming out his pores. He claimed not to have drunk alcohol that morning. It was possible. Perhaps he just sweats the stuff now.
No doubt the ulcers and depression was linked to his drinking. Google tells me heavy drinking may reduce your body's sensitivity to insulin, causing Type 2 diabetes. Funny, that.
He told me he had a hospital appointment that afternoon, having suffered hypo attacks recently, resulting in sudden collapses. I got him seen by the nurse.
I'm glad I did.
His blood sugar levels were in the thirties – I'm led to believe this is ridiculously high. Google would have be believe that he therefore meant 'hyper', not 'hypo', which is apparently when they're too low.
Nurse's orders were to give him food and drink. A few hours later, he'd come down to twelve, which I was told, was far more acceptable.

I'm responsible for these people's health and welfare whilst they're with us. But I'm no scientist or medical expert. Far from it. I'm a policeman. Never went to uni. Didn't finish my A-levels. I don't know the slightest thing about all these medical conditions people arrive with. I'm totally reliant on the HCPs that work in custody. This was another classic reminder that if in doubt, refer the DP. Better safe than sorry. I'd received a phone call that morning from a DC, who wanted to bring someone in for breaching court bail conditions. I hadn't read the statement, but was informed they'd contacted their ex partner since the conditions were imposed and a statement had been provided. The main reason for their call was that historic assaults and damage had also been disclosed in the statement, previously unreported. I was told the assaults were over six months old and were battery level, meaning the statute of limitations meant they could not be prosecuted.

There was a historic criminal damage that was minor in nature.

From the brief conversation we had, I considered the damage would unlikely meet the FCT and agreed the assaults were out of time, so suggested they arrest on the breach only. This meant no need for interview and a straight up remand to next available court.

They turned up shortly after midday. They'd already prepared their own booking in sheet, complete with screenshot of the bail conditions, prisoner details and so on. Rather useful really.

I had to keep them in the holding cell long enough for me to be sure the evidence was there, so I could lay the information on the DP as they were booked in.

I read the statement and the contact was bordering on witness intimidation. Though it was weak. I considered whether they should deal with that substantive offence but decided it unlikely it would go anywhere and stuck with the breach. I then noticed the vast majority of the contact occurred *before* the latest bail conditions were imposed by the court.
Anything prior to that would be null and void. Fortunately, there was one occasion on which the DP had contacted his ex since that date and so we were good to go.
I booked them in, laid the information and told them they'd either be in court that afternoon, or, more likely, the following morning. They seemed fine with this. I enquired as to their current state of mind, noting they'd wrapped clothing round their neck on the last visit to custody and they assured me they were in a better place, even apologising for previous behaviour.
The bail conditions were by the local Crown court. I was told to send DP to Crown court when setting the disposal. This was a new one on me, so I was grateful for the help.
One of my first jobs the next day was amending this. I was a bit annoyed, having specifically checked with colleagues, being unsure. I now understand breaches of Crown court bail get heard in the Magistrates court first. We live and learn.
The incorrect court on the charge sheet had caused all sorts of processing problems when the DP arrived at court. I was asked to produce a new charge sheet, specifying the Magistrates court.
I was half-minded to simply retype the text on the existing sheet. I decided this would likely cause problems internally with the criminal justice unit (CJU). I popped upstairs and asked them how best to proceed. Their go-to expert told me to create a duplicate charge, to enable me to create an additional disposal, on which I could specify the correct court. I'd done something similar before, so knew how to do this. Sorted.

I spent the morning reading up jobs. No interviews occurred before midday *at all*. This was completely ridiculous and meant we'd have the usual scrum situation early afternoon. The first update I took was a domestic assault, whereby the couple in question had been sat on a bench by a train station. A commuter witnessed the male hit the female in the face. They then walked off and he phoned police, providing descriptions and direction of travel. The couple were located a short distance away and the male was arrested.

The female had refused any statement, even saying it had been playful only and no assault had occurred. The independent witness was working out of area and would not be available for statement until eight that evening. I directed the OIC to contact them and see if there was any way a local unit could obtain this earlier, and to clarify exactly what was seen and whether it could have been playful. No, they couldn't provide it any earlier and it was a definite lunge and swing for her.

The DV appeared to be escalating between these two, with another recent assault awaiting CPS advice slow time. I decided to use the PACE clock and keep the DP in for the statement, believing we'd likely then be at the FCT to take to CPS, hopefully with the other matter too.

The solicitor made representations about this, expressing concerns we were keeping her client in for so long when we could bail. She claimed keeping them in was not necessary. I firstly reminded her of the change in bail legislation and that I did not believe it necessary or proportionate to bail when we could simply keep DP in for a few more hours and have the matter sorted that same day. I further explained that ultimately, we were trying to safeguard the victim and I believed this was the best way of achieving that. I assured her I would note her reps on the custody record and facilitated her seeing her client before she shot off.

The following update was a prolific burglar I'd had previous dealings with on response. He's provided a no comment interview to a pub burglary, whereby an officer had ID'd him from CCTV. All enquiries were complete. CCTV was very clear. I sent it to CPS on the FCT, advising of my intentions to remand.

The final update I took was a domestic assault, where the suspect had pinned down his partner and damaged items. On police arrival, he'd run upstairs and latched on to his partner in a kind of bear hug, interlocking his fingers and officers had to forcibly remove him from her. The victim provided a statement, in which she noted his increasingly bizarre behaviour of late. There were photographs of the damage. Officer statements covered the bizarre removal of the suspect from the address.

No risks had been identified on his arrival at custody the night before.

The PSI (police staff investigator) who interviewed him explained how his behaviour in interview had been erratic and she'd almost pushed the emergency button. She said on several occasions he'd called her by his partner's name, as if she was sat in the room with him accusing him of those things live time. He then got up towards the end of the interview, stormed round to her side of the table and then faced the wall for three minutes, crying. Not your usual interview.

I arranged for the in-house mental health worker to see him. They were satisfied there were no mental health concerns and the guy was just experiencing relationship problems. As such, I sent the job to CPS recommending a charge of assault and criminal damage.

I then assisted by releasing three people for jobs already reviewed by a DS and charged and remanded the burglar when the advice came through.

CPS did run the job but did so on the THT. I was initially confused by this, wondering whether I had completely misunderstood everything about the THT/FCT. From reading their comments, I gather this was because they wanted to view CCTV themselves before making a charging decision, however, acknowledging this guy needed remanding, agreed to charge there and then, knowing they'd view CCTV by an agreed date.

I often read other sergeant's reviews, some of which refer to a job meeting the THT but when all lines of enquiry are complete. I can't help but think they mean FCT. THT would be when there is other key evidence outstanding you believe can be obtained within a reasonable timescale to bring to the FCT. That is certainly my understanding but you doubt yourself and your understanding when you read other people's reviews.

It prompted me to research the THT/FCT on Google that evening and I'm certain I have it right based on what I've read. I bloody well hope so anyway.

The following shift was my first late. It also happened to be my worst experience of custody so far.

It was relentless. Non-stop. My stress levels were through the roof. My anxiety was at its worst – more on that later.

I took over eleven prisoners. My colleague took seven. There were already DPs queuing to be booked in once handover finished. I didn't book any of them in. In fact, of all the DPs that arrived that shift, I booked one in - just before handover to nights. Simply didn't get a chance, due to the demands of what I already had.

We were bang on MSL. Three sergeants but one was DO-ing. No-one doing solely disposals. This caused a headache for investigators. They weren't getting help from their own supervisors. Now, in fairness to them, I expect they were rammed too. But it meant they had nowhere else to go and loitered until I became free. That took well over an hour in some cases and I could feel their staring eyes burning into my back.

Three of my DPs were warrants the courts refused that afternoon. They all took this remarkably well. One was outstanding for a shoplifting and assault, which they should've really been nicked on instead of the warrant. Because the court refused them, it provided an opportunity to clear up that job. I was told on handover someone would be assigned and would crack straight on.

Two of my DPs and one of my colleague's were all linked to a theft of motor vehicle (TOMV) job. One of the outgoing days skippers had reviewed it but something I said made them doubt their decision. They mentioned they'd been seen only to push it along and one of them had been seen to tamper with the ignition.

I had no knowledge of the job, but from memory believed you needed to be sat astride the moped in order to be considered carried on it. I would have had to check legislation myself to be sure, but saying this caused them enough doubt to be concerned about their decision. They'd clearly had a horrific shift too, and were already late off and desperate to get home. I said to leave it with me, although I never got an opportunity to review the job myself. There was always something more important that cropped up that needed my immediate attention. People's safety has to come first in custody and the issues that arose were those types of considerations. The OIC's DS had knowledge, so I left it with them.

A DO appeared and informed me one of the TOMV DPs had threatened to punch the next person to enter his cell but was now requesting the toilet. None of the DOs wished to get hands-on, not having the same PPE (personal protection equipment) as officers. I got one of the other sergeants to join me. He wasn't happy but did his business without issue.

I took an update for a female in for administering a poison. What she'd actually done was disclose to her son's school teacher she'd been crushing up his medication and hiding it in his meals to help him sleep, due to having a sleep condition. For some reason, that prescription stopped and she was at the end of her tether. She had exactly the same medication prescribed to *her*, albeit a stronger dose. She'd therefore cut hers to match what dose *he'd* previously had and only gave him that amount.

It appeared she'd been doing what she believed best for her son, albeit, naively.

They'd sorted safeguarding with social services and arranged for the son's father (who claimed to have no knowledge of this) to supervise all contact with the children. He was her estranged husband, living under the same roof. A urine sample had been taken from the kid and they needed the results to determine what was in his system. If it was as she said, they intended on taking no further action. I released her under investigation.

The same DO then appeared and informed me the same TOMV punk had broken his zip and was trying to break the cell intercom from the wall. This same DP had successfully done exactly this a couple of weeks ago, so was certainly capable. By the time I got to the cell, he'd stopped but was sat on the bench self harming with the zip, cutting his arm.

I entered with the same sergeant and we took an arm each. No sign of the zip. He had superficial marks to his arm. No bleeding. I searched his pockets. No sign. A DO checked the cell. Nothing. We remained stood there holding an arm each. We requested a DO call up on the radio and request two officers for constants, otherwise two sergeants would have to cover it and custody would be at a complete standstill. The DP eventually spat out what remained of the zip, claiming to have swallowed the other half. We retreated out the cell and consulted the nurse, who had no concerns.

The PACE Inspector came and saw me, asking what my intentions were. Response had either argued they had nobody or it wasn't their place to provide resources to custody. As such, the PACE Inspector would have to escalate things to 'Force silver' - a Superintendent. He therefore needed to know the situation and why it required response to provide this cover. This is where the system falls down. We all need to help each other out. There was no way custody could cover this. We needed the help now, not later.

I had no idea whether I was remanding this guy or not. My colleagues views were if we don't want him there, get rid. However, I'd been told this guy had just come out of prison. I needed to research him, his previous convictions and have knowledge of the job before I could make any decision. I also needed the DS to make a charging decision on my behalf. I chased them and they agreed to stick a decision on the custody record 'shortly'.

Every time I opened up his previous convictions to research them, a DO would appear, alerting me to another ongoing situation requiring my immediate attention, quite often with the same moron.

He was seen trying to remove the intercom again. There was no point moving him cells. Every cell had one. We still didn't have officers available to sit watching him. I said we'd have to leave him to it and keep monitoring the CCTV and to update me if he managed to remove it.

I received an update that a domestic assault guy was to be charged, following CPS advice. He hadn't been processed, so I got a DO to take his prints and DNA.

I saw the DS update recommending the TOMV moron be charged with vehicle interference. I'd realise one of the others had already been released and had no idea why or what for. Things were a cluster fuck. There was too much going on for me to keep track of. This is where things turn serious quick. This was becoming *dangerous*.

I therefore returned to the previous convictions, however, the DO returned with the domestic prisoner and so I thought I'd get them charged and released quickly, so at least I had one less thing to worry about.

But sometimes in life, certainly in custody, things aren't quite that simple.

He had an AA present for charge. I read the wording out and started to explain the bail conditions. He wasn't to contact his partner (well, now 'ex') directly or indirectly. Ok, no problem he thought. The second would be the deal breaker. He was not to attend her address.

"That's my address", he said. He went on to explain he was agoraphobic and rarely left his address. As such, he hadn't seen friends or family in years and had nowhere else he could stay. He was adamant it was his name on the tenancy and that in interview, he'd learnt she was intending to move out and stay elsewhere.

I phoned the OIC. No answer. I looked at the time on their email, which was how they'd alerted me to the CPS result. A good couple hours had passed. I'd been so busy I hadn't noticed their email earlier. They'd quite clearly gone home. I phoned Investigations' main office and got someone to phone the victim. They phoned me back remarkably quick confirming the victim was adamant she was on the tenancy and was trying to get DP removed. She had no intentions of leaving and the DP had elsewhere to go.

I told the DP this. He remained adamant he had nowhere else. I got the AA to sit with them in an interview room whilst I flapped around.

I spoke with my colleague, who said I really only had one option – remand. I knew this, but this was such a ridiculous situation. I was *so* annoyed the OIC hadn't catered for this eventuality. I popped upstairs and updated the DS, who had to assign someone to complete a remand file in the OIC's absence.

I got the DP and AA back to the charge room and explained my decision. He suggested a friend who lived some distance away *may* be able to put him up. Apparently he'd babysat for her recently. Yes, I know what you're thinking – I thought it too. How would an agoraphobic manage that? I didn't even go there. I went to all the trouble of ripping open the evidence bag holding his property, so he could retrieve a number from his phone, only to be told she'd only be able to have him a couple nights. Court was in a month! I remanded him and he requested his solicitor.

Whilst I'd been sorting this, officers from response finally arrived to take on constants. Having remanded the domestic guy, a DO then appeared, informing me the cell intercom had now been ripped out and he was waving it about threatening to assault officers. I was told they had riot shields and were about to enter the cell.

My stress levels by this point were through the roof. I was aware of my anxiety but had kept it at the back of my mind, being too busy to deal with it. I found myself marching towards the cell but on route, realised my fist was clenched and I suddenly sensed how angered I was. Proceeding would be a bad career choice. There was no way I could go down there. For the first time in eleven years of policing, I was genuinely concerned I was about to beat the shit out of someone. I had lost control of my temper, fortunately only for a moment, and was able to turn around and focus. I'm just grateful I had that opportunity to realise the potential consequences of my actions. If I'd have already been down there, it may have been too late. The fact we were vastly overworked and put under considerable stress, would not have made any difference once the public were shown CCTV footage of the custody sergeant pummelling a prisoner.

In a perverse way, I was glad he'd destroyed that cell. It was one less we had available. In fact, it would probably remain that way for days to come, as repair jobs don't happen overnight.

He was moved elsewhere and kept on constant supervision. I took reps from the solicitor for the DV guy a while later. She was surprised he'd been charged at all, let alone remanded. I explained my predicament and that I was open to reversing my decision if he came up with someone who'd have him, provided I could verify it with that person.

She spoke with him and provided details of the friend he'd already spoken of, suggesting she could have him for a few days before he'd need to travel the length of the country and stay the remainder of the time with his nan. The catch being, he'd not spoken to his nan in years and only his mother would be able to contact her to okay this. This was a long shot but given the circs I wanted to be as reasonable as possible. The friend confirmed she could have him for a couple nights only but I couldn't get hold of his mother, despite trying several times.

Once I'd *finally* sorted that, I remanded the moron, adding an additional charge of criminal damage. He explained he'd only done it as he was fed up waiting to be charged. Twat.

CPS advice came back for another prisoner I'd missed the review for. He'd been in the day before – the guy behaving erratically in interview.

Having been charged and released the day before, with conditions not to enter the county or the victim's address, he went straight back to her house and kicked the door in.

He'd behaved in a similar fashion in interview again. The first solicitor was female and he started talking to her aggressively, believing she was his ex partner. It was too much for the solicitor to handle and she left. The firm had sent a replacement, only for them to be concerned about his state of mind too. Our mental health liaison had agreed he required an AA this time, but still didn't believe he was experiencing anything more than relationship problems.

I took the AA down to his cell to charge him. Clearly, I would be refusing bail. He'd breached bail conditions in any case and needed to be put before the next available court. Even the solicitor (who, amusingly, was the one I'd previously had a to-do with) had said as much, saying "New offences. Breach of bail...I'll see him in court tomorrow morning". Clearly no reps today then!

We arrived at the cell door and I could hear him having an animated conversation with himself. This guy was a fruitcake! How our mental health liaison considered him of sound mind, I don't know.

I charged him and halfway through reading the wording, he faced the wall and started crying loudly. He then walked over to the in-cell toilet and started urinating. I said I'd close the cell door to and give him some privacy until he'd finished. I said to the AA, "Well, he clearly doesn't experience stage fright!" – the AA, someone usually so professional and mindful of their clients sensibilities, lost control and started laughing. Things were far from normal that day and even he knew it.

I finished the charge and cautioned him. I asked if he wished to make any reply. He burst into a tirade of nonsense. He became aggressive and went to leave the cell. I went to close the door but he put his foot in the way. He kept it there, despite my demands for him to remove it. I ended up forcing the cell door shut, giving him no choice but to move his foot back. I was grateful to see that no toes had appeared, as the way my day was going, a toe amputation would've been just about right.

I'd remanded three. I'd dealt with god knows how much bullshit. Along the way, we'd been open, closed, open, closed. Not that I knew it – I'd still not taken in any prisoners. They'd all been diverted elsewhere.

Things were starting to settle. Of course, it would be then that the Superintendent arrives. I greeted him in the only fashion that fit the day I was having. I walked straight into him.

A prisoner arrived at the back door. We were clearly open again. I popped next door and told the others I'd take this one. With about an hour until handover to nights, I was *finally* in a position to accept a prisoner.

I started loading the custody record. As things had settled a bit, I became more aware of my anxiety. I started struggling to breathe. I took long, slow breaths in through my nose, held them for a few seconds, and then out through my mouth slowly.

It was a GBH with intent. She'd stabbed her partner in the face with a knife.

We had no dry cells available. I tasked a DO with swapping people round to free one up, otherwise she'd no doubt be on constants.

She was an alcoholic, last fitted that morning on withdrawal. Her solution had been to buy more alcohol. She slept rough in a tent with her partner.

She had various health issues and was a regular self harmer, having cut her wrist two days before. She explained it was a suicide attempt but the mark she showed me was superficial. She was compliant and I got through the process easily enough. I'd fobbed off an OIC before booking her in, asking them to return in a bit. Someone else appeared, wanting to give me an update. I said in all fairness to their colleague, it was only right I took theirs first and asked them to find them, which they did. The update was for the guy on warrant, also wanted for shoplifting and assault. I could not believe I was only just taking this update. Not that it mattered that much, as the guy wasn't going anywhere.

The job involved a prolific shoplifter stealing items from Debenhams. A security guard had watched on CCTV. An elderly lady saw him concealing items in his jacket and confronted him, saying (in old person croaky voice) "I don't think so" (with probably the stereotypical old person favourite "young man" tagged on), only to then be punched in the arm.

We had statements from the security guard, old lady and CCTV showing the incident. The DP had provided a 'no comment' interview. I authorised a charge of shoplifting and assault. I added my shortest ever remand rationale - he was in on a fail to appear warrant, so without even checking his previous, it made sense for these jobs to be heard in the morning, believing he'd likely fail to appear for them too.

I made a final attempt to contact the mother of the domestic guy I'd remanded. No answer.

The other OIC then appeared and I realised I was already late for handover and much to their annoyance, I said nights would have to deal. As it was, I also palmed off the actual charging and remanding of the warrant guy to nights too. Quite frankly, I'd had enough.

I left straight after handover. I was exhausted. Thoroughly fucked off, too. My chest was left feeling bruised. That was the anxiety. Custody is pretty stressful and relentless most of the time but we get by. This one was a killer. I'm becoming genuinely more and more concerned about the long term health effects of doing this role for a couple of years. Even experienced custody sergeants, with years under their belt, are saying things have become ridiculous and unmanageable. So many people are off sick with stress at the moment. Things *have* to improve.

I was extremely anxious the following morning. Couldn't stop thinking about the horrific shift. I could feel a full-blown panic attack coming on. I'd not experienced one properly in years. I couldn't believe how much I'd been affected. I was actually worried about going to work that afternoon. I was certain anything of the same level and I wouldn't cope.

Well, it was extremely busy but not the same level of intensity, so I got through it. Just.

Face stabber was still in. Her clock ran out at nine that evening.

I took over four others. Couldn't complain at that. I had a domestic violence to secure entry / public order guy in. A Lithuanian on suspicion of assisting the illegal entry of persons into the UK. One of the persons who'd come in on his truck. And a domestic harassment.

I went on to book five others in.

The first arrived soon after handover. It was the same twelve year old boy who I'd booked in before. Always cries. Intel for crack use and dealing. He'd been found in possession of a coat with security tag attached, and a pair of wire clippers.

Then in came a guy for sexual assault of a fourteen year old girl. He was further nicked in the charge room for child abduction and domestic assault. I was DO-less at that time and whilst searching his bag, located a cannabis joint.

At some point I reviewed the stabbing job for CPS. Homeless shelter workers had received a call from the DP during which she admitted the offence. Other homeless people had witnessed them arguing and left them to it as they felt uncomfortable. She'd been seen by a witness with a bag in a carrier bag earlier that day. The carrier bag she came into custody with had blood on it. I knew this as the evening before I saw the officer place it on the charge room desk and I remember thinking to myself how I sometimes place my lunch there. Mental note to self – don't eat your lunch there again. I also had an update from the officer dealing with the human-importer. I told her I was busy and would she kindly get her own supervisor to review for CPS, which they did.

There were enquiries outstanding. Her phones had been seized but awaited examination. There were forensics outstanding. But I was looking to remand her and sent it to CPS on the THT.

I booked in someone for robbery. They recognised me instantly, as I'd nicked them several times on response. He usually always kicked off but was the soberest I'd ever seen him that afternoon and was polite and jovial. He caused me no issues whatsoever and we had a bit of a laugh looking through his previous custody photos, even printing him out one to keep from when he was seventeen and sporting the most god-awful mop haircut.

Fourth in was a dwelling burglar. He lived in the same building as the victim and had simply booted in the other dude's door and taken some toiletries.

I received CPS results through in quick succession for the stabber and Lithuanian chap. Stabber was to be charged GBH with intent. Happy days. I'd been told the solicitor wished to make reps. I phoned him and he asked my grounds for refusing bail. I explained it was due to the seriousness of the offence and my belief that, if bailed, further violent offences would occur and the DP would interfere with witnesses in the case. In respect of the latter, he stated whilst he accepted the victim was a witness in the case, they had not supported the allegation and he doubted the prosecution would compel them to give evidence. His argument was therefore that the prosecution should be able to proceed without and as such, any interference that I was believing would occur would be irrelevant. I said it was still possible he'd be compelled. Simple as that.

In respect of further offences, he said (and this is where I could sense he was trying hard to remain professional and not laugh) that his client had suggested she had alternatives tents elsewhere in the area and could sleep in one of them. I explained it would be court in the morning and wished him well.

I remanded her and also the Lithuanian, although he required a telephone interpreter, which slowed that process somewhat. Throughout the afternoon, I'd been fobbing off investigators to go elsewhere for their reviews. Not because I didn't care but rather I simply had enough to concentrate on already. The system is broken. Management know this but will not provide further staff, as there is simply not the budget to do so.

The other immigration prisoner had an IS91 served, and the domestic DPs were released by a colleague, having been reviewed elsewhere. The twelve year old had also been NFA'd, though I never learnt why.

I popped upstairs with an hour to go to check the state of play with a couple of DPs I'd booked in. I chatted with the DS about how crazy things were getting. It was clear she was under extreme pressure too. She suggested one reason we'd been experiencing such a high footfall of late was a new priority arrest process in place with response. But then I can't blame officers for being proactive and getting out there nicking people. That's their job! The job itself needs to put enough resources in place to deal with those prisoners effectively.

I booked in a warrant when I popped downstairs and then released the robber under investigation for further enquiries. I handed over and shot home, staying up to watch Cujo 2. Well, actually Gerald's Game, but if you've seen it, you'll know where I'm coming from. Great movie.

I woke up late the following morning and decided it was time to go mattress shopping with the wife. I've been suffering some lower back pain and reckon the massive bulge in the mattress probably wasn't helping.

Whilst she got ready, I grabbed some breakfast. I was sat in our first floor living room in my boxers watching Red Dwarf. I suddenly heard someone entering the front door. Did the wife sneak past me without me realising?! I thought she was in the shower...

I started walking downstairs, only for the cleaner to look up in horror at her client in just his underwear. I felt like Harvey Weinstein, only not as fat and old.

We had success at the very first shop we went to. That is my kind of shopping. Done and dusted as quickly as possible. We went out for a mid afternoon lunch, before collecting the kids after school.

I have to say, I was fearing what the Friday night shift may have in store. But it was such a pleasant change of pace.

As soon as I arrived at work, two DOs collared me in the car park, saying how annoyed they've been by being made to feel guilty for taking meal breaks at work. They're not paid for them. They're entitled to them and have to take them. I reassured them I'd discuss with the skippers and get breaks allocated.

I did just that after handover, writing meal times up on the whiteboard.

I was DO-ing for the shift, making up MSL. It was nice not having direct responsibility for any DPs handed over. I did take the pressure off my colleague, by booking in three during the night.

First up straight after handover was a seventy-five year old for D&D. He was last in custody for drink driving eight years ago and had no remorse at all for his actions. He said he may as well go back to drink driving. He didn't give a shit.

I warned the others he had previous for assault police, though this was tongue-firmly-in-cheek, as it was from the 1960s.

I stuck in him a cell much to his disgust, and told him he'd be given a few hours to sober up before being released.

I did a bit of DO-ing in the form of searching people, booking property in, taking people to their cells, offering them food and drink, and so on, before there was another opportunity for me to help by booking someone in myself.

The next was a chap who'd threatened his neighbours with a hammer. He'd been nicked for a public order offence and possessing an offensive weapon.

He refused to sign the consent for photo and prints, stating he wouldn't do anything until he spoke to his solicitor. However he did then answer all my risk assessment questions and happily went through his rights. I asked whether he wanted his solicitor via telephone advice or whether he wanted them to attend the station. He said he may as well take the telephone advice, as there was no way we'd be getting him out his cell for an interview. That would be days' problem.

The last one I sorted was a crazy dude for possession of cannabis, assault police and ABH. However, this order of arrests confused me, given the circumstances were that a male had assaulted a female unknown to him in a completely random unprovoked attack. His description had been passed and he made off from officers. The officer and a special gave chase. The chap stopped running and confronted the officer, taking his top off and squaring up to him. The officer quite rightly gave him a taste of CS spray.
However, this had as much effect on the officer as it did the suspect.
I'm told that by chance, an off duty officer happened to be driving past, saw what was unfolding, mounted the curb damaging his own car and restrained the suspect, whilst the officer themselves was out of action and their special doing nothing more than observing.
The next officers on scene had assumed the chap had already been nicked, so searched him and found cannabis – hence the first arrest for this. They then realised he'd not been nicked for anything else and nicked assault police, due to the squaring up and causing the officer to apprehend immediate violence. He was later arrested in custody for the ABH once the female had been located and her assault confirmed.
The DP was either off his face on drugs, suffering severe mental health issues, or a mixture of both.
He became aggressive, threatening violence in the charge room, so was taken Route One to cell.
He immediately blocked the camera with his mattress and placed clothing round his neck, although removed the mattress and was then seen storming round his cell, using the clothing as a cape.
When he blocked the camera again, we entered and removed the mattress. He said he had pre-existing spinal injuries from a car crash and needed to see a nurse. He also said a whole load of shit that made no sense whatsoever.

I placed him on camera constants, due to his erratic and unpredictable, behaviour, aware he had previously self harmed in custody.

The nurse popped along to see him at one point, and was extremely frightened by him, enough to plead with me to ensure days were given a thorough briefing that should the nurse or mental health liaison see him, it be done in as cautious a way as possible for their safety.

Time came for me to bin the old dude. The evidence for D&D was there and I decided it in the public interest. He'd behaved like this on a bus full of people and had swung at the driver (no complaint made).

I'd written out a fixed penalty notice but he refused this, wanting his day in court! I charged him and officers gave him a lift home.

Then came the prisoner of the night, that my colleague booked in. A sixteen year old nicked sus attempt murder for stabbing someone several times in the back, leg and neck. He was threatening violence to officers and was taken to cell Route One.

I took the opportunity to write reports regarding the chaotic shift two days before. I submitted an injury report through the accident management system, for the injury of 'stress'. I'm sure this will likely raise a few eyebrows but my view is that this is a condition not talked about enough. And yet it seems to be the main reason people go off sick. The bosses needed to know quite how bad it was and how unsafe and dangerous a way of working it was, given the minimum staffing levels that day and the intensity of the work environment.

I had a pretty good sleep between nights. I did hear our new mattress being delivered and dumped in the room next to me but got back to sleep easily enough. When I was up, we swapped these over and my god the new one feels amazing! I look forward to sleeping on that. I'm actually working a third night this set. Hopefully this'll guarantee me plenty of rest and improve my back!

I woke up around three that afternoon to find a text from none other than the Chief Inspector of custody. He'd received my email and requested I call him – nothing to worry about, he said.

I phoned him and he explained he was worried about me and wanted to check in. I ranted, politely of course. It felt great to get it all off my chest. I told him how in eleven years of policing I'd never been concerned what I was about to do to a DP. He was really receptive to me being this honest and grateful for the feedback. I'm under no illusions that it'll get things changed. We still have ever tightening budgets, meaning it unlikely MSL will ever increase. I told him what I felt was causing the issue, particularly on lates and he explained there are plans afoot to get EROs to take on more disposal reviews, to get investigators to conduct interviews earlier and so on. Fingers crossed we see these things happening at our place of work sooner rather than later.

I started my second night slightly early - both sergeants were busy, so I assisted by taking a post interview update for a domestic violence to secure entry DP.

They were alleged to have attended their ex partner's address to retrieve their wallet. The ex had posted it through the letterbox. Not content his credit card was missing, he demanded she hand this over. She checked but couldn't find it. He became threatening and the victim and daughter then noticed he'd somehow jimmied the door and was forcing it open. They remained the other side pushing it shut and won the battle.

The victim had provided a statement. The daughter's was not possible until the morning. The DP denied the offence, stating neighbours could corroborate his account. I bedded him down for days to progress enquiries.

I then further assisted lates by booking in a Polish drink driver. She'd wiped out a set of traffic lights. Paramedics saw her and decided she didn't require hospital treatment.

She was diabetic, and had a heart condition, depression and sleep apnoea. She'd be on constants due to the latter. She'd need a nurse anyway as per policy for post-RTIs in custody. By the time I'd booked her in, it was time for handover. The officer took her to the Intox procedure, with instructions to remain on constants.

I took over an additional five on handover. A warrant, a domestic ABH (really a GBH stabbing), the DP I'd already reviewed, a burglar and a DP who'd been arrested attempt murder, having told the other guy from the night before to do the stabbing. It was once again just me and another sergeant on.

I went to check everyone was alive and well.

I was about to find out quite how unwell the Polish lady was. Tuberculosis.

Bollocks.

I distinctly remember asking her whether there were any other illnesses or injuries. Sod the depression. This is the sort of shit I needed to know about! She was an interpreter, so she blatently understood what I'd asked and it amazed me she'd not thought to tell me this and instead just dropped it into casual conversation with the poor dude on constants.

The nurse had already been made aware. She was on the phone, seeking advice from senior officials presumably at the hospital.

In the meantime, I updated the officers waiting in the holding cell it'd be some time yet and gave the reasons why.

I checked the other DPs and stuck my handover logs on.

"Telephone call for you Sergeant", one of my DOs said.

It was one of the other custody suites needing a DO. We had a spare, but I explained I needed to first ensure all was safe and we weren't simply going to spread infection to yet another custody suite.

We sealed off the charge room where she'd been booked in, the Intox room where she'd had her breath test and marked up her cell for a deep clean once vacated.

I updated the PACE Inspector of our predicament. Naturally, a backlog of prisoners built up. Any drink drivers were diverted elsewhere.

I kept popping back to speak to the nurse but she was usually always on the phone. The armed response officers who'd nicked her were waiting nervously outside her office for updates. A traffic officer told me his DP had used the machine straight after the Pole. Bad day to get nicked for drink driving, if ever there was a good one...

After a couple hours the crisis was over. Advice came through that unless you spend several hours in close confines, you are extremely unlikely to contract TB. She was shipped off to hospital in an ambulance, where she'd spend time on an isolation ward. I'd released her under investigation; to be interviewed at a later date.

The ARV officers wrote their car off for the night. It'd need a deep clean. They took themselves up the hospital for blood tests. The advice provided was only those in close proximity to the DP may wish to consider seeing their GP for a test. One of them was off on holiday the next day, so understandably wanted to set the ball rolling.

The other DP to have used the machine afterwards was informed of his luck and advised to see his GP if he had any concerns. The workings of the Intox machine was fully explained and that as such he should be fine. But then one must cover one's arse.

There was a backlog of around four to five DPs. My colleague was well and truly committed with a couple hours of paperwork, as the double handed attempt murder had resulted in CPS advice to charge both GBH with intent. He'd been asked to remand the stabber but to bail the other. The DS overseeing it had gone off duty and left no rationale for this, suggested conditions, etc. Brilliant.

There were around four investigators loitering in the corridor, wanting to update me. I simply couldn't do so. The backlog needed clearing, or it would only get far worse.

They were close to tears. The situation was ridiculous. It was my first late shift all over again in terms of stress levels through the roof. How I can be reasonably expected to be responsible for the safety of my DPs, along with all the other shit you have to deal with is beyond me. Ultimately, my primary job *has* to be ensuring nobody dies. When I'm unable to do that with confidence, the situation is dangerous.

As such, I contacted the PACE Inspector again. I explained the situation and that we needed an "operational pause". To his credit, he was fantastic. Rather than being cynical and questioning anything I said (as lots would), he instantly came up with an idea. He'd tell a couple response sergeants they'd either need to get down to custody and take those investigator updates, or custody would be "on pause" and prisoners would need to divert elsewhere.

Now, clearly the first option would be better for their officers, so they did just that.

This was brilliant. It enabled me to concentrate solely on booking in, of which there was a lot to do.

First in was an assault police. He'd been nicked to prevent a breach of the peace, following a domestic, and on being escorted out the address to the van, he kicked one of the officers. They took him to the ground and the DP hit his head causing a minor injury. However, given he'd been drinking and now had a head injury, all credit to them for taking him straight up the hospital first. The hospital were satisfied he was okay and they brought him in.

In the time he'd been up there and waiting in the holding cell, he'd calmed right down and was fairly pleasant. I instantly NFA'd the breach of the peace, deciding to proceed only with the assault police.

Next in was a domestic ABH, whereby the DP was alleged to have repeatedly kicked his partner. There was something about him. He stared at me intensely and had a slight grin. I stared back and won the contest – he looked away first. But it seemed an eternity.

I was prepared for him to suddenly flip. But he never did. He'd have been a handful too.

He was fixated on his shoes and the need for us to swab them. I explained my role and that I would not get involved in the investigation; but that I'd pop them in an evidence bag to preserve any evidence and leave them outside his cell should the OIC decide it necessary to seize them. He seemed happy with this. I seriously doubt they'd get seized but appeasing people, even if just a little bit, can make your life so much easier sometimes.

Another domestic ABH followed, though this one had an interesting twist to it.

As the circumstances were given, the officer said he had also received new information for which he needed to further arrest the DP. The ABH related to the fact he'd beat up his wife upon learning of an affair she'd been having. The further arrest was for kidnap – he was alleged to have sought out the man fucking his wife, put him in the boot of his car and dumped him off somewhere! As you do...

He came across as a really nice chap. I fully expect he's done this and may even admit to it. He seemed quite pleased with himself. When asked the self harm question, he said 'no' but he felt like it, but wouldn't as he was a rational man.

However then stated that given the chance, he would, so 'yes'. Given what he'd found out and was now under arrest for, I had serious concerns about what he may do once released and marked him up for a visit from the mental health liaison later that morning and ensured my feelings were passed to days.

The next DP was an eighteen year old who, I can only assume, was going for the 'goth in a wedding dress' look. She was perfectly pleasant, though the wedding dress was spoilt somewhat by vomit.

She was linked to someone still waiting in the holding cell. She'd tried to stop police arresting that person (a mate or boyfriend) by holding on to their arm and refusing to let go. Pressure points had been used on her to relinquish her grip and she'd then lashed out at the officer. She was in for assault and obstruct police.

She disclosed she was pregnant and was due an appointment soon to find out how far along. Bless. Little Jack Skellington Jnr will be so proud.

In came the mate or boyfriend next. Never did work out which. He'd been inside an ambulance and damaged items and thrown a sick bowl full of spit over a paramedic.

The escorting officers had no idea why he was in the ambulance in the first place. Neither did he. He was walking and talking, with no apparent injuries, so I accepted him. Sadly, I couldn't provide the codes of practice he'd requested, as all our copies were locked in the sealed off charge room.

The last prisoner of the night (for me anyway) was a local homeless man for GBH. He'd bottled someone, resulting in a nasty head injury that bled profusely.

He arrived throwing up over the holding cell floor. The strong smell of garlic made my DO retch.

I told the officers we'd take Route One to avoid the charge room being written off with vom. However, as we did, he kicked off and became aggressive. Four of us took him down. There were no camera cells available that were also dry cells and he needed the latter more due to the potential for forensics. We fought him for his clothing and I decided to take everything bar boxers, as the officers told me he'd threatened to place clothing round his neck. As we exited the cell, he threw his boxers at us, leaving himself starkers. I left an officer on constants with him as a means of managing the risk he posed to himself through self harming and also the potential for him to sleep-vom.

I used the remaining time that shift to submit yet another accident management form for stress and another email report to the boss detailing the shift we'd had and how things must change.

I handed over my prisoners to days and went home. I was exhausted, stressed and extremely anxious about having to work yet *another* night. I had this stupid extra night to work and I fretted about being in the same position again with just two sergeants and coming into a whole world of shit.

I barely slept. I simply couldn't switch off from work. I was worried about the TB incident and although I'd been vaccinated aged fourteen, whether there would be any comeback on my kids if I did happen to catch it. I would wake up in sweats thinking about how manic things had been. This wasn't healthy. I needed time to recover before next set.

I phoned in at lunchtime and told them I was going sick that night with stress.

"Will this likely impact on business?" the call taker asked. "I should certainly imagine so" I replied. "You best let the PACE Inspector know".

I received a text from my colleague later that evening. He'd heard I'd gone sick and offered his support, saying I'd well and truly arrived in custody, commenting on the run of challenging incidents for which I'd remained unflappable. He detailed how I'd taken the lead and control of the block that night and ran it like an experienced custody sergeant.

It's amazing the support you get from peers like this, compared to management. I'm not saying I didn't appreciate that phone call the day before from the boss. Of course I did. But they mainly speak management bollocks. It's not their fault. That's the way they have to speak to advance that far. It's become first nature.

But the real support came in carefully chosen words and that meant a lot.

I slept much better that night, making full use of the new mattress by around eight and a half hours. To clarify, I slept for that length of time, so maybe I should say standard use of the mattress. Full use only occurs on birthdays, anniversaries and the odd other day.

I went for a couple walks the following morning, getting my steps and active minutes up on my wrist gadget. I could've easily got in the car, but decided to do my chores on foot, for stress reduction. I received a text from my Inspector, in which he said he'd heard about my sickness and the stressful shift and wondered if I'd be up for a call. I wasn't really up to it at that time, wishing to focus instead on stress *reduction*.

I watched Atomic Blonde, starring the gorgeous Charlize Theron. She sported a sexy posh English accent, so I'm even more a fan now.

Around lunchtime I went to take a shit and decided that would be an ideal time to make the call to the boss. I dropped the kids off a nanosecond before he answered.

I couldn't wipe and chat, needing my right hand for both. He talked for so long I was concerned my ass would go crusty brown.

I kept things relaxed over the next two days and felt suitably recharged for my return to work.

Chapter Fourteen – Shit magnet

To my relief, there were four skippers sat on handover, me included. One looked like he was trying hard not to vom and he disclosed he'd been up all night with sick kids. He lasted another ten minutes before disappearing home. This still left three, meaning one could do disposals.

I took over seven prisoners. Two disappeared to court and my only involvement with the others that day was their welfare. My colleague took the disposals as and when they came.

I booked in four. Following my conversation with the boss, I told my DO I was going to authorise detention and be present as they completed the risk assessment, but would sit elsewhere for the remainder of the process to free me up to concentrate on other matters. I wasn't convinced I'd notice any difference in stress levels with this approach on days, given most disposals don't come until lunchtime, but was willing to start giving it a go.

The first in was a fail to appear warrant. He'd been found concealing drugs only a few days beforehand in custody, so I authorised a strip search, which was negative. The courts accepted him within a couple hours.

In came a domestic ABH. It was a hot handover, the job looked up together. He had those horrid ear lobe hoop things that make me shudder.

Around lunchtime, an ARV officer came and saw me regarding one in the holding cell. They explained the chap had been nicked for harassment, as he'd already been sent away from his ex's address once that morning by police, only to return. It was pretty weak – I gather there had been unwanted messages too, but the guy was outstanding for an ABH and coercive and controlling behaviour against the same female anyway, so I directed him to further nick for those to make things a bit more solid.

The DP was a first timer in custody, but you'd never have guessed it by his attitude.

Neither job was up together and had mention of a video recorded interview being required with the victim. I was pretty sure this would cause a headache for investigations and would later find out (when I checked the following day) that he ended up being released under investigation as they couldn't arrange it that shift.

Just before handover I booked in another warrant – this one a breach of court order. No issues there.

All in all, rather a pleasant shift to return to, given the set before.

The next day was somewhat of a mini-reunion. Three of us from the same custody intake. The other two were guesting from elsewhere, experiencing firsthand the utter chaos I was used to.

At their station, the investigator's supervisor takes *all* disposal reviews. This left them rather shell-shocked.

To confuse people attending custody, we all looked alike. I hadn't realised this until a DC pointed it out. Extremely CID of them, that was.

Several times throughout the shift, I'd get updates from people and would have to interrupt and say I'd no idea what they were talking about. It soon became clear they'd confused me with one of the others!

As predicted, the disposals all came at once around lunchtime. I therefore had to send investigators away to find the other sergeants or in some cases, their own supervisors to assist.

The first I took was a drink drive TWOC, where the DP had crashed a hire car that was in his mate's name. The mate was present in the vehicle, claiming they'd not given him permission to drive and had concocted an unlikely account that the DP had taken their keys and they'd quickly got in the car as they drove off to try and stop them.

The DP had proceeded to crash into six parked cars and on police attendance, he admitted he'd been the driver and provided a positive specimen of breath.

He provided a 'no comment' interview and his mate had refused to provide a statement for obvious reasons.

I initially said I'd charge but then realised it was aggravated TWOC, so given the lack of admission in interview, I could hardly anticipate a guilty plea, meaning as an either way offence it'd need CPS advice. The hire company had yet to provide a statement, so I directed the OIC to take one over the phone, to be signed by return of post, and hopefully CPS would accept that. I later found he'd been released under investigation, so can only assume they did not.

The only other case that came my way was a domestic ABH. Police attended a verbal domestic and whilst completing a risk assessment with the victim, she disclosed around five and a half months earlier, he'd hit her with a mobile phone, causing bruising to her eye.

To complicate matters, in her statement, the assault was only three months prior, so her account had already changed somewhat between initial disclosure and providing the statement. She'd taken photos of her injuries around the time, but these were not dated on her phone. Attributing them to the assault would therefore be difficult.

In his interview, the DP said he had never assaulted her and that her autistic five year old son had previously headbutted her, causing that injury. He said that children's services were already well aware.

The discrepancy in when the incident occurred, along with the difficulty in attributing the photos to an assault were the main issues undermining this case. However, given that CSD apparently had knowledge, I directed the OIC to contact them and enquire as to whether an assault or troublesome kid had been disclosed.

I was updated after handover that an assault had been disclosed involving a mobile phone but that the worker was not available that day. I wrote it up for a release under investigation, taking into account they were now ex partners, not living together.

Lates had three skippers on and I'd been booted off my computer, with no others free in custody. I found a terminal elsewhere and got some e-learning done, taking full advantage of this rare downtime.

I sat down in the handover room on the first late, expecting it to just be me and one colleague. I was relieved when another team's sergeant arrived, offering to do disposals. Three skippers on a late – thank god for that! However, my optimism was short lived, when I then realised the colleague I'd been expecting had been granted last minute leave.

I took over nine DPs. There were about nineteen total.

Two were NFA'd by a days skipper pretty much straight after handover, before I'd had chance to officially take them over.

I received an update a sixteen year old was to be released under investigation. He'd been arrested on a plane headed for Morocco and had a suitcase containing mostly new items of clothing, along with around three hundred quid of sterling and Euros.

I hadn't been told *anything* about his property and was about to release him when I got word a response Inspector wanted to speak to me. He said the property and cash needed seizing - this was a regular missing child and was clearly being exploited for drug importation.

Yep, I'd missed the memo on that one.

I asked him to send an officer straight down, as I was seconds from releasing him and had no power to keep him there any longer.

A frazzled investigator arrived minutes later, explaining she had been unfortunate enough to have answered the phone upstairs. I felt sorry for her – she was clearly extremely busy. The PACE Inspector caught her in the corner of his eye as he walked past our room and asked how her investigation was going, as he was about to review her DP. She explained not well, as she'd been collared by another Inspector and instructed to do this! You can't do two things at once and when two Inspectors are pulling you in different directions, you can't get *anything* done!

She seized the stuff and as I released the DP, I gave all his remaining property back to him, except for his passport, which I handed directly to his foster carer.

I released a domestic assault DP under investigation, and then reviewed a job.

It involved a shoplifting, turned assault, with a bit of cannabis possession and damage to police property for good measure. The shoplifting and assault were an easy NFA. There was no complaint from the shopkeeper, most likely as they'd been seen retrieving a weapon of some sort from the shop themselves to join whatever mayhem had unfolded outside their store! With only one witness to the fracas, I couldn't see a realistic prospect of conviction for even public order offences against this DP.

The cannabis was straight forward – he'd been found in possession of a little herbal on arrest and admitted this. Having already had a fixed penalty notice, and shown no remorse whatsoever, I charged that.

The damage to police property turned out to be a little spit to the holding cell window. With no specialist call-out cleaning required, I NFA'd that. I get it – as an officer stood with a DP in the holding cell, you feel powerless when they are insistent on spitting on the floor or walls. It's not at *you*, so you can hardly start using force on them but you still feel you need to do something about it. So you arrest them. But this almost always ends up causing you more work than it's worth.

In came my first prisoner – a fail to appear warrant. She disclosed a leg injury – an abscess no doubt from repeated heroin injections in the same spot. I had her checked by the nurse, who decided she needed hospital treatment for the infection and associated sky high temperature.

Next in was a recall to prison – he was an easy customer. Really nice bloke actually. A 'no' to everything on the risk assessment. This was slightly better than the other recall that got booked in almost simultaneously, who was causing no end of issues for my colleague, fighting in his cell on constant obs wanting to hurt himself.

I saw that a DP had been interviewed and had already pre-empted a review based on what I'd read. I went upstairs and found the officer, to add the interview content and sent it to CPS. Just as I stuck my log on, I noticed the ERO had duplicated this work and no one had thought to tell me. Slightly annoying, that.

I NFA'd a Romanian for criminal damage. No one had actually seen him damaging the window to an address – they'd only seen him inside and knew he was the former tenant. All we could really prove was a civil trespass.

A Nigerian gentleman arrived, suspecting of damaging his partner's property and assaulting her friend. The domestic related damage was weak – make up had been thrown and broken. At least there was an assault attached to it.

He arrived holding his throat. I considered he either had an injury or was about to start speaking like Donald Duck with a tracheotomy.

It was the former. He claimed it was *he* who had been assaulted, and had been strangled to the point of unconsciousness. The nurse came into the charge room and said if what he was saying was true, he needed to be checked out at hospital. So a second DP of mine disappeared.

I got word CPS advice had come back on a domestic to charge. I explained to the bloke I'd be imposing bail conditions, wanting to pre-empt any issues with where he would stay, rather than be faced with decisions on the spot when charged. He decided he'd spend the night at a hotel, and the remainder of the time at his mother's. Brill. I charged and released him. Fifty-five minutes after leaving for hospital, the neck man returned. The triage nurse had called BS.
I received update prior to handover the warrant lady was awaiting blood results, which would determine how long she'd likely remain at hospital. I handed this to nights, along with the other three prisoners I had by then.
I'd nothing to do after handover, so got a 1-2-1 done, before returning home.
I'd arrived at work the following late nice and early, only to be unable to turn right at the roundabout by the station due to a road closure. I therefore spent the next twenty odd minutes circumnavigating a dodgy part of town, only to arrive back at the same roundabout from the opposite direction, by which time they'd removed the closure. Fuckers.
Both the other sergeants were already in, noting down prisoners, so I took disposals.
After handover, I was asked to concentrate solely on dealing with a chap who had thirty minutes on his PACE clock. I was told they were awaiting CPS advice and if NFA'd, he'd be granted a DVPN.
Word came that CPS wouldn't run the job, so the officer arrived to serve the DVPN on his release.

Only problem was he was refusing to leave his cell, wanting to stay there and go to court the following morning. I tried explaining he was not being charged with any offences, so wouldn't be going to court in the morning and that continued detention would be unlawful. He said he'd be homeless as a result of the DVPN and he'd nowhere else to go. He said he'd make it lawful then, taking his top off and squaring up to me, intimating he'd become violent just so he could get nicked for assault and remanded.

I didn't fancy getting assaulted just as a means to an end.

He said the minute he left the nick he'd kill himself by any means possible. This was clearly another threat to get himself locked up but I did run it past the mental health liaison just to cover my arse – as expected, she refused to see him, stating she wouldn't escalate the process to a mental health assessment just for someone who clearly just wanted a roof over their head. They did, however, give me housing support literature, which helped with my pre-release risk assessment, as I was able to show we'd helped him as much as possible.

The DVPN was served in-cell, which he refused to sign. I then left him there and stuck a log on the custody record explaining he was free to leave but was refusing to do so, so as far as I was concerned he was not being unlawfully detained. Essentially, I had a squatter!

I updated the PACE Inspector, who recommended getting Level Two officers down to forcibly remove him from the station. Specialist trained officers from the support unit heard my request over the radio and gamely attended. By that time, he came willingly out his cell, spitting a few times in my charge room. Not wishing to bite, I simply ignored this and sure enough, the spitting stopped. He left, escorted to a nearby bus stop by those officers, well away from the staff car park!

Next on my list was to charge and remand an eastern European chap for domestic assault. In doing so, he had also breached court bail conditions, to do with a previous assault on the same woman. The breach of bail conditions made it an easy remand decision – he *had* to be put before the next available court.

I NFA'd a young woman for domestic assault and then released one under investigation.

There was a lull in terms of disposals but a queue developed at the back door, so I helped booking in.

To really cement my 'shit magnet' status, I, of course, chose the one that needed to go to hospital.

I'd heard I'd be booking in an old lady and to be fair, looking at the holding cell CCTV, she did look that way. But this was just another heroin addict, whose body looked weathered beyond their years.

She could barely talk, stand or open her eyes. Extremely drowsy was an understatement. Markers for conceals drugs in custody. Marker for overdosed in cell having been strip searched, requiring emergency medical treatment. That one showed that even if strip searched, you couldn't rule out the possibility of things plugged in intimate places.

I wasn't taking any chances with this one. Strip search authorised. Negative. No nurse on site. Hospital. Even the arresting officer said he'd become more and more concerned about her, given on arrest she was fully alert.

The queue continued, so I booked in another. This one was the complete opposite – extremely pleasant, polite and sober. She was a young woman, who'd phoned police to report an ongoing domestic between her and her heroin/alcohol dependant partner. What she – a 'no' to every question – was doing with someone like that was beyond me.

Despite being the one who contacted police, she disclosed she'd actually assaulted *him* by slapping him to the face and scratching his neck. He had injuries consistent with this and confirmed the assault, albeit, backtracking unconvincingly when she was then arrested.

Within an hour and a half of her arrival, the arresting officer cracked on with interview, during which she fully admitted the offence, stating she suspected her partner was back on the gear and was slapping a confession out of him! I directed the officer to seek CPS advice and updated nights on handover of this remarkably quick prisoner turnaround! This *never* happens!

We handed over a full cell block to nights. With the queues of prisoners, we'd actually declared ourselves full by half eight that evening.

Despite days and lates being *so* much better than last set, for some reason, my anxiety was playing havoc with me that evening. On returning home, I could barely catch my breath and was controlling my breathing by inhaling slowly through my nose and breathing out slowly through pursed lips. The beginning part of the shift had been stressful, what with the dickhead refusing to leave, but otherwise it had been busy but relatively easy. Yet, it appears the custody environment in general has a stressful impact on me, causing me to feel this way. It's bizarre – I shouldn't have been feeling that way after a manageable shift (and set thus far). Perhaps the slower pace simply meant that I was more aware of the stress that had been manifesting itself inside me. I don't know. It's so frustrating, as I don't feel in control of myself when I'm like this. I get an impending sense of doom, feel like I'm about to have a heart attack, being aware of this makes you more worried. Your breathing goes haywire. I get hot, clammy, can feel the sweat on my palms, often get numbness in limbs...its rather unpleasant. Just writing this makes me feel like a right head-case. No wonder people don't talk about things like this – people think you're mad. I'm starting to think I am. I know I'm not really, as I meet people that are *way* more fucked up than me.

I'm done with keeping my anxiety private. I've started talking about it more. Especially to my wife. It's helped so much. I never used to, and arguments developed but now she realises what I'm going through and helps me recognise the signs of when I'm stressed and this helps calm me down.

When I got home after that second late shift, I walked in to a full dishwasher load, waiting to be put away. The draining board was full of stuff waiting to be put away. This caused a stress overload and I started banging and crashing things around as I put them away. She came down and saw what I was doing. Probably saw my body language. My fingers clutching my lips, my hair, my chin. Stress hands.

She gave me a hug and whilst this should've made things so much better, I was still having breathing difficulties. Couldn't calm myself down.

As a general rule, I've stopped drinking alcohol during the working set, as I'd noticed I was drinking a lot more after stressful shifts. But she'd bought some ginger beer, stating she'd heard it goes really well with rum. I fancied one. We both had one, watching some Russell Howard, before she disappeared off to bed. I had another. Whilst this is clearly not an ideal long term solution, the second did the job and I felt more relaxed as I went off to bed.

We took the kids to a wildlife park the following day. The wife was keen on getting me out and about, rather than cooped up in the house. The exercise did me good and I felt refreshed for the first night shift.

There were only two of us on but we had very little handed over. I took three, my colleague about double.

The first chap I booked in remained silent, only answering or even acknowledging my presence when asked if he wanted a solicitor and whether he wanted any food or drink. As I placed him in his cell, he asked me how long he'd be there for. As tempting as it was to give him the silent treatment back, I thought better of it. However, it was my pleasure to be realistic with him.

A grandmother followed! No, not an old dear but a middle-aged lady. I can't mock that – if my eldest has a kid when I had my first, I'll be a grandparent at forty-eight. Although doing the maths with this one, I think she'd have been in her thirties! I think mocking *that* is fair.

Police had been called to a scrap outside her flat. She'd assaulted her daughter and threw a can of deodorant at her, but missed, hitting her teenage grandchild in the face, causing injuries.

She was highly emotional. I did my sensitive bit, offering her a tissue.

In the early hours, I devoured an out of date egg and cress sandwich. A doughnut followed.
A first timer arrived, accused of stealing *from* a car, stealing *a* car and *going equipped* to steal from cars.
Someone had phoned in youths trying door handles. When the first police unit arrived on scene, they spotted a van driving erratically, which then quickly parked on a driveway and seemingly a whole school class exited and made off. This young lad was unfortunate enough to be one of the slower ones.
He had a bit of an attitude but was otherwise no trouble.
We experienced a bit of a lull and I took full advantage by having a meal break, watching the first forty minutes of *Judge Dredd*. Not a patch on the later version, but still fun.
Another first timer arrived and it was clearly a night for vehicle-crime related cherry-popping.
A member of public reported an abandoned vehicle, which turned out to be stolen. A dog unit tracked from this to the DP and a friend. They had a multi-tool between them.
He was extremely polite. I told him to stop calling me 'Sir!', although he kept doing so and then apologised every time! He lived with his grandparents, as his mother worked abroad. I couldn't get them on the phone and he said they'd almost definitely be out for the count. No wonder they'd no idea what he was getting up to.
Not long before handover, two prisoners arrived. They'd both been nicked following threats made with a knife at a 24-hour shop.

Mine was a sous-chef, who'd been on his way to work. I was told he matched the description of the offender, although soon after I booked him in another DP arrived and it appeared they too matched the description! One of these had been unfortunate enough to be in the wrong place, at the wrong time clearly! I suspected mine was the unlucky one, but he'd made a remark about a female with blood on her hands approaching him and kept asking how badly hurt the shopkeeper was, so if he was innocent, he'd unfortunately linked himself enough to warrant further enquiries! I permitted him a call to work so he could explain his absence. I left my DO loading the next custody record whilst I handed over to days.

Apart from waking for a piss around nine that morning, I slept through to just gone four in the afternoon. I only woke *then* as the same annoying motorcyclist kept revving his engine. This is an ongoing problem of late – it's usually a wakeup call around half six each morning but being a shift worker, his thoughtlessness has the potential to affect my sleep at any time of day. If I wasn't a copper, I'd be tempted to kick it over. But it's not worth my pension.

That night, I sorted my emails, before booking in a prisoner for domestic assault and damage. The assault was four months old - an ashtray had been thrown at the victim's head, leaving a scar. The damage was only a couple days old, involving items thrown at a wall and mugs being smashed. I authorised detention and was halfway through booking in when a DO said there was a phone call for me that couldn't wait. I left them with the DP and took the call from the DS in investigations.

They explained the job had already been filed by another DS and they'd already had an argument with the arresting officer as they were on route to custody. It seemed to me the other DS had already decided there was insufficient evidence and an admission was unlikely. The person I spoke with said she'd told the arresting officer they'd be lucky to get them into custody. I said I was more than happy to authorise based on the circs I'd been passed – it was a domestic after all. If it'd just been the historical matter perhaps I'd have asked more questions, but there'd been a much more recent incident. Apparently this job had been up through the ranks, each sergeant and inspector had a different view as to how best to proceed. Some saying it should be filed, some saying he should be invited in for interview under caution, others saying he should be arrested. Not all those persons had actually put their name on the job, so some of this was hearsay.

It was a right mess. Bottom line, they were in now. I was happy. He needed interviewing. I was told investigations had no one and so I requested they liaise with response for him to be dealt with overnight, given I was told all lines of enquiry were as complete as they'd ever be.

I had taken over four prisoners.

One of these involved a shoplifting, two public order offences and cannabis.

The evidence showed it was actually his mate who committed the theft. The public orders were sound but I went for lower level offences, as the fear or provocation of violence was weak but they'd clearly intentionally caused two members of staff alarm by the insults thrown at them. The cannabis was straight forward.

This young lad had already entered the court system, as there was nothing further the local youth offending team could do with him. I charged him for three offences.

Another early hours lull occurred, during which I caught another forty minutes of Sly Stallone grunting and declaring he was the law.

As I emerged from my break, I realised I'd missed two DPs, one of which was still being booked in by my DO. He'd been stopped driving a vehicle that'd been involved in a road rage incident the night before involving weapons. The officer had therefore searched his vehicle and located metal poles etc in the boot. He'd been nicked off-wep.

Another lull occurred, during which I familiarised myself with how to access custody CCTV. I'd not had chance to do this before and it was easy enough. I watched the last chap get booked in and realised he'd been a bit of a chopper when he first arrived but as soon as the arresting officer disappeared, leaving just the female DO, the bravado disappeared.

I heard a guy arrive, shouting and swearing. He'd been restrained by door staff upon being ejected from a nightclub. As police arrived, he started threatening to kill pretty much everyone present and made a gun with his hand and shot at those present. He came in for threats to kill, though it was clearly more of a public order offence.

I was told to go fuck myself for many of the questions asked but I persevered anyway. He answered some questions, telling me he was a Bangladeshi gentleman and had a seizure through drug use a couple months beforehand.

We took him to his cell, where he continued swearing but otherwise offered little resistance as we searched him.

As we left him there, he began threatening to blow himself up and told staff he was being trained to kill people. An email was sent off to Special Branch in case he was of interest; though I doubt he'd been trained particularly well, blurting out this information.

He proceeded to sing (poorly), providing us with at least some form of entertainment as we worked.

The response officers finally arrived to interview the domestic chap, having been roped into completing two house searches first. Interviewing someone at around five in the morning is far from ideal, but I didn't want to hand this one over to days given the circs.

He denied the historic assault and made partial admissions to the damage, only admitting to having smashed a couple of drinking glasses, valued at around £1 to £2.

There was no complaint from the victim. No photographs of any injuries, only of the recent damage, which was minor. I wrote a spiel on the job about how I did not believe it to be in the public interest to prosecute given the low value of damage and that there was insufficient evidence to proceed with anything else.

My cover arrived just in time for me to scoot home on time. Rest days had come. That was a much better set after the one before. Had that been a set of the same intensity, I think I'd have broken. Yet, I'd still struggled with my anxiety. One thing was for sure – I'd become known as the shift's shit magnet!

Rest days were relaxing. With Halloween approaching, I was keen to introduce my daughter to the horror genre, but do so in an age appropriate manner, so showed her films like The Burbs, Death Becomes Her and Arachnophobia. I saved the likes of IT and A Nightmare on Elm Street for when a mate came over. Depending on whether I can be arsed that particular year, I sometimes put decorations out; I opted for minimal this year, sticking to a ceramic pumpkin containing tea lights, ghost and spider lights and skeletons hung from the ceiling. Oh, and my five year old is now obsessed with greeting people by a shake of the hand, leaving them holding the fake bloodied limb.

Chapter Fifteen – Zut alors!

I took on nine prisoners first day back. My colleague took more. It was a full cell block. If the control room was to be believed, we only had three spaces in the whole Force. Something was clearly in the water, or Halloween had brought out all the ghouls.

There was one familiar face among mine, being the chap who keeps breaching his criminal behaviour order by being drunk on public transport. I had two on constants, one quite simply wanting to kill herself and the other due to erratic behaviour. The one wanting to kill herself had two epileptic fits fairly soon after I visited her and was taken to hospital with officers. I never saw her again that shift.

At least three of my bunch requested solicitors as I walked round, which I had to then call through.

I amended a couple of care plans from thirty minute checks to sixty, believing that to be more proportionate to (lack of) risks identified. Whilst more favourable for DOs, I did amend one from sixties to thirties, believing the self harm history warranted a higher level of check.

I helped a colleague with a strip search. Their DP had been in for seventeen hours and were still not sober. The nurse was convinced he'd been topping himself up with something. Sure enough, I located one of those coin bags in his left trouser pocket, which contained white powder and a single white tablet. The latter could've been paracetamol for all I knew. I suspected the powder was cocaine. I seized this and booked it into the drug safe.

Apart from interviews predictably not happening until late morning and therefore only being able to shift one prisoner before handover (a bog standard assault with no complaint), the only issue I really had was with one prisoner in particular. The erratic one on constants. She just couldn't stop assaulting people.

She'd been in custody the day before, for arson. Upon being released into the care of her parents, she proceeded to thank them by throwing a mug at her elderly mother's forehead. When police arrived, she threw multiple mugs at officers (let's pretend one was called Celine), hitting one on the arm and the other in the neck. She was arrested for three ABHs and criminal damage – including poor Celine I presume (thank you).

I asked our mental health liaison to see her, as I'd been told she clearly needed a full mental health assessment. She did see her, although spoke through the hatch due to her unpredictable violent behaviour. The DP still managed to throw a shoe at her, hitting her on the nose.

Despite this, she was still in two minds as to whether to call a full assessment. Apparently, the DP was doing things you'd not expect someone with mental health to be doing. I was told a whole bunch of shit that meant nothing to me, being too sciencey for me, a mere custody sergeant, but I believe the gist of what I was being told was that there was every chance this lady was faking it. But there was something about her that caused doubt, so they set a full assessment in motion.

Just prior to this decision being reached, she assaulted the DO I'd placed on constants. She chucked a hot chocolate drink over her, causing slight burning to her upper chest. Fortunately, they'd had the sense to keep the drink from being boiling hot, so this *only* left reddening to her skin. I wrote *only* in italics, as nobody wants to get assaulted, by any means, and this was still extremely unpleasant and caught my colleague off guard and caused considerable upset. It made me want to do the same to her (DP, not colleague), only my pension-alarm sounded again, as reliable as ever. Got to ensure the batteries never run out in that thing, like they almost did the other set!

Amongst the mayhem, I did book one in for a domestic assault, turned theft of mobile phone. The chap was accused of pushing his ex partner the night before and then stealing her phone. I was told he'd been found in possession of said phone on arrest. Apart from being a bit annoyed by the manner of the arresting officer, they were fine and caused no issues. I permitted a phone call to keep them sweet and provided them a bible on request. I half wondered whether that was a ploy to show they were angelic and couldn't possibly have committed the offences. Having dealt with him on response, I know he can be an annoying prick, so angelic, even as a guise, was a welcome alternative.

Just prior to handover, I realised one of my DPs had been written up for charge and remand some two hours beforehand, yet the skipper making that decision had not had opportunity to do so, with all that had occurred. I was expecting lates request I stay on to sort it but thankfully, the skipper I handed over to had knowledge and said it'd be their pleasure to deal. Happy days.

I checked the welfare of the assaulted members of staff before going home to have my lunch.

That evening, the kids settled remarkably quick considering the amount of fireworks going off, meaning I could enjoy a few episodes of the latest Stranger Things.

I took disposals the next day, as did another skipper, having a grand total of four sergeants on.

Knowing it would likely be quite some time before the first came, I read jobs, creating reviews I could simply add to later. I dealt with three, one of which caused me more headaches than the others.

The first update came in the form of a domestic assault. She had attacked her estranged husband she still lives with. Never a good idea that, living with the person you are trying to divorce.

There was a statement from him. Photos of his injuries in the form of cuts to forehead, eyelid and nose from where she'd allegedly pushed his glasses into his face, scratching him with her nails in the process too. She provided a no comment interview.

I sent the job to CPS, believing they'd charge it. I asked the OIC to check with the DP where else she could go should they authorise a charge, as I'd be looking to bail with conditions. It'd been graded high risk and she'd been cautioned only a few months beforehand for the same thing.

They returned saying "well that went well". She'd become extremely emotional, stating there was nowhere else.

I got the mental health liaison to see her again, as she'd already done a face to face to gauge her state of mind. The interview process had upset her. I wanted to ensure she was well supported and was planning where else she could stay. They returned stating she'd simply said if she wasn't going home, she wasn't going anywhere. I was fairly convinced I'd be remanding her at that rate.

The next update was another domestic, this was adult son versus father. Son had hit father in the face during an argument. Neither parent wanted to criminalise him and refused statements. There was no injury. All we had was a statement from the attending officer detailing disclosure. The DP made admissions and I sent the job to CPS. Funnily enough, he had no legal rep.

The third and final update was a GBH, whereby there were several enquiries outstanding and the officer requesting they be released under investigation. I rushed through that review, agreeing a charging decision couldn't be brought until those enquiries were complete, forgetting to even ask what the DP had to say about it! But then we weren't looking to remand him and even with an admission CPS would no doubt require medical evidence to determine level of assault.

The advice for the emotional DP came back quicker than expected. Charge assault by beating. I saw her brother had phoned in, offering to collect her. I phoned him and he was willing to look after her on release and allow her to stay at his. He lived some distance away, so would take a few hours to arrive. He suggested her twenty year old daughter could attend in the first instance. I phoned her and she agreed.
I got the liaison worker to join me in delivering this news, so we could explain what her brother was willing to do and that her daughter would meet her on release. She was extremely tearful still but appeared to be delighted in her daughter and did agree to stay with her brother. She said she had no plans to harm herself on release, though stated when asked that if she did, she wouldn't tell us. This didn't fill me with much confidence but she was saying all the right things by then. With the support from brother, I decided to release her. I added a clause to the condition of non contact, allowing for indirect contact via a third party for the purposes of child contact. She seemed to appreciate this and I am hopeful that by trying to be as flexible as possible, she may not kill herself! Sadly, I would class this DP as another pension roulette scenario. I ensured a good log went on justifying my decision. Advice came back on the other domestic. Before I could deal, they needed their prints and DNA taken. However, I then noticed they were marked as having an AA. The custody record indicated they'd not had their rights reissued in the presence of any AA. I couldn't see any mention of whether there'd been one present for interview, or why one was actually required in the first place!
Lates hadn't taken over this DP, knowing I was disposing. It was a balls up. Presumably, the OIC removed the DP for interview without even checking whether an AA was required.

Despite the DP appearing to fully understand the process, I decided to proceed using mum as AA (she'd arrived to collect him) just in case. At least this covered the DO taking prints and DNA. As he appeared to understand the process, I was satisfied that proceeding was morally right, though accept any later challenge may succeed on technical grounds.

I then contacted the OIC, who was suitably embarrassed and apologetic.

Once I'd sorted that, it was home time.

I took a charge room the following day, taking over four prisoners. One of the best possible starts to a late shift, that. My colleague took over slightly more. There were an additional two skippers on disposals. Typical we had so many sergeants on when the DP numbers were low, but hey ho.

I booked in three in quick succession.

The first was a guy I've dealt with before. Heroin and crack dependant, he'd been wanted for some time in relation to a shoplifting gone wrong, whereby he'd been challenged and caused damage and verbally abused staff. There was a warrant outstanding but I kept that up my sleeve.

I asked him to remove his shoes for a search. As if by magic, an ID card in another name appeared by his feet. It had either fallen out his shoes or, more likely, dropped out his trouser legs, as he had a 'conceals' marker for hiding property in his underwear.

I therefore authorised a strip search, much to his annoyance. Nothing further was found.

In next was an elderly gent for sexual assault and indecent images of children. He'd been on a coach sat next to the aggrieved, boasting of his relationship abroad with a thirteen year old girl. He'd clearly felt comfortable enough to show her photographs of the girl which were said to have been indecent in nature. During the journey, he'd touched the passenger's thigh in a sexual manner. Reckon next time, she'll opt to drive instead.

He was denying the allegations, believing the process to be absolutely ridiculous. He reminded me of John Hammond from Jurassic Park, complete with white beard and walking stick, except in the case of little Tim and Lex, I hope the dinosaur man only fiddled with fossils.

The following DP was a slightly unusual arrest circumstance. He'd actually turned up voluntarily for an interview, however, took his partner along. His partner was the victim of the domestic ABH he was to be questioned about. He refused to attend any interview without her present. Alarm bells understandably sounded and the decision was made to arrest him to prevent any witness intimidation.

He caused me no issues and appeared to accept why plans had changed. I gather even his solicitor wasn't surprised, when usually they'd challenge any decision to arrest when a voluntary attendance had been arranged.

My DO informed me she'd found herself in the awkward position of popping out to the front office, only to be handed some chocolates by a lady wishing to thank custody for taking such good care of her the day before. She said the lady's name and I realised it was the pension roulette DP I released hoping she wouldn't kill herself!

As nice a gesture as this was, the Inspector reminded us they'd need to be declared to professional standards and he would store them in 'a safe place' until we received direction back.

We experienced a bit of a lull, during which I decided to take a meal break. I finished watching Judge Dredd, which was still in the machine from nights! I'm clearly the only person that uses the DVD player on a meal break.

Returning from Mega-City One, I realised things had become rather busy.

Someone had been booked in and my DO was logging property.

I liaised with the skipper next door, who'd authorised but not been present for the risk assessment. I'm of the belief a sergeant should be present for the risk assessment process, but that hadn't happened here. I set a care plan based on what risks had been identified, which in the case of this chap, was only that he was Army and he was a first timer in custody. In fact, he was still in full camouflage attire, as if he'd been nicked out at war.

The last DP that evening was a breach of bail, or rather, likely to breach bail. You have to be careful with those, as the particular circs have to cause you to believe there was no way they'd be able to complete the conditions of their bail through whatever actions they'd taken. In this case, he'd been reported as buying a last minute one-way fare abroad, so the attending officers believed it highly unlikely he'd be able to sign on the following morning. Seemed fair enough to me.

I asked him to place all property on the desk. He then took off his hat and I was shocked by what I saw. He was bald and had numerous tattoos covering his scalp. Such a bizarre sight. He felt let down by mental health services in this country and that was why he'd tried travelling abroad – to utilise services elsewhere. This is a common theme when in policing we meet people suffering with their mental health. An awful lot of the time, they are frustrated with not having the right support. I'm quite sure as with anything, including policing, once again it comes down to budgets.

I told him to settle for the night and expect to be sent off to court in the morning.

On handover, I learnt that the smackhead, Jurassic coach and domestic dudes were at CPS, whilst GI Joe had been NFA'd. All the others I'd inherited had long since been released.

After handover, prior to leaving, I took on a disposal for a domestic assault, sending it to CPS.

The following morning I finished Stranger Things. Absolutely fantastic.

Work that afternoon was fairly Q to start with, as there were four sergeants in. Two of us did disposals, though when my colleague disappeared leaving just me taking updates, I became rather busy.

The first review was for a Romanian chap, accused of drink driving, having crashed his father's car and been seen by witnesses trying to drive off. They'd stopped him from doing so and chased him as he made off. Statements from witnesses covered the continuity and I was satisfied there was sufficient evidence for a RPOC. However, the DP's father was in Romania and could not be contacted. The OIC had no idea when he would return and so we had no evidence the car had been taken without consent. The interview was all no comment. I decided to forget any TWOC and charge the drink drive, no insurance and licence offences.

The Romanian interpreter had hung fire, having been advised we were close to charging. I charged him and handed over the paperwork. He pointed out that his surname was completely wrong. His first name had been recorded as his surname, and his middle name as his first name! He provided the correct surname, which we did not have at all until that point. Annoyingly, that meant I had to get a DO to quickly contact Immigration to redo the relevant checks, before he could be released. Thankfully, they came back fine and he was shown out.

I was asked to review a domestic assault, whereby the DP was accused to throwing a shirt in the victim's face. Now, this may sound all a bit pathetic to you. And it is to be fair. "You are under a vest", I joked. But then we have a pretty strict domestic policy at present, where officers are heavily criticised for not arresting. Often for good reason, too I should add. It has therefore become far easier to arrest than to spend ages typing up a detailed NDM justifying your decision not to arrest, which, despite your efforts, will likely be ignored anyway.

Hand up – I have thrown items of clothing at my wife before. She has thrown clothing at me. I dare not drop this into casual conversation at work, as no doubt one of us will end up spending hours in a cell.

This guy had already been in for six or seven hours. The victim did not support. The only evidence was the attending officer statement, detailing the victim's disclosure. I was pretty sure I knew where this one was going...

Only the DP admitted throwing it at her in frustration!

I was fully aware of how ridiculous this job was. It wasn't as if she'd been punched or slapped. She hadn't been whipped or flogged with this item of clothing. It had been thrown at her from across a room. Anything of significant weight thrown – fair enough. But this was a cotton shirt. I'd have understood if someone had been fleeced...

But here he was, in police custody. After six or seven hours. His arrest had been deemed necessary. It had been reviewed by the attending officer's sergeant, ratifying the decision to arrest. An arrest strategy had been created. He'd been accepted into custody. He had admitted what was alleged! After all that work, after all that time in custody, I could hardly now decide to NFA the job...

So I sent it to CPS. The OIC laughed, understanding my predicament but appreciating how farcical things had become. I was pretty sure CPS would NFA it, which they later did. I was told the prosecutor was close to actually charging it, but spoke with their manager who thought otherwise.

When they got the written decision back, I released the DP. That was one collar that went nowhere...

One of the other sergeants had reviewed a job and authorised three charges. The DP was wanted on warrant for failing to appear at court. I went and broke the news, refusing him bail on grounds of deciding it highly likely he would fail to appear given he was wanted for this! He also had extensive offending history linked to heroin use.

I released a guy under investigation for assaulting his partner's four year old daughter. She'd told her teacher step dad had punched her arm, causing bruising. Children's services had contacted police and he was arrested when he went to collect her from school. The mum had refused to provide consent for any medical or otherwise protect the kids from further harm, so they were taken into police protection. He'd provided various suggestions as to how the injuries could've been caused. The child had yet to be interviewed by specialist officers. RUI was really the only option.

Another job that came my way was a community support officer who'd been assaulted. They'd challenged a guy selling counterfeit goods and been pushed several times. It sounded like they'd done a cracking job of taking the guy to the ground and restraining them until officers arrived to arrest him. PCSOs don't carry asps, cuffs or CS/pava spray, yet they often end up detaining people until joined by a copper. So fair play to this one for getting stuck in to the extent they did. We only had the victim statement, which given their role, I was happy to take as reliable. However, the assault had been outright denied in interview, and there was mention of an independent witness who could possibly corroborate the victim. I therefore directed the OIC to obtain that statement before I made a decision.

This was obtained and whilst they hadn't witnessed the actual pushing, they'd seen the DP try and snatch the carrier bag of goods back from the officer. I charged and released him.

The last review I did was a threats to kill / threats to cause criminal damage, whereby the DP had left a threatening voicemail on a friend's phone. They'd met via social media but never in person. They'd recently exchanged addresses with a view to meeting. So he did know where he lived. The threat was he'd burn her house down, killing everyone inside.

He'd never been in trouble before. He was suicidal of late, going as far as leaving his mother (who he lived with) a suicide note before being reported as a high risk missing person. He returned home of his own accord and was arrested, being wanted for the above matter.

The threat came about as a result of the online pal revoking their friendship, having become fed up of the DP dumping all his troubles on her constantly. This led him to get drunk and leave the message.

He admitted it in interview, denying any intent to carry it out but accepted it was always going to at least cause her considerable upset.

I considered an out of court disposal for a malicious communications offence involving the intent to cause anxiety or distress, however, the OIC informed me they were in the early stages of examining his mobile phone and realised he'd made several more calls to the victim that day, none of which were detailed in her statement. The incident was a few days old and nobody had spoken to her since to ascertain whether there'd been trouble since.

Rather than rush into a decision, I therefore decided to RUI him, so they could continue the phone work and re-contact the victim, in case there was more to this.

My main concern was therefore releasing him, given he had just been a high risk suicidal missing person.

I arranged for his mother to attend, so he could be released into her care. He did not disclose any suicidal or self harm thoughts on departure. He'd been left support information by the mental health liaison and advised to contact his GP.

Away from her son, his mother asked whether we could get him assessed. I explained he'd already been seen by the liaison who did not believe there was any requirement to call for a full mental health assessment.

She understood my situation, however, clearly felt the system failed her son. She explained she'd tried getting him to see his GP but he refuses to do so. He did not appear distressed or unsettled on leaving, but was very quiet and subdued.

This was yet another 'pension roulette' release. I certainly wasn't getting the vibe this one would bother with chocolates the next day.

And then it was nights.

I took over twelve DPs, whilst my colleague took around half that number.

I had a warrant and a recall. The other ten were live prisoners.

Two were linked, both in for concerned in the supply of class A. It was a well known address, which transient dealers were cuckooing. They'd allowed the vulnerable occupant a rare trip out to walk his dog and he took his opportunity to phone police. Officers entered the address and found both males sat on a sofa, with a knife between them. They eventually gained compliance by red-dotting the males with taser. One was taking the feathered role too literally – he was sat on the drugs like a broody hen with her eggs.

One had served four years in prison already for heroin and crack supply, so no doubt they'd want to make a decent job of these two in the morning. I bedded them down, to allow for house searches and phone work.

A third sergeant took disposals that night, so some of mine (not many) disappeared come morning.

I booked in three all night.

A young lad had failed to stop for police and drove dangerously in a car he'd taken without permission. He was calm, compliant and annoyed with himself. Statements were being obtained as I booked him in. I contacted the response sergeant and requested he be interviewed overnight, knowing otherwise he'd be released the following afternoon.

He fully admitted the offences, though the disposing sergeant decided evidence supported due care better than dangerous.

I booked in a woman in her mid twenties for assaulting her mother. She'd allegedly dragged mum round the room by her hair.
She was quite tearful and had suffered with her mental health of late, having only just been released from a facility following a recent suicide attempt.
She disclosed no allergies during the risk assessment, only stating that she was very hungry.
She was provided some food and I learnt she'd soon started throwing those up, declaring she was allergic to mushrooms.
I got the nurse to see her as a precaution and she then decided she wasn't allergic, just didn't like them. Much the same as me. Mushrooms…urgh.
I'd spotted on a previous risk assessment she was bulimic. I put the vomiting down to that, as did the nurse.
The last DP that night was a Latvian gentleman on suspicion of GBH. Before I booked him in, I liaised with my colleague, realising one of his DPs were related. I was told that my DP was in fact the victim of the alleged assault for which his mother had already been arrested.
I was therefore concerned it may be the far-from-ideal case of arresting both parties, having had counter-allegations made at the scene.
This turned out not to be the case. During the same incident earlier, my chap was alleged to have pushed yet another female to the ground, causing a suspected broken arm. Attending officers had not been aware of this at the time, but rather later got called to hospital when a female presented there with those injuries. Back they went and in he came. Whereas his mother spoke no English and required an interpreter, mine conversed brilliantly.
I felt sick towards the end of that shift and as I went to bed, but resurfaced that afternoon feeling a new man, whereas I received a text from my colleague, stating he'd clearly caught whatever it was and wouldn't make work that night!
Perhaps mushroom lady set us off. Who knows.

The last night arrived. I clocked on early to assist lates, booking one in straight away.

The officer had stopped a car due to recent intelligence linking the driver to supply of drugs. They themselves had also previously stopped the same person, and had a crown court case pending for PWITS.

On this occasion, he found Class A & B hidden, along with £200 cash on the driver himself. To top things off, there was no insurance on the car.

I squeezed in another prisoner before handover. It was a breach of non-mol order, whereby the DP had been outstanding for about ten months. It was clear numerous arrest attempts had been made during that time, so I was happy to accept him in.

However, he was bent over himself as he walked in, clearly in a tremendous amount of pain. I'd seen from a previous custody record on that occasion he'd not been fit to detain overnight, so wanted the nurse to see him straight away. She took one look at him and decided his level of pain could not be managed in the custody environment, so I turned him away. I believe the officers dropped him at another station, for the OIC to deal outside of custody.

On handover, I only inherited two other DPs. One was remanded for burglary, driving offences and cannabis possession. He'd intimated wishes to kill himself on being charged and bail refused, so remained on camera constants. When I went to check him, he appeared settled, wanting to go to sleep. I stood down the constants.

The other was a breach of criminal behaviour order. The lates DS came and saw me after handover, offering to review and send to CPS. I gratefully accepted, explaining there were only two sergeants on and a big queue at the back door. I'd already booked in two that night and would go on to authorise another six.

I got a drink driver in first, keen to get him on the machine as quickly as possible. He expressed a desire to end his life, but thankfully not in custody. He'd not been seen driving by police, so witness statements and CCTV enquiries were required. This was ideal, as once he'd blown over, I bedded him down to the morning, which allowed an opportunity for him to get relevant support for his issues prior to release.

In next was a guy for shoplifting and assault. He'd tried leaving a Tesco with two hundred-and-something quid's worth of goods, assaulting a staff member when challenged. He'd refused all details. He was clearly a foreign national and didn't appear to speak any English. Frustratingly, he refused to divulge what language he *did* speak, or cooperate by pointing the relevant language out from a wall chart.

He kept squaring up and acted aggressively, so I took him straight to cell. There, he kept stopping just short of doing enough to justify taking him to ground, which would've been an easier and safer way of getting the corded clothing from him. He'd apparently told the attending officers he spoke French and Romanian, but failed to converse with either interpreter at the scene when attempts were made.

I know fuck all Romanian but got an A at GCSE French. These days, I can really only remember things like how to order a table for four people, something that is not particularly useful in this situation. I recalled that 'vetements' meant 'clothes', or thereabouts, so kept saying this as I pointed at his hoodie. We took the cuffs off and he kept tensing but eventually took his top off in a strop. I pointed at the cord in his trousers, explaining (albeit in English) they'd need to come off.

One of the escorting officers had a French revelation of his own, recalling 'pantalon' to be 'trousers'. I'm not convinced the DP really spoke much French himself, but after a while of pointing he eventually grabbed hold of the cord and threw it at us.

Knowing absolutely bugger all about him and any risks, I kept him on camera constants for a good few hours until he settled. Next in was a massive lump of a guy sus domestic assault. I'd nicked him a few times on response, so knew he had the potential to suddenly flare-up.

It was clear he wasn't interested in the booking in process and he kept trying to walk out the room. Knowing how difficult it is to wrestle someone many times heavier than you, with little assistance, I decided to perform what was essentially a voluntary Route One!

The next chap was much easier. He'd assaulted his mother but was nice and compliant with us. I built a rapport with him early on, commenting on how awesome I thought his skull tee was!

He showed me scars on his left arm from where he'd self harmed with a blunt knife that evening. He confirmed he did so for release, hence the *blunt* knife. He had a full sleeve of tatts down one arm, explaining he gets those for the same reason.

We got his prints done and he settled for the night.

The penultimate DP was one of two youths in for GBH, having been accused of stamping on the victim's head. The other was sent straight to hospital by my colleague, for a nasty cut on his hand.

Mine was relatively straight forward. Parents already aware. I stuck him in a dry cell until such time as we heard otherwise.

A seventeen year old drink driver rounded off my night.

He'd crashed his car, wiping out a lamppost. He'd no obvious injuries and wasn't seen by ambulance at the scene.

I checked the policy, and believed I should accept him into custody but request the nurse assess for 'fit to detain' at the earliest opportunity.

Halfway through the procedure, the nurse updated me that he should be taken to hospital, as she was unable to properly assess and be certain what internal injuries he may have from such a crash.

As the procedure was ongoing, I decided it be finished and afterwards, as the reading was not massively over the limit, I released him under investigation, instructing the officers to drop him at hospital, where his mum met him. This saved them sitting up there but meant they'd need to arrange an interview later. From what I gathered, he'd already coughed it several times to them.

And that was pretty much that for the shift.

Epilogue

I had the next set off as leave. During that time, I hit my six months as custody sergeant. This includes the four week course but it was pleasing to consider I'd already done quarter of the generally accepted two year minimum.

I would then go two years without writing another word here, only occasionally revisiting the book to edit. The word count was well over 100k and its now just over 97k. Thanks for bearing with me!

The reason I'd abandoned the book was because I'd discovered the thing I'd wanted for some time – a hobby! I won't say what here, as I'm after some level of anonymity. The project I'd been working on outside of work is now more or less complete. It came with stresses of its own but was a bucket list tick box of mine, so ultimately was rewarding and worthwhile.

I'm also about to escape back to response, after two and a half years in the dungeons. It's been stressful at times; *extremely* so on occasion, but has flown by.

I'm often asked by people if I enjoy it. I think the word 'enjoy' is a bit strong. I think I've been able to *tolerate* it more than expected. I was expecting shifts to drag but the opposite happens.

There is much to like. You're almost *always* off on time (this does, of course, mean you don't build up much time-off-in-lieu). But you have minimal staff to supervise; meaning less PDRs to write, less welfare issues to manage, more time to concentrate on the job in hand...

You don't get cold and wet, stuck at a scene or road accident for hours on end. You're not chasing mispers round all day. You have no workload that carries forward day to day and no jobs to review and file.

You're in charge. Inspectors will offer their point of view but ultimately they respect that it's *your* domain and *your* final call on most matters. *You're* the expert on the subject matter and several times I've had to correct (or advise) visiting Inspectors. Some are better than others – usually the ex-custody sergeant ones! I would definitely agree with those who say for promotion to Inspector to be considered, you must have done time in custody. The experience is invaluable and will serve you well in the next rank.

I also enjoy making disposal decisions. Loads of sergeants I know *hate* this side of the job. But I like it. It tests my brain. Tests my knowledge. I get to apply myself. But it's making those critical decisions under pressure I dislike. Pressure of queues at the back door. Pressure of queues of investigators waiting to give you updates. Pressure of DPs trying to harm themselves in their cells or smearing shit all over the walls. Pressure of the ICVs turning up unannounced. Pressure of nurses, mental health workers and other partners loitering as there's nobody else available to take them to the cells to see a detainee...

The good news is that the job is starting to listen to our concerns. Working practices are improving. Truth be told, things have almost improved to the point where I was tempted to stay. But I'm a response copper at heart and need to get back. Custody is an important role, so I don't want to make light of it, but I joined the job to hunt and lock up baddies, not babysit them. Ultimately, that's what you do.

Custody is an extremely stressful environment. So much responsibility. I think of it as a ticking time bomb. There's only so much one can take before they lose their shit or become mentally unwell. I've experienced both. I've suffered with anxiety since my teens. It was very bad then and it's reared its ugly head again in custody. Since arriving in the cell block, I've been prescribed meds. The first medication worked for a while but needed changing. The few weeks within which I weaned myself off one drug and introduced the next was a real low point. But touch wood, the current meds work.

I'm much more open about my mental health. We all have to be. The police are one giant family and we need to support one another. Only by talking about your issues will you get the help you need. A few years ago people would take the piss but these days it's recognised how severe the issue is within the service and people are far more supportive. Keep an eye on your colleagues and if you think someone is struggling, talk to them, or tell their supervisor.

Physical exercise has also helped no end. I've joined the gym during my time in custody – something I vowed never to do! I *hate* exercise but force myself to go once during rest days and once before my first late. I do an hour cardio – mix it up with 25mins cross trainer, 25mins cycle and 10mins treadmill, usually followed by some weights. I get self conscious in the gym – don't really know what I'm doing, especially with the weights, so I have some at home too.

I've also bought a bicycle under the cycle to work scheme. I must confess, I've *never* actually cycled it to work! Well, I did once on rest days, just to see how long it would take. But I've really got into it. I don't do crazy miles – think 30 is the most I've done so far, but that is something I like doing. I don't see cycling as exercise but rather as sweat-inducing exploring! I certainly don't go out to set any personal bests. And I'm a weather dependant cyclist! No sun, no fun!

I end this book thinking of those that will be coming into custody. The new course is underway. My replacement soon joins us. I'll be mentoring them before I'm off. With improved working practices, I'm hopeful they'll have a better start than I did. It's weird to think I'm the most experienced on the team now. The other sergeants I joined have all long gone. Soon the newbie will be the expert. The custody sergeant circle of life is complete.

The End.